THE DANCE OF THE MERRYMAKERS

With thanks for your help in the
Confirmation preparation.

+ James J McGuinness
  Bishop of Nottingham.

5th July 1992

JOSEPH O'HANLON

THE DANCE OF
THE MERRYMAKERS

A journey through the Scriptures

 St Paul Publications

Cover photo by Lorenzo Lees

St Paul Publications
Middlegreen, Slough SL3 6BT, United Kingdom

Copyright © St Paul Publications 1991

ISBN 085439 331 5

Printed by The Guernsey Press Co., Guernsey C.I.

St Paul Publications is an activity of the priests and brothers
of the Society of St Paul who proclaim the Gospel through the media
of social communication

Contents

Acknowledgements

There are many teachers and friends to whom thanks must be made for whatever good is in these pages. Without their help and encouragement my journey to and through the Scriptures would not have been possible. To all my students over the years I owe a great debt. Their persistent desire to know the word of the Lord has confirmed my romance with the pages of Scripture. Thanks from the heart to "my brother", Kenneth O'Riordan, and "my sister", Ellen McGrath, for walking, argumentatively, much of the way. To my students and friends, Tracy Hansen and Judith Carpenter, for help with preparing the manuscript for publication. To Dr Elizabeth Taylor, without whose loving badgering the enterprise might not have been undertaken. I would like to dedicate this book to my mother and my late father in gratitude for more than can be expressed.

Joseph O'Hanlon

Books of the Bible

The order and division of books according to Jewish tradition is as follows:

TORAH (Teaching)

Genesis	Numbers
Exodus	Deuteronomy
Leviticus	

NEVI'IM (Prophets)

Joshua	Obadiah
Judges	Jonah
1 and 2 Samuel	Micah
1 and 2 Kings	Nahum
Isaiah	Habakkuk
Jeremiah	Zephaniah
Ezekiel	Haggai
Hosea	Zacariah
Joel	Malachi
Amos	

KETHUB'IM (Writings)

Ruth	Lamentations
Psalms	Daniel
Job	Esther
Proverbs	Ezra and Nehemiah
Qohelet (Ecclesiastes)	1 Chronicles
Song of Songs	2 Chronicles

Christians of the Orthodox and Catholic Churches, as well as accepting the books of the New Testament, add to the Old Testament some books which have survived only in the Greek language. They order their Bibles in this way:

OLD TESTAMENT

THE PENTATEUCH

Genesis
Exodus
Leviticus

Numbers
Deuteronomy

HISTORICAL BOOKS

Joshua
Judges
Ruth
1 and 2 Samuel
1 and 2 Kings
1 and 2 Chronicles

Ezra
Nehemiah
Tobit
Judith
Esther
1 and 2 Maccabees

THE WISDOM BOOKS

Job
Psalms
The Proverbs
Eccliastes

Song of Songs
Book of Wisdom
Ecclesiasticus

THE PROPHETS

Isaih
Jeremiah
Lamentations
Baruch
Ezekiel
Daniel
Hosea
Joel
Amos

Obadiah
Jonah
Micah
Nahum
Habukkuk
Zephaniah
Haggai
Zechariah
Malachi

NEW TESTAMENT

Matthew
Mark

Luke
John

Acts of the Apostles
Letter to the Romans
First Letter to the
   Corinthians
Second Letter to the
   Corinthians
Letter to the Galatian
Letter to the Ephesians
Letter to the Philippians
Letter to the Colossians
First Letter to the
   Thessalonians
Second Letter to the
   Thessalonians

First Letter to Timothy
Second Letter to
   Timothy
Letter to Titus
Letter to Philemon
Letter to the Hebrews
Letter of James
First Letter of Peter
Second Letter of Peter
First Letter of John
Second Letter of John
Third Letter of John
Letter of Jude

Book of Revelation

The Chuches of the Reformation accept as their Old Testament those books found in the Hebrew Bible. They order them thus:

THE PENTATEUCH

Genesis	Numbers
Exodus	Deuteronomy
Leviticus	

HISTORICAL BOOKS

Joshua	1 and 2 Chronicles
Judges	Ezra
Ruth	Nehemiah
1 and 2 Samuel	Esther
1 and 2 Kings	

WISDOM BOOKS

Job	Ecclestiastes
Psalms	Song of Solomon (Song
Proverbs	of Songs)

THE PROPHETS

Isaiah	Obadiah
Jeremiah	Jonah
Lamentations	Micah
Ezekiel	Habakkuk
Daniel	Zephaniah
Hosea	Haggai
Joel	Zechariah
Amos	Malachi
Nahum	

Happily, the Churches of the Reformation agree with the Catholic and Orthodox Churches on the number and order of the books of the New Testament.

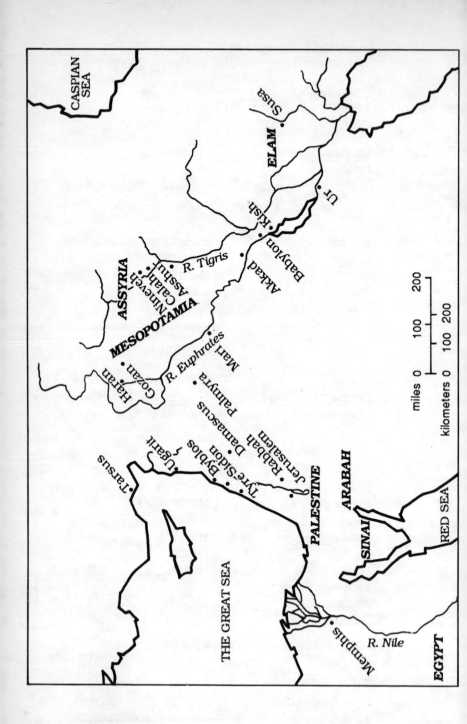

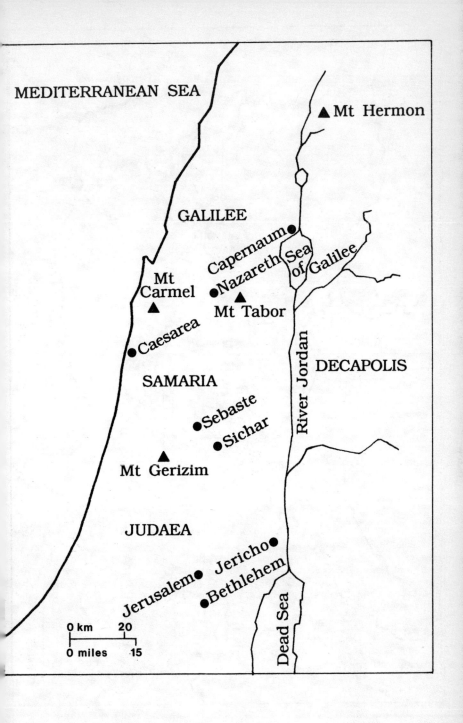

MEDITERRANEAN SEA

▲ Mt Hermon

GALILEE

Capernaum ●
Nazareth Sea of Galilee

Mt Carmel
● Nazareth
▲
Mt Tabor

▲

● Caesarea

River Jordan

DECAPOLIS

SAMARIA

● Sebaste
● Sichar

▲ Mt Gerizim

JUDAEA

Jericho ●
Jerusalem ●
● Bethlehem

Dead Sea

0 km   20

0 miles   15

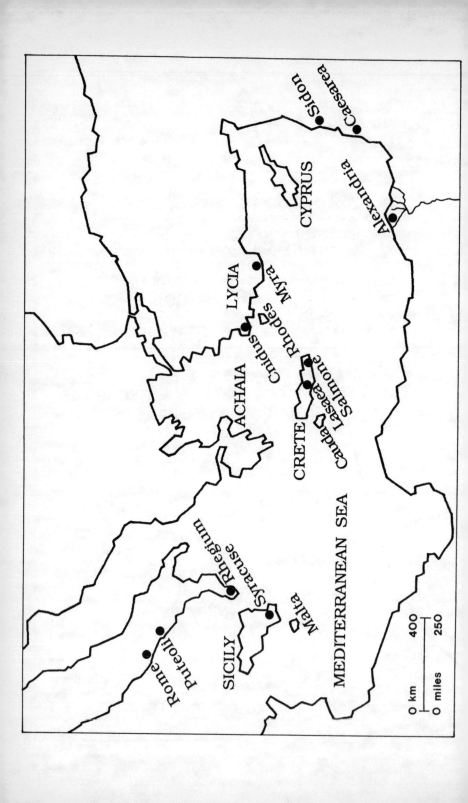

Thus says the Lord:
The people who survived the sword
found grace in the wilderness;
when Israel sought for rest,
the Lord appeared to him from afar.

I have loved you with an everlasting love;
therefore I have continued my faithfulness to you.
Again I build you, and you shall be built,
O virgin Israel!

Again you shall adorn yourself with timbrels,
and shall go forth
in the dance of the merrymakers

Jeremiah 31:2-4

Preface

How can we sing the Lord's songs in a strange land? Jeremiah looked to the day when his beloved people would return from exile to the land of Judah. Joy would replace mourning, music the silence of despair, all step out in the dance of the merrymakers.

We have been exiled from the Bible for far too long. For a variety of religious (irreligious?), cultural, social and political reasons, some of which will be delved into in this book, the Bible has been closed, walled off from Christian people. Especially is this true of Christians of the Roman Catholic tradition. For centuries, by deliberate act of ecclesiastical policy, neither priest nor people were allowed freedom to explore the word of the Lord, to taste and see that it is good. Latterly, with all the enthusiasm of a reformed addict, policy now declares the Scriptures open and available. All are invited, even constrained, to come and see.

But priests and people, long accustomed to a Bible at the periphery of their lives, cannot easily turn top over tail. The exhortation of the last thirty years has not, of itself, accomplished the desired conversion. Not everyone on the Damascus road falls off a horse.

Thankfully, official encouragement and new awakenings in prayer have led to a multitude of books designed to help win priest and people back to the Scriptures. This book is but one of many. But it does attempt something new: it begins at the beginning. We cannot assume that most priests and many people know what the Bible is, how it came to be and what on earth it is for. Biblical vocabulary, the vocabulary of revelation (what's that?), is not the vocabulary of the street. Redemption, salvation, reconciliation, atonement, covenant, Eucharist, sacrifice, resurrection – these are not Christian buzz words. They are Christian dead words. Only by realising the radical nature of the task confronting biblical renewal (as

17

distinct from the easy option of fundamentalist trivialisation) will these words undergo a resuscitation.

Can these bones live? Yes. If pastor and people sit down, preferably together, acknowledging that we must begin at the beginning. There is no need to be afraid; there is no need for pretence; there is no need for saving face. We can make a start with reading together, with sharing thoughts, with a common search, with prayer. Books about the Bible may discourage for it may appear that first one must know a thousand things. There is only one thing necessary: read the stories. The method followed in this book – and this is one of its unique features – is to learn by reading, not before reading.

The journey through the Scriptures proposed in these pages will travel through Jonah, Ruth, Genesis and selected passages from most other areas of both Old and New Testaments. Should the individual reader or the study group take pains to look up texts to which reference is made, then a very considerable part of the Bible will become familiar. Familiarity breeds love.

Joseph O'Hanlon

Feast of Mary Magdalene, 1990

Chapter 1

Journey through the Scriptures

Like the poor, the Scriptures are always with us. Indeed, they are with us rather more now than they used to be. In our Sunday worship we are presented with readings from various parts of the Bible. We sing songs of praise from the Book of Psalms. We are encouraged to read our Bible and to make it the basis of our prayer.

Yet there is unease about. How can we listen attentively to so many words, understand them, and keep them in our hearts as Mary did (Luke 2:51), in order to make them live in the turmoil of our lives? We believe that the Bible is God's word; we stand in church and declare, "This is the word of the Lord". Yet many people find the Bible strange, unhelpful, even boring. Hand on heart, do you believe that most people in the ordinary Sunday congregation are excited by what is read? Recently, a friend told me that she never opens her Bible unless she happens to be struggling with a biblical clue in her daily crossword!

Spelling out the difficulties

Some people might say that they have little or no difficulty with the New Testament, or, at least, that it is not as puzzling as the Old Testament. I suspect that what such people mean is that they are familiar with some of the Gospel stories, the Christmas stories, perhaps, and some of the parables such as the Good Samaritan and the Prodigal Son and that, of course, they know something about the death of Jesus. But, without looking up the answer, how many wise men were there? Which Gospel reports the story of the "Agony in the Garden"? The answer to the last question is "none of them"! (To be fair, three Gospels report the agony of Jesus on the evening before his death; one Gospel mentions that Jesus was in a garden on that night, but it does not mention the agony.) I have never met anyone who found St Paul's letters anything but difficult. The New Testament is not as familiar to us as we think it is. I would

19

agree, however, that it is the Old Testament which seems so unrelated to our lives and so unnecessary to our worship.

There are many reasons for our difficulties with the Bible. Some are to do with the kind of society in which we live, the kind of education we receive and, indeed, with the kind of Church we have become. But two reasons are of particular importance. First, the Bible comes from long ago and from distant lands. It is not one book, though the word "bible" means "a book". It is, in fact, a small library of books, seventy-three in all, assembled over a period of 1,200 years, the last of which was written nearly two thousand years ago. The Bible was put together by people who spoke strange languages, lived lives totally different from ours and whose cultural and religious values seem very strange. To emphasise the last point, for nearly one thousand years (say, from 1400 to 400 B.C.E.), the Jewish people lived among the Canaanite people in Palestine. The Canaanite religion encouraged male and female prostitution in their temples as part of religious worship. Sometimes the Jewish people adopted the religious practices of their neighbours. And this was going on while these same people were making and shaping the stories and tales, the poetry and prayers which, in God's good time, came to be what we call the Old Testament.

Secondly, we misunderstand the Old and New Testaments because we read them in the wrong way. A simple example will help you to see what I mean. The newspaper you read every day is made up of news pages, editorial comment, feature articles, sports news, gossip columns and cartoons. The sports page is not written in the same way as the editorial comment and the news pages are not written in the same way as the gossip columns. As we get used to a particular newspaper, we become familiar with the different kinds of writing it contains. We learn to discriminate between one kind of writing and another. No one is daft enough to take a tip for the two-thirty at Epsom on the sport's page as if it were an official announcement of the winner. So it is with the Bible. We find there short stories, poems and prayers, lists of laws, bits of history, proverbs and wise sayings, sermons and songs. But we read all the Bible as if it were history. Consequently, we make a difficult task quite impossible.

Suggesting a solution

It is going to take a long time for us to get familiar with our Bible and even longer to acquire an understanding of its contents. But it is not an impossible task and, with good will and energy, it can be done. Remember the story of the two followers of Jesus who were walking to the village of Emmaus on the day of Jesus' resurrection (Luke 24:13-35)? On the seven-mile journey, they were sharing their bitter sadness and disappointment over the death of their friend. They had had such high hopes! Now all they had was the body of a crucified criminal. Jesus joined them, though they did not recognise him. He asked them to explain their despair. They told of their hopes for the "prophet mighty in deed and word before God and all the people" (Luke 24:19) and of a death that brought an end to all hope. But Jesus opened for them the Scriptures and showed them how all that had happened had, after all, been in accordance with God's will. A little later, two very excited human beings shouted to each other, "Did not our hearts burn within us while he talked to us on the road, while he opened to us the Scriptures?" (Luke 24:32). Two lessons suggest themselves. One is that the will of God is given to us in the strange writings of the Bible. The other is that the effort to discover God's will in the pages of the Scriptures can cause our hearts to burn within us, burn with new faith, with new hope, with new vision.

So let's begin our journey through Scripture!

Step 1

Buy a Bible. Not just a New Testament. There are many excellent translations available and, unlike older Catholic and Protestant versions, they are, for the most part, reliable. I use the *Revised Standard Version* because it is accurate and I like it (recently this has again been revised and published as the *New Revised Standard Version*). The *Jerusalem Bible* and *The New Jerusalem Bible* are popular and the versions which have introductions, maps and notes are excellent for beginners. The *New International Version* has won many friends since its publication. The *Good News Bible* is published in many colourful and helpful editions but it is not noted for the accuracy of its translation. The *Revised English Bible* and its predecessor, the *New English Bible*, are accurate but hardly elegant. Whatever translation you prefer, make sure that you buy an edition with extensive notes and good maps. Most modern translations are published in a large print edition for those with imperfect eye-sight.

Step 2

Go on a tour of your Bible. Look at the Table of Contents. Count the number of books in the Old Testament and in the New Testament. Catholics recognise forty-six books in the Old Testament. Protestants follow the Jewish tradition of thirty-nine books, omitting the books of Tobit, Judith, Wisdom, Sirach (Ecclesiasticus), Baruch and 1 and 2 Maccabees. Happily, both Protestants and Catholics agree on the twenty-seven books of the New Testament.

On this initial lightning tour, it is important to get the basic division of the Bible firmly in our heads. There is an Old Testament collection of books and a New Testament collection of books. The Old Testament is the Jewish Bible. It was put together over a long period of time and all the books which make up the Old Testament were completed about one hundred years before the birth of Jesus. The Jewish people call their holy book Tanach. Christians "borrowed" it. It is of the utmost importance, therefore, to remember that the Old Testament was not written by Christians and it was not written for Christians.

The New Testament writings were composed in the seventy years after the death of Jesus, though it took Christians three or four hundred years to make up their minds which books they regarded as "the word of the Lord".

We shall examine the meaning of the word "testament" when we come to the story of Noah and the Flood.

Step 3

Start a Bible group. Making a journey is more pleasant with good companions. A group of about twelve is ideal – Adlous Huxley once remarked, "Not for nothing limit fixed on twelve apostles". Try to find someone who can help with difficulties, someone who has some professional training in biblical studies. Cast your net wide and deep. There may be somebody in a local university, college or school who is willing to help. Some of the other churches in your locality may be able to help.

Step 4

It is time to start on a book of the Bible. There is one golden rule for beginners: start small. Pick a short book. Shortness does not, of course, guarantee simplicity but it is hopeful to see the light at the end of the tunnel. We shall begin our journey through scripture with the Book of Jonah which, in my Bible, has just three pages.

A METHOD

Before we begin, however, we must agree on a method. It isn't possible to tackle every book in the same way. Different kinds of writings require different approaches. But, on the first stages of our journey, I suggest the following procedure:

1. Read the book through from beginning to end. Note down the names of people and places mentioned.

2. Find out what you can about the people and places mentioned. Here is where the Bible with good notes and maps will prove its worth.

3. Go through the book again, this time in manageable sections, noting down any difficulties, obscurities and perplexities. If you have managed to find someone to help with problems, he or she should be able to clear things up. Be patient – we don't have all the answers. If you have no guardian angel, then you will have to rely on the information given in your Bible and what you can get from books. The snag is that you may not know which books and where to find them. Your clergy should be able to help here and, of course, your local schools and libraries will have some books.

4. Try to sum up the message of the book. Clearly, a group which has worked together will have an advantage here over the one who has ploughed a lone furrow. And remember that opinions and views will differ. Don't try to crucify the book into one neat package. There is no one "Catholic" meaning so long as we keep within the boundaries of faith.

5. What image of God emerges from the book? Try to see how the book enriches your understanding of God.

6. It is a good idea to begin and end your Bible study with a prayer. Pick one from the Bible itself.

Chapter 2

Jonah: A reluctant preacher

The Old Testament seems remote from our lives and an unnecessary distraction in our worship. But the plain fact of the matter is that we cánnot understand the New Testament without the Old. Without the Old Testament, the life and teaching of Jesus would be incomprehensible. The Bible is like an iceberg, one-tenth of which appears above the water and nine-tenths below. The Old Testament is the nine-tenths without which the New Testament would simply melt away. In any case, all the books of the Bible contain the word of God, the Book of Genesis as much as St John's Gospel. The gospel according to Isaiah is no less inspired than that of St Luke. We need the Old Testament for its own inherent religious worth as much as we need the New Testament for its witness to Jesus. Therefore, we will start with a book of the Old Testament and step out there. I propose to start with the Book of Jonah which takes up two pages in my Bible. It is not quite the shortest book in the Scriptures but it meets perfectly the requirement to start small.

READING THROUGH

On first reading, characters need to be identified, cities and towns found on a map and difficulties noted. On reading through this little story, I noted down Jonah, Amittai, Nineveh, Joppa and Tarshish.

Jonah was a prophet who lived during the time of King Jeroboam II who reigned over the northern kingdom of Israel about 750 years before the time of Jesus. And, like Jesus, Jonah the prophet came from Galilee, from a small village three miles north-east of Nazareth. (Try to find these places on a map.) He is mentioned in the Second Book of Kings (14:25) as a prophet who gave good advice to the king. However, the Book of Jonah was written over three hundred years later by an unknown author who composed this fictional short story and made an otherwise obscure Galilean prophet his reluctant hero. The meaning of the name Jonah is very suggestive. It means "dove" and there are many references to this bird in the Bible. In some instances, the dove is a metaphor for Israel, as in Hosea 7:11 and 11:11. In the Song of Songs (= Song of Solomon), it is loyalty to its mate that makes the bird a symbol of love – see 1:15; 4:1; 5:12. But, perhaps, the reference which Jonah mostly clearly had in mind is Psalm 55:8-9. (See also Ps 74:19; 68:13).

Amittai is said to be the father of Jonah. Nothing else is known about him.

Nineveh was, for a time, the capital city of the Assyrians, a people who lived in what is now Iraq but whose empire sometimes extended to Egypt, Cyprus and Asia Minor. In the many wars fought by this aggressive and cruel empire, the tiny land of Israel was frequently involved, either forced to pay tribute or pressured into disastrous alliances against the might of the empire. Indeed, in 724 B.C.E., the king of Israel revolted against Assyria but the imperial troops swept into the land and, by 721, had reduced it and its capital to rubble. The Assyrians deported the tribes of Israel who occupied that part of the country and scattered them to the four corners of the empire where they disappeared from history. "None was left but the tribe of Judah only", the Second Book of Kings relates (17:18). The holy land of Israel was given to pagan planters (who were later called Samaritans). When news reached Jerusalem in 612 that the Babylonians had destroyed Nineveh, not many tears were shed. When the Book of Jonah was written, Nineveh had been in ruin for centuries.

Tarshish has not been positively identified but many think that it was in south-west Spain. In the Bible it is regarded as a source of gold, silver and ivory and it became, in popular imagination, a distant paradise.

Joppa, now called Jaffa, is the southern extension of the modern city of Tel Aviv. But at the time of our story, it was a flourishing port. You will recall that St Peter stayed there in the house of Simon the tanner (Acts 9:39-46).

Jonah 1:1-3

God commands his spokesman, the prophet Jonah, to deliver a message to the pagan, cruel and hated city of Nineveh. He is to go and "cry against that great city" but he is not told precisely what he must say (that will become clear later at 3:4). The reason for his mission is given: "for their wickedness has come up before me". Here the author imagines God sitting on his heavenly throne and receiving a report of the evil-doings of the citizens of Nineveh. A similar imaginary picture can be found in Job 1:6-12. Jonah's reaction is amazing for it is unthinkable that a prophet would run away from God or refuse to carry his word to the intended recipients. If Tarshish was in south-west Spain, our reluctant prophet is going as far away from God and Nineveh as he can. Presumably, Jonah believed that he could escape God's presence by fleeing as far as possible from the place where the command of the Lord first came to him. Notice that in these opening verses Tarshish is mentioned three times, and "from the presence of the Lord" occurs twice; this repetition and the details concerning payment of the fare and embarkation emphasise Jonah's determination to disobey and the speed with which he does so. God says, "Go east!" And Jonah heads west for the Costa del Sol!

Why does Jonah disobey? The reason is not given to the reader until 4:2 but the prophet knows from the start:

> I pray thee, Lord, is not this what I said when I was yet in my own country? That is why I made haste to flee to Tarshish; for I knew that thou art a gracious God and merciful, slow to anger, and abounding in steadfast love, and that you repent of evil.

Jonah knows well the kind of God he is dealing with and that God's love and patience would cause the Ninevites to repent. He does not wish to be the messenger who warns these hated pagans and thus be instrumental in saving them. What Jonah wants for Nineveh is fire and brimstone. Even that would be too good for the cruel Assyrians whose holocaust almost wiped the Jewish people off the face of the earth.

Jonah 1:4-6

There is no escape from God. He stirs up a fierce Mediterranean storm and the ship is in danger. The sailors pray to their gods, in contrast to Jonah who has nothing more to say to his God and is asleep in the hold. Cargo is thrown overboard as panic sets in. The captain discovers Jonah and commands him to pray to his God. What a scene! The pagan captain ordering this spokesman, this prophet of the one true God, to pray!

Jonah 1:7-12

The storm is so fierce that the sailors come to the conclusion that it is being caused by some god who wishes to punish someone on the ship. They cast lots (dice) which, so it was believed (Acts 1:26), would reveal the intentions of the gods. The lot fell on Jonah and he is forced to confess that he is a Hebrew, one of God's people, a worshipper of the Lord who made the land and the sea. He is not an ignorant pagan who doesn't know his right hand from his left! When the sailors learn that Jonah is running away from the very God who made the land and the sea (and so the one responsible for the storm), they fear greatly and ask the prophet what is to be done. The game is up for Jonah. He is a prophet; he knows God's will; he knows what has to be done. The only solution is to cast him overboard.

Jonah 1:13-17

The sailors hesitate lest they shed innocent blood. They try to reach land; perhaps, all God wants is to get Jonah ashore. But the storm increases. Then an amazing thing happens: the heathen sailors turn to pray to the Lord God. They acknowledge his law that punishment is due to those who kill the innocent. They beg that what they are about to do is God's will. How ironic! These pagans are praying that they be obedient to God's will and do what is right with the disobedient prophet of the Lord!

Jonah is cast into the sea and the storm ceases. The men on board ship fear God with a great fear and offer sacrifices to him. They make vows. We are not told what they vowed. Perhaps, it is now their intention to become worshippers of the God of the land and the sea?

God is not a God of destruction. He appoints a great fish to swallow Jonah and the fish obeys. Don't worry about how the fish manages to swallow a man whole or how Jonah survived three days and three nights in its belly. This is a story and imagination governs what happens in stories. I know of a lion called Wallace who swallowed a little lad whole! What we need to notice is that the fish is obedient to God's will, like the wind, the sea, the sailors and, later on, the castor-oil plant: all in marked contrast to disobedient Jonah.

Jonah 2

It is generally considered that the Psalm of Thanksgiving is out of place and may have been added to the story at a later stage than the original composition. Some would point out that it would be more appropriate after Jonah is spewed up on dry land. Be that as it may, we can imagine the time spent in the fish's belly as a time of retreat for Jonah during which he discovers his God again and re-dedicates himself to his service. First, we notice that Jonah "prayed to the Lord his God". He is no longer running away from his God; he is running to him. Secondly, the psalm is full of gratitude for the God who is saving Jonah. No one else can. "Deliverance belongs to the Lord", he sings. A few details need explanation.

Jonah 2:2

Sheol was regarded as the region of darkness where all the dead, good and bad, exist in ghostly fashion. We must remember that for most of the Old Testament period there was no belief in life with God after death, no belief in eternal joy or eternal punishment, for that matter; good and bad alike went to the misery of Sheol.

Jonah 2:4-7

While God is present everywhere (indeed, this is one of the lessons of the Book of Jonah), Jonah speaks of the presence of God in the Temple in Jerusalem, for that was where God was especially present among his people.

Jonah 3:1-5

God does not reprimand Jonah but quietly repeats the command. The content of the message is not yet given. But this time the "Arise" of God is followed quickly by "Jonah arose and went to Nineveh". The author exaggerates the size of the city; in fact, the length of the walls measured seven and a half miles, hardly a three days journey. But the larger the city, the larger the marvel at its conversion. Jonah journeys to the centre of the city and preaches a sermon of five words (in Hebrew). At last, we have the content of the message God intends for the people of Nineveh. The evil ways of the citizens will cause the city to be destroyed totally. And – surprise, surprise! – the people of Nineveh accept God's message instantly and proclaim a fast and dress in sack-cloth and ashes (the traditional signs of mourning and repentance). This immediate acceptance of God's warning by these pagans stands in contrast to the indifference shown by the people of Israel to the messages of their many prophets.

Jonah 3:6-9

Just as God was sitting on his throne at the beginning of our story, so now the mighty king of Nineveh is seated on his throne in his royal robes. On hearing of the prophet's proclamation, the king and all his nobles adopt the sack-cloth and ashes of repentance and decree that everyone else shall do the same. Just as Jonah was to "cry against" the great city, so now the whole population is urged to "cry mightily to God" to avert disaster. The prayer is that God will repent and turn from his fierce anger. There is no more startling idea in the Bible than the idea that God changes his mind in our regard.

Jonah 4:1-5

In order to understand what happens in this chapter, we must realise that Jonah knows well from the beginning what the outcome is going to be. That is why he runs away. He knows what God is like and, in his angry prayer, he points to those qualities of God which ensure forgiveness even for the wicked, pagan citizens of Nineveh. Jonah is angry, for two reasons. First, as one of God's Chosen People, he does not wish that God's mercy and forgiveness should be granted to any other than the Jewish people. Secondly, what Jonah and every other Jew wish for Nineveh is destruction and doom, as the Book of Nahum declares. Jonah does not want to be an instrument of saving Nineveh from what it richly deserves. "Make me an instrument of your peace" is not his prayer.

30

Revenge is what he wants. Jonah is so angry that he wishes to die.

Jonah 4:6-11

Though Jonah provides a shade for himself, verse 6 states that God provides a broad-leafed plant to save him from discomfort. It is clear from verse 8 that Jonah had no shade except that given by God's plant. There is some confusion in the text but the main outline is clear. Without being asked, God gives the angry prophet a plant to shade him from the burning sun. But God takes the plant away and Jonah's anger and death-wish return. Again, God's question is, "Why are you angry?". The lesson of the plant incident ought to be clear to the prophet. If God in his kindness provides the plant for Jonah without the latter's effort or merit, how much more is he likely to show mercy and forgiveness to all people, yes, even to the hated Assyrians of Nineveh? If Jonah is angry at the destruction of a mere plant, how much more ought he to be angry at the thought of the destruction of a great city and its people? God's final question is addressed to Jonah and the reader. Who are we to limit the mercy of God?

THE MESSAGE

All sorts of riches are presented in this little book. There is the lesson that we ought to listen to God's word even when it conflicts with our own views. But the essential message is, surely, that we must not restrict the mercy of God by our own narrow-mindedness. When this book was written, the people of Israel had turned in upon themselves and begun to regard the rest of the world, the Gentiles, as beneath contempt. Because they were God's chosen people, many of them adopted an intolerant, nationalistic spirit which limited the love and mercy of God to themselves. All that was due to the non-Jewish world was God's anger and wrath, as the attitude of Jonah shows so clearly. But the writer of this humorous tale – and it is funny – gently but firmly reminds his countrymen that all people belong to God and he cares for all. The story contains the gospel message that God's mercy extends to all creation, that what God creates, he does not destroy.

31

Incidentally, Jonah's sermon has five words. Preachers, please note. Short sermons are best.

IMAGES OF GOD

Briefly, the book is about the image of God and hinges around the description of God in 4:2. This description occurs frequently in the Old Testament (see, for example, Exodus 34:6; Numbers 14:18; Nehemiah 9:17; Psalm 103:8; Psalm 136; Jeremiah 32:18). "Steadfast love" is the Old Testament's final word on the meaning of God. The challenge to Jonah and to his contemporaries was to take that image seriously, to believe it rather than to pay lip-service to it. The challenge is there for everyone who would seek to limit God's mercy and forgiveness in any way. Those who used to say that outside the Catholic Church there was no salvation had not read the Book of Jonah. Jesus had. He taught that God "makes the sun to rise on the evil and on the good, and sends rain to fall on the just and unjust alike" (Matthew 5:45).

PRAYER

Psalm 136 is a prayer of thanks to the God whose steadfast love endures forever.

Chapter 3

Ruth: A woman of worth

We promised ourselves that we would begin our journey through the Scriptures with short steps. So, for our second step, we will read the Book of Ruth which has four pages in my Bible. This delightful short story is intended for our entertainment and our instruction. Though it is a work of fiction, it reflects the lives of ordinary people in Old Testament times. We don't know when the book was written (more about this later) or why it was written. We don't know who wrote it but whoever it was possessed an amazing talent. The Book of Ruth is a gem!

READING THROUGH

Keeping an eye out for names and places, I have noted down Bethlehem, Moab, Elimelech, Naomi, Mahlon, Chilion, Orpah, Ruth and Boaz.

Bethlehem of Judah is a small town, about five miles south-west of Jerusalem. King David came from around Bethlehem and, of course, over nine hundred and fifty years after David's time, Jesus was born there. Bethlehem is situated in the southern region of Israel called Judah. The name means "House of Bread" or "Storehouse for Food".

Moab is part of modern Jordan and is the name of the territory east of the River Jordan and rising from the shores of the Dead Sea. Hills rise steeply from the sea-shore and form a plateau which is excellent for grass crops and for pasturage. The people of Moab and the Jewish people were at war fairly frequently and could be regarded as traditional enemies but there were times of peace and friendship. Indeed, when King Saul was pursuing his son-in-law David and his band of rebels, David asked the king of Moab to look after his parents until more settled times came along.

Elimelech is the husband of Naomi. His name, which means "My God is King", occurs only in this book of the Bible.

Naomi is a key character in our story. The name "Naomi" may mean "the delight of God" or "My lovely one". In view of the fact that Naomi is a famine victim who has to emigrate to find food, and that she loses her husband and two sons and becomes a penniless widow, makes her name sound somewhat ironic. Surely a woman of sorrows and acquainted with grief!

Mahlon and Chilion, the sons of Naomi, marry Orpah and Ruth, two Moabite women. It is important to note that these marriages were mixed marriages from the religious and racial points of view. There is no satisfactory explanation of the meaning of these four names. Ruth, of course, is the heroine of our story. Boaz is a well-to-do farmer of Bethlehem and a relative of Naomi. He is a kind-hearted man, generous and fair, with an eye for a pretty woman and lucky enough to find Ruth, "a woman of worth".

READING THROUGH AGAIN

Ruth 1

Bethlehem is on the edge of the Wilderness (desert) of Judah, the land around it is poor and famine is not unheard of. Naomi, with her husband and two sons, must emigrate to survive. The immigrant family is received with friendliness in Moab for Mahlon and Chilion marry local girls. But tragedy strikes and Naomi loses her husband and her two sons. She decides to return to her own people. She tells her daughters-in-law to return to their own families and prays that each "may find a home" (1:9) and a husband. The two women wish to go to Bethlehem with Naomi but she explains that they must return to their people. The reason she gives is important for our story. Naomi is too old to marry again and, even if she were to marry and have sons, would it be fair to ask Orpah and Ruth to wait until they were grown? Better by far that these young, childless widows return to their families and find a home and a husband. Orpah kisses her mother-in-law and goes back to her people and her gods.

Not so Ruth! She refuses to abandon Naomi. Her plea to be allowed to accompany the older woman is very moving:

Where you go, I will go, where you lodge, I will lodge. Your people shall be my people, and your God my God. Where you die, I will die, and there I will be buried. May the Lord do so-and-so to me and more also, if even death parts me from you!

1:16-17

The last sentence is an old formula for swearing and one probably drew one's index finger across one's throat when saying the words. It means something like, "May God strike me dead if I don't do as I've promised".

Notice what is involved here: Ruth is leaving her own country, her own family, her own religion, her chances of getting a husband and children. Of her it should be said, "She has loved much" (Luke 7:47).

The women of Bethlehem welcome Naomi but she is now an embittered woman and she bewails her misfortune, blaming God for all that has happened to her. She declares that her name should be changed from "Delight of God" (= Naomi) to "Bitter One" (= Mara). Is this the God Ruth has taken into her life? Will she, too, be abandoned by the Lord and become an embittered, desolate and childless woman? Well, they arrive at harvest time and that may be a sign of hope.

Ruth 2

Our story-teller introduces Boaz, a wealthy man, related to Naomi by marriage. Will this prosperous kinsman be of any help to his poverty-stricken in-laws? Time will tell. Ruth decides to take matters into her own hands and seeks to provide for herself and for Naomi. Picking the crumbs that fall from the tables of the rich is ever the fate of the poor (Luke 16:21) so, because it is harvest time, Ruth sets out to glean. "To glean", my dictionary tells me, is "to gather corn left by the reapers." The Book of Leviticus lays down:

When you reap the harvest of your land, you shall not reap your field to its very border, neither shall you gather gleanings after your harvest. And you shall not strip your vineyard bare, neither shall you gather the fallen grapes of your harvest; you shall leave them for the poor and the sojourner: I am the Lord your God.

Leviticus 19:9-10

In this way, God says, the poor and the landless are to receive a share in the harvest. Note that Ruth is not only poor but she is a sojourner as well, that is, a resident alien, an immigrant who has no land.

By chance (or is it God's doing?), Ruth comes to that part of the field belonging to Boaz and makes an immediate impression on those who are reaping the harvest and on Boaz himself when he arrives. Notice the number of times the writer emphasises that Ruth is a foreigner (count them!); even so, Boaz is attracted to her. He explains that he has heard of her care of Naomi and is sure that God will reward her, the God "under whose wings you have come to take refuge" (2:12). The idea of taking shelter under God's protective wings is a very beautiful image of God's care. Jesus spoke of his love for the city of Jerusalem in the same way when he said,

> O Jerusalem, Jerusalem! How often would I have gathered your children together, as a hen gathers her brood under her wings, and you would not!
>
> *Luke 13:34*

To speak of being safe under the enfolding wings of God is common in the Book of Psalms (look up Psalms 17:8; 36:7; 46:6; 57:1; 61:2). Will Ruth find protection under the wings of her new God?

Boaz is obviously very taken with Ruth and goes out of his way to help her, even to the extent of a little deception (2:16). When Ruth reports all that has happened to her mother-in-law, Naomi blesses God, recognising that, after all, his "loving kindness has not forsaken the living or the dead". The older woman's faith in God's steadfast love is restored by the caring attention of "one of our nearest of kin", that is, by Boaz, a kind and generous man (2:20). No wonder Naomi advises her daughter-in-law to keep close to Boaz. Who knows what might happen?

Ruth 3

It appears that both Naomi and Ruth think that Boaz will marry Ruth with a little encouragement! Naomi advises Ruth on how best to move matters along. She is to put on her most alluring clothes and go to the threshing-floor where an end-of-

36

harvest party is in full swing. There she is to wait until Boaz's heart is merry with wine and he lies down to sleep. Ruth is "to go and uncover his feet and lie down".

Ruth obeys Naomi's instructions immediately and, when Boaz is asleep in the corner of the threshing-floor, she comes softly, uncovers his feet and lies down. Her action is highly ambiguous, deliberately so, it seems to me, and the suggestion is clearly there that Ruth lay down alongside of Boaz. The explanation of this "forward" behaviour may be found if we turn our attention now to the word "kinsman", so frequently used in our story.

In Old Testament times, should a young woman be left a childless widow, one of her husband's family was obliged to marry her and the first son of that marriage was regarded as the son and heir of the dead man. You may read about this strange custom in Deuteronomy 25:15-10. There was a technical term for the one who was supposed to marry the widow and it is this word which is translated "kinsman" (except at 2:1, where a different word is used). The idea was that one must fulfil one's obligations as a kinsman in order to preserve the integrity of the family. The widow and the land she inherited from her dead husband must not be allowed out of the family and the dead man must be allowed to live on in the life and memory of a son. The Hebrew word is often translated as "redeemer" and lies behind the idea of Jesus as our redeemer. More on this later. For the moment, notice that when the word occurs, either as a noun or as a verb in Ruth's story, it refers to one who has to fulfil family obligations and ensure that Ruth and the little bit of land belonging to her and Naomi remains in the family and that she is not left a helpless widow. Look up 2:20; 3:9; 4:1; 4:6; 4:8; 4:12.

To return to the story, when Boaz discovers Ruth, she asks him "to spread his skirt over her", which is a proposal that he marry her! Boaz again blesses her and praises her for not running after young men (is Boaz getting on a bit?) but rather honouring her widowhood and proving to all in the town that she is "a woman of worth". Then he tells her that he is not her nearest kinsman, not her redeemer, but that, given the opportunity, he would gladly marry her. Here, I think, lies the explanation of Ruth's behaviour (apart from the fact that she was a girl who didn't let the grass grow under her feet!). It is clear from 3:2 that Naomi was aware of a number of relatives but did not know who was the nearest and, therefore, did not know which one had the duty to marry the widow of Chilion. Wrongly, she assumed it was Boaz. And, perhaps, because Boaz does not appear to be in the first flush of youth, she advised the pretty woman to further the romance by placing the man in a compromising situation. Be that as it may, Boaz announces that he is not the kinsman and Naomi's plans seem to have badly misfired. But Boaz says that he will see the matter through and either compel the nearer relative to marry Ruth or to marry her himself. The present he gives her would seem to suggest that all will turn out right.

Ruth 4

Our story hastens to joyful conclusions. A meeting is held at the city gate, the usual place for conducting legal affairs. The nearer relative waives his right with respect to the widow and the parcel of land which goes with her. The reason for this decision is not clear but the man may have been holding out for a more prosperous woman! Boaz is now clear to marry Ruth and this he is most happy to do. The people at the gate and the influential citizens ("the elders", not necessarily old men but wise ones) who witness the agreement bless Ruth (count the number of times she is blessed in the story). They pray that she may be like the beautiful sisters, Leah and Rachel, the wives of Jacob, who had eight sons and one daughter between them. The reference to Perez, Tamar and Judah becomes clear to those who read Genesis 38, another story involving a reluctant redeemer/kinsman.

The story ends with great joy. Naomi is blessed because, in the end, God does not leave her outside the family but provides a kinsman for her. Boaz restores her to life by enriching her old age with children. The grandmother takes the child to her bosom and nurses it. It is as if her own sons had been given back to her: "Unto her a child is born, in the city of David" (Luke 2:11). Indeed, the foreign immigrant, the pagan-born, poverty- stricken Ruth becomes the great-grand-mother of King David and the mother-ancestor of another child born in the city of David, Jesus who is Christ our Lord.

The book abounds with kindnesses done, over and above the call of duty. The pagan people of Moab accept the famine-stricken immigrants from Bethlehem. Elimelech and Naomi are made welcome in a foreign land; their sons marry into local families. Ruth stays with Naomi when prudence would recommend that she return to her own people. Boaz is exceedingly kind to Ruth, though he is under no obligation to her. He provides her with food and protection; and kindness leads to love, love to a wedding and a child. Above all, behind the story lies the guiding hand of God, the one who is blessed because he turns the bitter heart of Mara and she becomes Naomi again, the delight of God.

The idea of kinsman/redeemer ought to remind us of what we mean when we call Jesus our redeemer. What Boaz did for Ruth, Jesus does for all. He brings us back into the family. Jesus shouts (if we would listen) that God has one family and he won't allow any strays. Even one sheep wandering off is a headache for God. He must be up and scouring the countryside. Jesus, God-with-us, is our kinsman who sees that no one is left outside.

By the way, did you notice that Boaz made Naomi welcome with bread and wine? Ring any bells?

Some would say that this story was written after some of the Jews returned from the Exile, around 530 B.C.E. (Fifty years before the country had been devastated and the people carried off to foreign lands.) The few thousand who returned to Jerusalem were afraid that, if they married with neighbouring peoples (such as the Moabites), they would be absorbed and God's people would disappear. So marriages to foreign women were forbidden (see Ezra 10). Our story-teller may be reminding his audience that hostility to other people, looking down on them and refusing to associate with them, is not the way. If Israel is to be "a light to the nations" (Isaiah 49:6), then she must adopt a broader view. Gently, our author points out that, after all, the great-grandmother of King David was a foreign woman. The Christian reader will want to share the view of the writer because he will recall that from the foreign blood of Ruth came Jesus of Nazareth (Matthew 1:5).

The Book of Ruth provides an excellent basis on which to

begin discussion on such important subjects as bereavement, widowhood, childlessness, mixed marriages, emigration and immigration and women's plight in a man's world.

IMAGES OF GOD

When we read a Bible story, we should always ask the question, "What kind of God is in there?". So, what kind of God had Naomi and Ruth to deal with? Is Naomi right? Has God given her the back of his hand? – "the hand of the Lord has gone forth against me" (1:13). Is she right to blame God for the death of her husband, the deaths of her sons, her childless and lonely widowhood? – "the Almighty has dealt very bitterly with me" (1:20). It is fine and even easy to find God in the smile of the new-born child, to see God in the happy ending, to praise him when all is well. But where is God in the suffering of the world, in the lonely passion of a bitter woman, in the childless poverty of a pagan girl? Where is God when we need him? Does the God of this story ask you to re-examine your notion of God? Does he call on you to look again at your views on the issues noted in the last paragraph?

PRAYER

Perhaps, a prayer for children, that they may be "nourishers of our old age" (3:15) and for all, that God may be to us, as to Naomi, "a restorer of life".

40

Chapter 4

Creation stories

We have started our journey through the pages of Scripture with small steps. Now we must lengthen our stride. We will tackle the Book of Genesis, a tall order indeed, but we shall proceed with care and, gradually, build up an understanding of one of the greatest and most important books of the Bible.

Explanation

A word of explanation before we start. The word "Genesis" is a Greek word meaning "beginnings" and is not the original Hebrew title of the book. But it is a good one because it summarises its main teaching, namely, that God constantly seeks new beginnings for the people of the world when violence threatens to overwhelm them.

Genesis is really a collection of stories from the rich tradition of Jewish story-telling. Over many centuries, these stories were handed down by word of mouth, passed on from parents to children. Gradually, some stories were written down, perhaps, to make sure that they were not lost or forgotten. This means, of course, that a book such as Genesis may be assembled at a late date, yet contain material that is very much older than the final product. It may be that the Book of Genesis did not reach its final form until about 400 years before the time of Jesus but it contains material from many centuries before. Collections of written stories from various parts of the Holy Land were lovingly made and lovingly stitched together by some unknown genius to form a new story which we call the Book of Genesis. I say "a new story" because, although the raw materials of his book were old, yet the author, in putting these old stories together, gave them a new meaning. This is inevitable. Suppose you have lots of colourful patches, bits and pieces collected over the years, and you decide to make a patch-work quilt. Out of the small pieces, you create something new. Now you have a quilt, whereas before all you had was a jumble of odds and ends. The example (though we shall use it again) is not perfect. But you can see that, by joining originally separate stories together, the author of Genesis must arrange them according to his own pattern, put on them his own particular stamp and use them to promote his own ideas.

Caution

The Book of Genesis is a difficult book, not made easier by the fact that many adult Christians have the impression that it was composed primarily for children and contains rather quaint fairy tales. I have a Sunday School leaflet which informs me that Noah's ship was 145 metres long and that no longer ship was built in the world until Cunard built the *Etruria* in 1884!

Worse still, there are those who would isolate the story of the Fall of Adam and Eve from the rest of Genesis and, indeed, the rest of the Bible, and point to that as the essential message of the book. Such readers manage to make sin the be-all and end-all of the human story. We shall strive, on the one hand, to avoid trivialising some of the most profound passages of Scripture and, on the other hand, we shall endeavour to keep God (and not sin) at the centre of things.

GENESIS 1

Creation stories

There are two accounts of the creation of the world and of men and women in the Book of Genesis, accounts which are very different and, indeed, contradictory. For example, in the first account, God creates men and women by his word, out of nothing; in the second account, man is made out of the dust of the ground and woman is fashioned from one of the man's ribs. Many other irreconcilable differences will be apparent, even to the inattentive reader. However, there is no cause for alarm. What we have are two fictional stories which are presented to convey great truths. They are not scientific accounts of how the universe came to be. The writers of these tales were not scientists but teachers of religious insights who used stories much in the way that Jesus did to convey his teaching.

Every people of the ancient world had stories about the origin of peoples and things and the Jews were no exception. Not only did they have their own stories but they knew and borrowed from the creation stories of their neighbours in the Near East. Indeed, the two creation accounts in Genesis have been influenced in some details by other stories that have come down to us from that part of the world. Nevertheless, the accounts of creation in the Bible are unlike the tales of their pagan neighbours. Indeed, they were written to oppose pagan ideas and to assert fundamental truths of the faith of Israel.

The first creation story

There are few finer pieces of writing in the Bible than the magnificent first chapter. It opens with the sentence, "In the beginning God created the heavens and the earth" and concludes, "these are the generations of the heavens and the earth when they were created". Between these two statements we have a very carefully constructed account of God's creative activity within a seven-day framework. The reader must understand that this framework is artificial and tells us nothing about when or how our world was created. The story is not based on human memory (the world is too old for that) but on human imagination.

READING THROUGH

The following important elements call for comment: the nature of God, the spirit of God, man made in God's image, the blessing of humankind, the goodness of "everything that he had made", the origin of the Sabbath.

God

It is God and God alone who creates. Pagan creation stories present many gods and goddesses as creators but the Bible is clear that there is only one God. (The plural, "us", in 1:26 does not mean that God was addressing some other god or gods; nor does it refer to the Trinity. It is a plural of deliberation, used to indicate the profound seriousness with which God determines to create men and women.) This God is not part of the universe; he is independent of it and is its sovereign ruler. He is all-powerful so that a mere word ("let there be light!") is enough to bring things into being. Though distinct from his creation, God is deeply concerned for it. This is clear from the fact that he confers something of his own goodness on all that he makes. On men and women and animals he gives the special gift of his blessing.

Spirit of God

The spirit of God moving over the face of the waters is not the Holy Spirit of the Blessed Trinity, as the Revised Standard Version seems to suggest. Other translations have "a mighty wind", "an awesome wind", or "God's breath". The author imaginatively envisages God's breath as the source of life and order which utters the word that overcomes chaos. In the Hebrew language the same word is used for breath, wind and spirit.

In God's image

Man and woman are made in the image of God. We must not seek the image of God exclusively in our spiritual nature. The image of God is not to be found in the soul but in the whole person. We must note, too, that it is not lost by sin, original or otherwise (see Genesis 5:1 and 9:6 for evidence that God's image remains even after the fall of Adam). In fact, the text supplies the answer. As God creates men and women in his own image, he gives them dominion over all creation. We are like God in that he shares with us his sovereignty over all that he had made; we receive responsibility from God for creation: "He granted them authority over the things upon the earth" (Sirach 17:2). Psalm 8 expresses the matter with great beauty:

When I look at thy heavens, the work of thy fingers,
the moon and the stars which thou hast established;
what is man that thou art mindful of him,
and the son of man that thou dost care for him?
Yet thou hast made him little less than God,
and dost crown him with glory and honour.
Thou has given him dominion over the works of thy
   hands;

thou hast put all things under his feet,
all sheep and oxen, and also the beasts of the field,
the birds of the air, and the fish of the sea.
O Lord, our Lord, how majestic is thy name
in all the earth!

The blessing

Again and again, in the Old Testament, we are reminded
that God is the one whose steadfast love endures forever. The
New Testament declares simply, yet astonishingly, that God is
love (First Letter of John 4:8). There is never a time when God
ceases to love us; his love is constant, forever. It is in the
context of God's enduring love for us that we must locate the
idea of blessings.

Blessings are of three kinds. First, there are occasions when
we bless God. Obviously, such blessing does not confer any
benefit on God; rather, the blessing is an act of faith and
thanksgiving, a recognition of God's constant love. A beautiful
example of such a blessing is to be found in Ephesians 1:3-10,
where God is blessed for all that he has done through his Son
Jesus Christ.

Secondly, there are instances where God declares people
to be blessed. These are declarations that God's steadfast love
is shown in a particular way. Such blessings are a participation
in the very love of God itself, manifest in a particular gift. The
Beatitudes (which means "the blessings") in Matthew 5:1-11
are of this kind. It is worth noting that all the gifts mentioned
in the Beatitudes really amount to the same thing: all who are
blessed live in the heart of God.

Thirdly, there are blessings we confer on each other, on our
food, our homes, our livestock, and on ourselves. Such
blessings are prayers, hopes and wishes that God's goodness
and love surround what we bless. Our simple "God bless!" is
a prayer that God's constant love may envelop the one we
bless. When we bless ourselves we are praying that we may
experience God's steadfast love every moment of the day and
reminding ourselves that even in dark moments we are never
beyond the pale of God's love.

There are two blessings in the first creation story; at verse
22, God blesses "all creatures great and small" and, at verse 28,
he blesses the man and the woman. God's blessing is,

therefore, effective for all living creatures, for everything that has the breath of life. For the man and woman, it consists in begetting, conception, birth and the succession of one generation after another. God is promising his continuous, creative power, his active presence in the process of multiplying and filling the earth. We are invited to see in the fertility of creation, in our own fertility, a sure sign of God's ever-present steadfast love. It should be noted, however, that the blessing to increase and multiply and fill the earth goes hand in hand with dominion over all creation. We must exercise dominion with responsibility. The blessing is that we fill the earth, not overcrowd it. And, perhaps, it is necessary to add that the blessing of fertility and the responsibility for dominion are conferred equally on women and men.

It was very good

After each act of creation God "sees" that what he has made is good. When all has been created, he observes that it is very good. What is created is good in the eyes of God. Creation is good simply because God regards it as good. We might say that the goodness of creation consists in God keeping an eye on it. The constantly recurring sentence, "And God saw that it was good", is telling us that God constantly recognises the goodness of all that he has made. The final verdict that all creation is very good invites us to join in praise, not only of creation, but of its creator. The basis for all praise in the Bible is the recognition that all that God does for us is very good.

The word for "good" in Hebrew contains the idea that something is good, not only if it is beautiful, but if it is suitable for the purpose for which it is made. In declaring creation to be very good, God is not only attesting to its beauty but also affirming its fittingness for fulfilling its purpose.

The Sabbath

The origins of observing a rest-day, a Sabbath, are obscure. So, too, are the reasons for its observance. In some parts of the Bible, the Sabbath is seen as a reminder of deliverance from slavery in Egypt (Deuteronomy 5:15); in others, it is seen as a time for reflection so that the devout Jew may know "that I am the Lord your God" (Ezekiel 20:20) or the one who gives holiness to his people (Ezekiel 20:12). Other texts, like Genesis

2:3, point out that the Sabbath rest is observed in imitation of God's rest after creation (Exodus 20:11). What is clear is that the Sabbath is a gift to us from the Jewish people and their religious traditions (no other ancient peoples had a day of rest) and we should treasure it. By observing the Sabbath, we recognise God as our creator; we live by his enduring love; we proclaim that we intend to direct our lives according to his holy will.

PRAYER

Psalm 148 is a prayer in praise of the God of creation.

Chapter 5

Adam and Eve
and original blessings (1)
Genesis 2:4-25

Did you know that the Bible was divided into chapters by an Englishman? The ancient texts of both the Old and New Testaments were not written in neat paragraphs or chapters, nor had they verse or sentence divisions as our modern Bibles do. The ancient reader was confronted with a hand-written scroll or book with no chapter divisions, no paragraphs, no verse divisions, no commas, no full-stops! When, for example, Jesus wished to refer to a passage of Scripture, he had to supply as much detail as possible so that his listeners could identify the passage. In Mark 2:25 (notice how easy it is for us to refer to a passage), in response to a question of some Pharisees, Jesus answers,

> Have you never read what David did when he was in need and hungry, he and those who were with him; how he entered the house of God, when Abiathar was high-priest, and ate the bread of the Presence... and also gave it to those who were with him?

Notice that, in order to recall the incident to the Pharisees, Jesus had to supply numerous details – that the incident occurred in the time of David, more precisely when Abiathar was high-priest (of a temple at Nob, not Jerusalem), that David and his soldiers ate the holy bread.

How much simpler the procedure is today! For in the thirteenth century the Bible was divided into chapters of approximately equal length. The system was devised by Stephen Langton (?1150-1228) who was a professor at the University of Paris and who later became Archbishop of Canterbury and a Cardinal and had a hand in drawing up the Magna Carta. He introduced the system of chapter divisions

48

into a new edition of the Bible called the Parisian Bible about 1206. The modern chapter divisions do not differ very much from those of Stephen Langton.

The division of chapters into verses is more recent. After some experimentation, Robert Stephanus (or Étienne), a Frenchman, in 1551, produced a New Testament and, in 1555, an Old Testament, with a system of verse divisions, that has become standard and is now employed in every edition of the Bible.

Thanks to these two scholars, and to the invention of printing, we have very readable and convenient Bibles. Had Jesus our advantage, he would have said to the Pharisees, "Look up the First Book of Samuel, chapter 21 and read verses 1 to 6". (By the way, if you compare the story in 1 Samuel with the summary given by Jesus in St Mark's Gospel, you will notice that the priest in question was Ahimelech and not Abiathar.)

I mention these matters because our journey through the Book of Genesis begins with familiar ground. The creation of Adam and Eve and their expulsion from the Garden of Eden are stories well known to all Christians, even to those who never read the Bible. It is unlikely that, in the case of Scripture, familiarity breathes contempt but it may result in complacency. Because we know the stories, we may be in danger of taking their meaning for granted rather as we do our convenient chapter and verse divisions. We are in danger on two fronts. First, we may isolate chapters 2 and 3 and seek to understand them independently of the rest of the Book of Genesis and, indeed, of the rest of the Bible. Secondly, we may so concentrate our attention on original sin that we forget original grace. Yes, ORIGINAL GRACE!

We must realise that what is really original is God's graciousness, his steadfast love (grace) in creating a world which reflects his own goodness, in creating men and women who are blessed with divine authority and responsible fruitfulness. None of this outpouring of God's love is lost by what we call "original sin". That is why the first chapter of the Bible is first – to remind us that what is original, and what endures forever, is not sin, but goodness and love and blessing.

The following matters call for explanation: Adam and Eve, the tree of life, the tree of knowledge of good and evil, the four rivers and the serpent.

Adam and Eve

It is noticeable that the names of the man and the woman are not given until the end of chapter 3. Yet it is clear that the "man" of chapters 2 and 3 is Adam and that the woman is Eve. It is the meaning of the names that is important. The word *adam* is related to the Hebrew word *adamah*. In Genesis 2:7, we read that "the Lord God formed the *adam* out of the dust from the *adamah*. Two things are clear.

First, the writer is not referring to an individual. The word *adam* occurs 555 times in the Old Testament with a variety of meanings. The word tends to be used to describe a human being, without any further qualification, when a writer wishes to speak of what we might call "humanity in general". The word does not mean a person, a particular man or a particular woman. It does not refer to an individual but to the species, to humankind. The Adam of chapters 2 and 3 of Genesis is humanity.

A second consideration is equally clear. The man (*adam*, humanity) is formed out of the dust of the *adamah*. The word *adamah* means the face or the skin of the earth. The writer wishes to highlight the bond between humankind and the earth, between *adam* and *adamah* (which is a feminine noun, by the way). The play on words points to a relationship: human beings and earth belong together; the earth is there for humanity and human beings are there to be responsible for it and to populate it:

> For thus says the Lord,
> who created the heavens
> (he is God!),
> who formed the earth and made it
> (he established it:
> he did not create it a chaos,
> he formed it to be inhabited!)
>
> *Isaiah 45:18*

Humanity is dust and will return to dust (the Old Testament and its people, for the most part, did not believe in life after death; when it says we return to dust, that is precisely what it means - body, soul, mind, spirit, return to the dust of the earth). Having spent its days tilling the ground, the *adam*/humanity, returns from whence it came (compare Genesis 2:7 and 3:19). Thus, even before the expulsion from Eden, we have emphasis on the frailty, the limitations of humanity's earthly existence. It is clear, too, that human beings are directed to the earth in their work and that the earth is directed towards the work of human hands. The man in the Garden of Eden is placed there "to till it and keep it" (Genesis 2:15); he must work the soil and maintain it, if he is to live, even in Eden.

The author imagines (and this is a story of imagination, not of human history) God forming a "mud pie" and shaping it into a human figure and, as it were, giving a kiss of life to the inanimate statue, causing it to become a living being (Genesis 2:7). There is great danger here that the reader will believe that the sentence "and breathed into his nostrils the breath of life" means "God created the human soul". In the view of the Bible, a human being does not consist of a number of parts (like body and soul and so on). To exist as a human being is to exist as an undivided unity, a unity that cannot be sundered, even by death. It is not correct, either, to read into the sentence that something of the divine was given to human beings at creation, any more than it is to think of "the breath of life" as "the human soul".

The breath of life means simply being alive; it means that God gave life to human beings – and nothing more. Nor does 2:7 give any grounds for the opinion that God created human beings to be immortal; those who would maintain that Adam and Eve received the gift of immortality must come to terms with the fact that the Old Testament has no belief in such a doctrine.

In a rather odd verse, Genesis 3:20, Adam names the woman Eve, "because she was the mother of all the living". By giving a name to the woman, the man is saying what she means to him, for the name in Hebrew resembles the word for living. The woman means life to him. The odd thing about the verse is that Adam names Eve "the mother of all the living" before she has borne any children. It may be that the naming should come after the birth of Cain in chapter 4 and the text may have undergone some accidental alteration. Whatever the explanation, the man recognises what his wife means to him: she is the bearer of life.

Eden

The word *Eden* occurs 17 times in the Old Testament and there seem to have been many stories concerning a garden of/ in Eden, and of the same or another garden called "the garden of God". The diligent reader may wish to look at the following texts outside the Book of Genesis: Ezekiel 28:13; 31:9,16,18; 36:35; Joel 2:3; Isaiah 51:3. The attentive reader will note that chapter 2 speaks of "a garden in Eden" and that chapter 3 refers to "the garden of Eden".

It is quite clear that Genesis 2:8 intends to refer to an actual region, a definite land. But this land cannot be located geographically; it cannot be shown to exist outside the Bible. It is probable that the name "Eden" means "delight". By telling us that Eden is "in the east", the writer wishes to convey that the garden of delight is far, far away, as far away as the mythical Land of Youth.

The tree of life

The idea of the "tree of life" was well-known in Israel in ancient times, and not just on the basis of chapters 2 and 3 of Genesis. The reader may wish to examine the New Testament use of the idea in the Book of Revelation (2:7; 22:1-4; 22:14-19). Nor was the idea confined to Israel but is to be found in many stories of the ancient Near East. In the famous Epic of Gilgamesh, composed before the Book of Genesis, the hero discovers a plant which confers immortality and which is named "Man becomes young in old age". He is confident that on eating it he will return "to the state of my youth". Unfortunately, a serpent (yes, a serpent!) steals the plant and the hero is destined to die as all mortals are. It is likely that the tree of life in the Genesis story is meant to be understood as signifying immortality.

The tree of the knowledge of good and evil

The tree of the knowledge of good and evil is that which is forbidden to the man in Genesis 2:17. The tree of life is mentioned only in 2:9 and 3:24 and, apparently, is not specifically forbidden. It assumes great importance at the end of the story.

The tree of the knowledge of good and evil is said to produce fruit "to make one wise", and this wisdom is said to consist of "the knowledge of good and evil". We may note, for the moment, that the capacity to distinguish good from evil is seen as a prerogative of God, for should the man and woman eat of the tree, they "will be like God, knowing good and evil". In the First Book of Kings 3:9, Solomon prays to God for an understanding mind so that he may "discern between good and evil". In Isaiah 7:16, the prophet speaks of a child growing up and says "before the child knows how to refuse the evil and choose the good ...". It would appear that while knowing good and evil is God's concern, yet human beings need to share in this capacity and are not grown up until they can do so. We shall have to tread carefully!

The four rivers

Of the four rivers which flow from the garden, two are well-known, the Tigris and the Euphrates. The Pishon and the Gihon are unknown (but the Second Book of Chronicles 32:30 refers to "the waters of Gihon", a well-known Jerusalem spring) and, most probably, are imaginary. As we use the number 4 to speak of the whole world ("the four corners of the earth"), so the ancient writer speaks of four great rivers which water the whole of the earth. The intention is to highlight God's loving care for humankind in Eden. So plentiful is the water that waters this oasis of delight that it spills over into four great rivers and waters the face of the earth – an indication that God is mindful, not only of Eden, but of the whole of the earth in which man and woman will soon have to make a home.

The serpent

In the world of Eden there are only two people in the midst of all the animals named by man. So if our story requires a "tempter", then, an animal it will have to be. Of all the creatures that the Lord had made, the serpent was the most subtle, astute, clever. The cunning of the serpent is proverbial: Jesus advised his disciples to be as wise as serpents (Matthew 10:16). The man and the woman will be led astray by listening to the words of a clever-talking snake, a creature of God.

We must be careful not to read into the story what is not there. The serpent is not Satan in disguise; it is not Satan who is cursed in Genesis 3:15 (see Job 1 for an Old Testament understanding of Satan). The serpent is not to be confused with the devil who, in Christian tradition, is the tempter and source of evil. There is some evidence in the Bible that ancient Hebrews (the proper name for early Jewish people) regarded the serpent as the animal of life and death (Numbers 21:4-9 and 2 Kings 18:4) and, indeed, many ancient religions regarded the serpent as divine or as possessing divine powers. In the religion of the Canaanite peoples, who occupied the land of Israel before and along with the Jewish people, the serpent was the symbol of fertility. Whatever the role of the serpent in ancient religions, in Genesis 3 our main concern should be not with what the snake is but rather with what it says.

PRAYER

Count your blessings, consider all the wonderful things God has done for you and give thanks for such steadfast love with Psalm 136.

Count the number of times God is described as the one whose steadfast love endures for ever in this psalm. We might call it a psalm for the slow learner!

Chapter 6

Adam and Eve
and original blessings (2)
Genesis 2:4-3:24

The Bible is a collection of books, consisting, in Catholic editions, of seventy-three books. Suppose you had these seventy-three books, not bound together, but each in its own separate binding. Suppose further that you are a librarian and you must decide on which shelf you should place each book. Where would you put the Book of Jonah? Into the history section? Or, perhaps, it really belongs in the fiction department? What of the Book of Ruth? A fictional love story? Or is it a piece of propaganda, arguing that racially mixed marriages are permissible? The Book of Psalms will not cause you much trouble – you may put it in the poetry section or in the prayer section. But what are you going to do with the Book of Revelation? Is it fact or fiction? Clearly, it is important to decide what kind of writing a particular book is, if we are to understand it properly. Even within a single book, we may find different kinds of writing. When we read the Gospels, we find some historical facts concerning Jesus but we find lots of fiction as well. The parables are fictitious stories, composed by Jesus, to make some point or other. Consider, for a moment, the most famous parable of all, the Parable of the Prodigal Son. This is a fictitious tale composed by Jesus in order to explain something of the nature of God's mercy. It never really happened; it is a story. But that does not mean that it is not true! If it is perfectly acceptable for Jesus of Nazareth to invent stories (parables and the like) in order to teach profound truth about God and about ourselves, then why can't the writer of the Book of Genesis do the same? With this consideration in mind, we can now return to chapters 2 and 3 of Genesis.

The second creation story

The very careful reader will have noticed many differences between the first creation story and the second. One very noticeable fact is that each account has different names for the creator. In the first account, the creator is called "God" and, in the second, he is called "Lord God". The image of God which emerges from each story is quite different, too. We shall see more about this later; for the moment, we may note that, in the first account, God is aloof from creation and creates by the power of his word alone, whereas, in the second account, we have a much more "homely" picture of God, a picture of a God who walks in his garden in the cool of the day. From these, and other reasons, scholars believe that, at one time, these two creation stories existed separately. In fact, it is widely believed, and for very good reasons, that the first story was written some five-hundred years after the second, which is thought to have been composed about one thousand years before the time of Jesus. At some later stage, the two stories were combined, along with a host of other stories from Israel's rich traditions, to form what we know to be the Book of Genesis. It is important for readers of Genesis to have some awareness of the complex history of its composition. We must not think of one author, sitting down one day to write a book. What we must realise is that the book was put together from material that already existed, some of it very old indeed. The Adam and Eve story is among the oldest of biblical stories, whereas the first creation story is among the "youngest" of Old Testament stories. What we must endeavour to do is to try to understand what an author might have hoped to achieve by placing both side by side. We must try to balance what we learn from the first story with what we learn from the second. The two stories complement each other.

READING THROUGH AGAIN

Genesis 2

The second story of creation, as we have seen previously, pictures God making man out of the dust of the earth and bringing his clay model to life. Needing to find a place for the man, the Lord God planted a garden in Eden, in the east, and placed him there to till it and keep it. Concerned that it was bad for man to be alone, God created all the beasts of the field and the birds of the air (but no fish!) and brought them to the man to name. However, God's plan didn't work for, among the birds and animals, "there was not found a helper fit for him". For the Lord God, it was back to the drawing-board! And so out of the man's rib, the Lord God created a woman and brought her to the man. When he awoke and saw the lovely new creature, he burst into song:

This at last is bone of my bones
and flesh of my flesh;
She shall be called Woman,
because she was taken out of Man.

Genesis 2:23

Among the more important issues in the story so far, we need to comment more extensively on four:

(i)   men and women and their relationship;
(ii)   the value of work;
(iii) the naming of the animals;
(iv) the role of the two trees.

Men and women and their relationship
Is the second creation story the work of the world's first male chauvinist? After all, is not the man created first? Does not God offer all the animals to man as possible social companions? Is not Eve an afterthought, a second best, when God's first plan proved unacceptable to the man? Is not the woman created simply as "a helper fit for him"?

In the first creation story human beings were created last to highlight the fact that they are the pinnacle of creation. So it could be argued that, in the second creation story, woman is created last because she is the pinnacle of all creation! The English translation, "a helper fit for him", is not very accurate. The Hebrew would be more properly rendered by something like "the one opposite to him", or "the one counter to him". Even if the idea of "helper" cannot be excised from the text, it should be noted that the Hebrew word translated "helper" is used elsewhere in the Old Testament exclusively for God. For example:

Our soul waits for the Lord;
he is our help and our shield.

Psalm 33:20

What is remarkable is that the Old Testament uses the Hebrew word for "helper" only of God (in such phrases as "the Lord is my help and my protection") and of the woman whom the Lord brings to the man in Eden. And when the woman conceives, she exclaims, "I have gotten a man with the help of the Lord" (Genesis 4:1). So there is something very special about this "helper". She is a helper as the Lord (and only the Lord!) may be called a helper! While I do not mean that women are divine, it is quite clear that women are not inferior to men. It is to be with a woman that a man leaves his father and mother and cleaves to his wife. Of all the beings which the Lord God has made, a man is most near to God when he is with the "bone of my bones and flesh of my flesh".

The two human beings stood before each other naked and unashamed. The Bible affirms that the sexual relationship of the couple is at the heart of God's plan for humanity, a relationship which is a gift from creator to creatures for their mutual pleasure and self-giving.

The value of work

The Garden of Eden is not heaven. It is not the dwelling-place of God. It is the place assigned to human beings and it must be worked and cared for if it is to be of benefit to them. Work is not the result of the Fall and it is not a consequence of sin. It is part of God's order for creation; it is of the essence of human dignity.

Naming the animals

In chapter 5 of St Mark's Gospel, Jesus demands to know the name of a demon who has taken possession of a man and he is told that the demon's name is Legion. The point of seeking to know the name is that, in the understanding of the time, to know someone's name somehow gave one intimate knowledge of the other person, even to the extent of conferring a measure of control over the one named. What the writer of the first creation story calls "dominion", the composer of the second story conveys by the act of naming the birds and the animals. It should be noted, however, that when the man names the woman (Genesis 3:20), he is not claiming dominion over her. Rather, he is acknowledging that she, like God, gives life to the living.

The role of the two trees

The tree of life, as we have seen, represents immortality. In the Genesis story, immortality does not mean the immortality of the soul; it means everlasting life, life without death.

The tree of the knowledge of good and evil would appear to be a symbol of the capacity to distinguish good from evil. It is not clear how human beings, before or after the Fall, could function without such capacity. King David is praised for his ability "to discern good and evil", a power which makes the king "like an angel of God". But this should not be taken to mean that the king possesses divine power; the text (2 Samuel 14:17) is a piece of blatant flattery, not doctrine. In the famous Emmanuel text of Isaiah 7:14, the child to be born would know "how to refuse the evil and choose the good". The implication would seem to be that the child would have a more discerning mind than that of the faithless King Ahaz. However, the serpent tells the woman that, if she eats the fruit of the tree of the knowledge of good and evil, she "will be like God, knowing good and evil". It seems that some divine quality is forbidden to men and women. Human freedom is limited by God's command. There is a separation between the human and the divine. God is God and the creature is creature. Any stepping over the boundaries drawn by God is to invite disaster.

READING THROUGH AGAIN

Before we read through again the story of Adam and Eve in Genesis 3, we need to take a broad sweep through Scripture so that we may come to this first story with the last story, the story of Jesus, firm in our minds and hearts.

Of the seventy-three books of the Bible, forty-six belong to the Old Testament and twenty-seven to the New. Unlike the books of the Old Testament, all of which were written over a long period of time before the birth of Jesus, the books of the New Testament were written within a period of less than one hundred years after his death. Four of the books of the New Testament are called Gospels, and it is worth paying attention to the meaning of the word. We can trace it back from modern English to Anglo-Saxon (the language spoken by most people in Britain from the fifth century to the arrival of the Normans in 1066), from Anglo-Saxon to Latin, and from Latin to Greek, the language in which the Gospels were written. It is worth recalling the salient facts.

The word "gospel" is derived from the Anglo-Saxon "god-spell", meaning "good story", "good tidings", "good news". The Anglo-Saxon word is a translation of a Latin word "*evangelium*" which, in turn, is based on two Greek words, "*eu*" meaning "good" and "*angellion*" meaning "message" or "news"; (the word "angel" comes from "*angelos*", a messenger). So the word "gospel" means "a good message".

In the New Testament, it has two points of reference. First, it refers to the news concerning the birth, baptism, ministry and teaching, death and resurrection of Jesus. That is the way St Paul uses the word. He opens his great letter to the Jewish and Gentile Christian people of the city of Rome like this:

> Paul, a servant of Jesus Christ, called to be an apostle, set apart for the gospel of God which he promised beforehand through his prophets in the holy scriptures, the gospel concerning his Son.
>
> *Romans 1:1-3*

He declares,

> I am not ashamed of the gospel: it is the power of God for salvation to everyone who has faith.
>
> *Romans 1:16*

So the first meaning of the word refers to a message concerning what God has done through Jesus Christ. But, later, the meaning was extended to include four books, particularly treasured by Christians because they recorded, as did no other New Testament books, some of the words and deeds of Jesus, interpreted to show the great things God had done through his Son.

Yet it must be borne in mind that all Scripture, both the Old and New Testaments, is gospel, good News for the human family. Every book, from the Book of Genesis to the Book of Revelation, bears witness to the God who is for us (Romans 8:31), to the God whose steadfast love for us endures forever. The God who liberated the people of Israel from the tyranny of the Pharaohs is the same God who, through Jesus Christ, works for the freedom of all peoples. If God has chosen one people, is it not thereby to show that he has chosen all peoples? If God has made one day holy, is it not to teach that all days are holy? If God has raised one man from the dead, is it not to show that he will raise all men and women from the dead? The revelation of God's loving kindness is a seamless garment. It is not enough to speak of the Gospel according to Matthew or Mark or Luke or John. It is not enough to listen to the Good News in Paul or James or Peter. We must hear the Gospel of Isaiah, of Jeremiah, of the Books of Kings, of the Book of Genesis. And must we not say, too, that in the midst of the disaster of the disobedience told in the second creation story, we must look for good news, for gospel, for all humanity? It is not enough to witness the work of the serpent; we must trace the hand of God in the story, unbinding and setting free. It is not enough – and it is not good news – to speak of the sin of Adam and Eve; we must hear of their salvation.

Genesis 3

The story of Adam and Eve is not a unique human experience; it is the story of every man and woman. It is of the utmost importance to understand that when you read about Adam and Eve, you are reading about yourself. "All have sinned and fall short of the glory of God", says Paul (Romans 3:23).

When we set out on our journey through the two creation stories, a warning was sounded that they should not be read in isolation from the rest of the Book of Genesis, nor, indeed, from the rest of the Bible. We must now pay heed to that warning and see Genesis 3 as part of a wide canvas, sketching in broad strokes the sad tale of human rebellion and the signs of human hope, from the Garden of Eden to the Tower of Babel, from the Ark of Noah to the Cross of Jesus.

The whole of the Bible's teaching about God may be summed up in two statements. On the one hand, God is with us. On the other hand, he is distant. Theologians speak of God's immanence (his presence throughout the universe) and of his transcendence (his existence outside and apart from the universe). To put it another way, we know God, yet, at the same time, we don't. The Bible is clear that God is God and creature is creature and we must not confuse the One with the other. While blessings in abundance are given to Adam and Eve, they remain creatures. The tree of knowledge of good and evil stands in the Garden of Eden as a symbol of the domain of God; of every tree the humans may eat, they may enjoy all that is given to them. But they may not cross the dividing line between that which is theirs and that which is God's. To do so is to court disaster.

To that disaster the serpent lures Eve with the promise that she and her husband will be like God (or, perhaps, like "gods", for the text is not clear). The humans will be like God (or, gods) in that they will know good and evil. According to 2 Samuel 14:17, the ability to discern good and evil belongs to "the angel of God", that is, to God himself (angels, in the Old Testament, are not beings distinct from God, rather a respectful way of speaking about God). Whatever the precise meaning, the rebellion of Adam and Eve is an attempt to go beyond the limits of human freedom, to break down the distinction between creator and creature.

The rebellion is partly successful and God has to admit that "the man has become like one of us, knowing good and evil" (Genesis 3:22). But the creatures fail to "take also the tree of life, and eat, and live forever" (Genesis 3:22). Some elements in the story are deeply puzzling. In what, precisely, lay the (partial) success of the rebellion? Having eaten of the forbidden fruit, why do the man and woman not die, as God threatened?

Perhaps, the writer reflected on human experience in this way. Children, he sees, are not capable of serious moral choices because they have no experience of life. They live in blissful innocence (Garden of Eden) and are cared for by their parents (God providing for the needs of the couple). All that is required is that they obey their parents and they will be safe in the paradise of childhood (God commands obedience). Such innocent children do not have to make decisions which can bring them into conflict with God. But children grow up and painfully discover an adult world where difficult choices must be made and responsible decisions taken. The sad experience of every man and woman is that good people make bad mistakes, often for good reasons. Many Christians supported Hitler because they wished to see an economic recovery in Germany and thereby they became implicated in the death of millions of people. Growing up inevitably brings us into conflict with God (we are all sinners), but we must grow up. The tragedy is that our capacity to make decisions is limited by our lack of wisdom. If we had immortality, we would have the time to learn from our mistakes, to recover from our short-sightedness.

Perhaps, that is what our writer saw as he looked on life. In some sense, we do share with God an instinct for the good and the bad. In some way, we are "like gods". But we are not God. We strive for the good but we fail. We soar to the heavens as saints, only to fall to the ground as sinners. We have not wings; we have feet of clay. This turmoil in the human condition our writer describes as a rebellion, as a tragic flaw in our make up. Humanity's problem is not that Adam and Eve took too much; it is that they took too little. They failed to eat of the tree of life.

Consequences

The consequences of the sinful disobedience are immediate. The eyes of both are opened and they know that they are naked. The Hebrew verb "to know" involves much more than the possession of intellectual awareness or knowledge; it means to experience with all one's being. When the Bible wants to say that a husband and wife make love, it says (as does Genesis 4:1) that the man "knew his wife" (notice that Mary says to the angel, "I don't know a man", meaning, "I have not experienced sexual relations": Luke 1:34). The Bible does not speak of sexual relations in this way because of shyness or false modesty. It does so because "to know" embraces physical, psychological, spiritual and emotional awareness. In some way, the rebellion of Adam and Eve damages humanity itself; men and women no longer relate to each other without guilt, embarrassment and even shame. Genesis is saying that our befuddlement over good and evil finds its way into the most intimate areas of our lives and leaves its scars even there.

– for the serpent

The serpent is condemned to crawl on his belly and eat the dust of the earth. Since the writer chose to make the serpent the villain of the piece, he had to be punished. Crawling about on one's belly is the least dignified of postures for the most subtle of all the wild creatures (Genesis 3:1) and dangerous, too, because of perpetual and instinctive human hostility. The enmity between the woman and the serpent should not be taken to refer to antagonism between the devil and humanity. There is no devil in this story and no amount of pious thinking can turn the serpent into one. Nor, therefore, does Genesis 3:15 refer to Christ or to Mary, as Martin Luther, for example, believed. Precisely what the writer meant remains obscure. We can't know everything.

What is clear is that God curses the serpent - and no one else!

– for the woman

God does not curse the woman. But he does point out the consequences of her action. For the woman child-bearing is to be a painful experience. Of course, bearing children and giving birth may not be, for many women, a distressing experience. But to the ancient (male?) writer of Genesis 3, it would have appeared so (read the poignant story of the death of Rachel in giving birth to a child she called "Ben-oni", "the son of my sorrow", in Genesis 35). Further, the woman is to be subject to her husband. But women's subjection is not, it should be noted, due to God's intention but to man's invention. Christ's victory over sin restored equality between women and men:

There is neither Jew nor Greek,
there is neither slave or free,
there is neither male nor female;
for you are all one in Christ Jesus.

Galatians 3:28

Unfortunately, this teaching of the apostle Paul, the Church's finest mind, was quietly and quickly abandoned.

– for the man

For the man, no curse either. But his keeping and tilling of the soil out of which he was made is reduced to drudgery. Thorns and thistles mar the landscape of trees "pleasant to the sight and good for food" (Genesis 2:9). Man's harsh relationship with the soil is resolved only in death. Again, notice, as in the pain of child-bearing, how limited the view of the writer is. Farming is not always soul-destroying and work not always a curse. The writer pictures human limitations in his terms, not ours. A reminder not to take the story too literally!

Gospel

There is good news here for those who have ears to hear. Yes, life is harsh betimes, the consequences of our decisions are beyond our control, our limited vision does not stretch to the horizon. We walk but haltingly. But we do not walk alone.

The care with which the Lord God made garments of skin and clothed the man and the woman speaks of a partner on life's journey. We are not abandoned. Unto Eve a child is given with the help of the Lord: the blessing of fruitfulness is the hope of humanity. There is a future and we are brought to it by a God who blesses us on our way. That is the good news for Adam and Eve and for all their children throughout the ages.

The gospel of the Fall is the good news that, in our tragic human condition, God is with us. It is the same gospel told to us by Jesus: "behold, I am with you always, to the close of the age" (Matthew 28:20).

PRAYER

A prayerful reflection on Psalm 53 provides a salutary reminder of how, without wisdom, we turn away from the God who looks down from his heavens upon his people.

Chapter 7

To Adam and Eve – A son
Genesis 4-5

The Book of Ecclesiasticus is not, I suspect, everyone's cup of tea. But it has its interesting aspects. For one thing, it is one of the few books of the Bible the name of whose author is known. The author was Joshua ben Sirach, which is Hebrew for "Jesus, son of Sirach". We know something about the man, too. He was a Jewish scribe, that is, a professional teacher of the Torah (what we would call the teaching of the Old Testament) and he conducted a school, probably in Jerusalem, where he lectured young men on moral behaviour and other religious subjects. He wrote down his teaching in the Hebrew language around 180 B.C.E. and his grandson translated it into Greek fifty years later.

The reason for calling attention to the teaching of ben Sirach at this point on our journey through the Book of Genesis is to be found in one sentence:

From a woman sin had its beginning,
and because of her we all die.

Ecclesiasticus 25:24

Is Eve to blame? Scholars are almost unanimous in agreeing that ben Sirach here attributes the origin of sin and death to Eve. Blaming the woman has had a long and popular run; it is time to set the record straight. In the opinion of ben Sirach, death is part of the lot of humanity from the beginning: death is "the decree of the Lord for all flesh, the good pleasure of the Most High" (Ecclesiasticus 41:3-4). God created death when he created the world!

The Lord created man out of the earth, and turned him back to it again. He gave them a few days, a limited time, but granted them authority over the things upon the earth.

Ecclesiasticus 17:1-2

So, for ben Sirach, Adam and Eve, the Garden of Eden, forbidden fruit and rebellion, do not enter the picture. Death is not due to sin. Death is not the creation of sinners. Death is, from the outset, God's good pleasure!

This is a view not shared by other biblical writers but it can't be dismissed. And, if it is a legitimate view, then, it seems all the more unfair to blame the woman for sin and death and all the other consequences which appear to flow from the failure of Eve to resist the serpent.

What, then, does ben Sirach mean when he teaches that sin had its beginning in a woman and that "because of her we all die"? The fact of the matter is that he is speaking, not about Eve, but of an evil wife. This is clear from a proper consideration of the whole section (Sirach 25:16-26) which concerns itself with the effects of marrying the wrong woman: she'll be the death of you! The writer is a misogynist, a hater of women, and, as far as he is concerned, "no wickedness comes anywhere near the wickedness of a woman". Behind every evil man is a woman who led him astray!

And that is what he means when he says that sin has its beginning in a woman. This may be a piece of crass male chauvinism but it does not blame Eve for sin and death – as most people seem to think. In *The Jerusalem Bible*, a footnote to Ecclesiasticus 25:24 informs us that the writer is alluding to the first sin and to the guilt of Eve in the matter. We are further referred to St Paul to confirm, by the weightiest authority, woman's responsibility for sin and death in our world. But when we turn to Paul, we find no such thing! The text to which appeal is made reads:

> But I am afraid that as the serpent deceived Eve by his cunning, your thoughts will be led astray from a sincere and pure devotion to Christ.
>
> *2 Corinthians 11:3*

To be sure, Paul says that Eve was deceived by the serpent but he does not say that she is, therefore, guilty of bringing sin and death to our world. In fact, when he thinks about the matter, he reaches quite a different conclusion: "sin came into the world through a man" (Romans 5:12). Perhaps, it needs to be said, and with some bluntness, that there is no mention of sin in chapters 2 and 3 of the Book of Genesis! Not of Original Sin nor of any other kind of sin!

The misunderstanding of ben Sirach's teaching and the rush to make even St Paul say what he never thought are clear warnings of the dangers of taking one sentence from the Bible and forcing on it a meaning it does not have in its context. As we make our way through the story of Adam and Eve, we must be careful not to trivialise its presentation of human tragedy with childish notions and downright prejudice.

What was the sin?

Much ink has been spilt on the matter and not a few people seem to think that Adam and Eve committed some kind of sexual sin. Most jokes about the matter adopt this view. While unhappy with the usefulness of the word "sin" as an aid to understanding the tragedy of the Genesis story, nonetheless, one must face the question. Let it be said straightaway, there is not the slightest evidence to suggest that Adam and Eve were driven from Eden for some sexual offence. All we know, and all we need to know, is that the couple disobeyed a direct command of God because of their desire "to be like God". The man and the woman together attempted to overcome the distinction between the divine and the human; they sought to cross the boundaries drawn by God. As we have remarked before, the tree of the knowledge of good and evil stands in the Garden as a symbol of the domain of God. Disaster awaits those who seek to storm that domain. It is the teaching of the Book of Genesis that humans constantly seek to devise ways and means to further their selfish desires rather than to live as the creatures God made. The story of Adam and Eve is the story of every human being: "All have sinned and fall short of the glory of God" (Romans 3:23).

The rebellion spreads

Cain and Abel are the first children. In their story we see again the story of their parents. The story-teller does not explain why God accepted the animal offering of Abel and not the fruit offering of Cain and the reason for God's preference must remain without explanation. What is clear is that God's regard of the one and rejection of the other provides the motive for conflict between the brothers. In other words, God's decision to act as he pleases is opposed by Cain. The first child becomes the first murderer.

The Lord asks of Cain the whereabouts of his brother and receives the reply, "I do not know; am I my brother's keeper?" God does not answer Cain's question, at least, not yet. Much will happen in human experience before the truth emerges. If we are to live in peace, if we are to live at all, we must learn to say to the whole world, "I am your brother! I am your sister!" But there is much to be learned before we can pass from the story of Cain to the story of Joseph.

We must not isolate the rebellion of Adam and Eve from the rebellion of Cain. Genesis 3, as we have seen, deals with crime and punishment. The story of Cain follows the same pattern. Just as in Genesis 3, there is a trial, face to face; questions are asked and inadequate, evasive answers are given. Punishment is meted out but it is tempered by mercy. As Adam and Eve were expelled from the Garden, so Cain is expelled from the land and becomes a wanderer.

There is a pattern here which ought to be observed. Note carefully:

1. God gives the blessing of children to Adam and Eve.
2. Cain refuses to accept the divine order of things, namely, that he is his brother's keeper.
3. Cain rebels and kills his brother.
4. God punishes Cain.
5. God saves Cain.

Try to trace this pattern in the story of Adam and Eve.

It is particularly important to notice that the mark of Cain is a sign of God's care and protection. It is this mark which will prevent the murder of Cain. In all the stories of human rebellion, Cain's, yours and mine, there are signs of God's determination not to write us off. God's love will not be outdone by sin. Original grace will always triumph over original sin.

There are many things in the Book of Genesis which should claim our attention. But we set out on our journey through its pages as beginners and we must not try to satisfy our curiosity on every point. So we will not explore every detail of chapter 4. But notice the Song of Lamech in verses 23-24. Violence is spreading. Lamech has been done a wrong and adopts a future policy – from now on he will revenge any wrong done to him seventy-sevenfold. You will recall that Jesus recommends forgiveness seventy-seven times, a divine reminder that it is mercy and not murder that blesses the face of the earth. Lamech's story is the same as Cain's, the same as Adam's, the same as Eve's. The refusal to live in the world on God's terms brings disaster. The flood-waters are held at bay by forgiveness, mercy, compassion. The flood-barriers are everywhere breached by violence.

PRAYER

If we would live in our world as God wishes, if we would live in peace and harmony, brothers and sisters together, we must live on God's terms, not ours. Psalm 96 is a song which puts the right perspective on creation.

Chapter 8

God and Noah
and Dr Woolley's telegram

There wasn't always a Bible. When Abraham journeyed from Ur of the Chaldees, he had no Bible in his baggage. When Joseph was sold into slavery in Egypt, he had no book to remind him of his God. Many hundreds of years later, in the time of (say) Isaiah the prophet, there was no written Sacred Scripture and the great prophet never speaks of there being one. The Old Testament, as we know it, was finally put together not very long before the time of Jesus. The people of the Old Testament and their religious beliefs were long in existence before their religious books were written.

And the same is true of the New Testament, though, to be sure, it was produced more rapidly than the Old. St Paul came to believe that Jesus had risen and was Lord not because he read about it in any written Gospel. Paul and all the first Christians believed, not because of what they read, but because of what they heard. The Church existed long before its holy books. In the beginning was the word, the spoken word.

In other words, the books of the Bible express the faith of a people, a faith which existed first in a people before it came to be written down. When most people could not read, when there were few books for anyone to read, faith in God was passed on from one generation to the next by story-tellers. These tellers-of-tales told of who God is, of what he does for the human family he created, of the hope he holds out for all who are born into the world. Children were not taught to read; they were taught to listen. Their hearts burned within them, set alight by the wonderful stories of their God and they, in turn, retold the tales, stirring and nurturing faith in their children. And, of course, stories didn't lose in the telling.

Many stories: One God

A famous Jewish rabbi (teacher) once said that God created people because he loves stories. When Jewish and, later, Christian peoples came to write down their faith, for the most part they wrote stories. The Bible, both the Old and the New Testaments, is a story-book. It is full of stories about good people and bad people (a lot of these), simple people, clever people, brave women and men, cowards and fools, rich and poor, winners and losers, believers and unbelievers. No matter how simple, no matter how complex, Bible stories tell one tale: God is in love with his creatures and his creation; he looks on all that he makes and what he sees is very good. We may think our world is in a very sorry state and, indeed, it is. But, so the Bible goes, God doesn't see us for what we are: he sees the potential.

The journey through Scripture is a testing one. We have to try to build our portrait of God from a great variety of stories. Sometimes, what is essentially the same story is given in various versions and it can be difficult to see the wood for the trees. The two Books of Chronicles, for example, go over much the same ground as the two Books of Kings, yet the attitudes and insights of each are dissimilar. We have come across two stories of creation (Genesis 1 and 2) and noted the different portraits of God in each. Such is the case in the accounts of the Flood and the matter is further complicated because the two versions are told, not one after another, but mixed up together. More about this later.

A telegram

In 1929, a famous British archaeologist, Sir Charles Leonard Woolley, was excavating in the Tigris-Euphrates Valley, that is, in the area of the world, more or less, where the Iraqi/Iranian war took place in the last decade. While sinking some shafts into hilly ground to discover what might have been buried beneath the surface, he came across the usual rubbish - broken pottery and the like – which one expects to find. (In a few thousand years, future archaeologists will be similarly exasperated digging up our plastic bags and empty coke cans.) However, in Woolley's case, as the shafts went deeper, something remarkable began to happen:

The shafts went deeper and suddenly the character of the soil changed. Instead of stratified pottery and rubbish we were in perfectly clean clay, uniform throughout, the texture of which showed that it had been laid there by water... the clean clay continued until it attained a thickness of a little over eight feet... no ordinary rising of the rivers would leave behind it anything approaching the bulk of this clay bank; eight feet of sediment imply a very great depth of water, and the flood which deposited it must have been of a magnitude unparalleled in local history.

From Dr Woolley's Ur of the Chaldees

Soon a telegram was winging its way to the newspapers of the world: "We have found the Flood!" There was much excitement. And when some old timbers were unearthed on the mountains of Ararat in Turkey, some years ago, there were those who claimed that Noah's ark had been found. But scientific examination revealed that the timber was no more than seven or eight hundred years old. Sir Leonard's further excavations were to show that he had stumbled on the remains, not of a universal flood, but of a local disaster. There is no evidence to lead us to believe in a catastrophic worldwide flood or that one solitary vessel once contained all that was left of humanity, birds, beasts and reptiles. The story of the Flood is a product of human imagination, not a history of the day the rains came!

Once upon a time

If we have no evidence of a universal flood, we have an abundance of universal flood stories. There are nearly three hundred stories that tell of a great flood which destroyed the whole world, stories which come from all parts of the world. The question arises, therefore, if we have no reason to believe that there ever was a universal flood, why are there so many stories, from so many different peoples and places, telling of a worldwide disaster when the heavens opened and the rains came down?

Once upon a time... That's how many of our stories begin and "once upon a time" really means that our story doesn't belong to any time. You can't put a date on a story which happened "once upon a time". The importance of such stories lies not in when something happened but why it happened. The hundreds of flood stories around the world do not answer "when" questions; they answer "why" questions. Basically, they answer three "why" questions.

We shall explore these questions in the next chapter. In the meantime, a careful reading of the Bible story of the Flood (Genesis 6:1-9:18) is recommended. The alert reader will notice that two stories have been interwoven in intricate fashion. For example, in 7:12 we are told that rain fell upon the earth forty days and forty nights. However, verse 24 of the same chapter reports that the waters prevailed upon the earth a hundred and fifty days. In 6:19, Noah is commanded to take two of every kind of creature into the ark, whereas in 7:2 the command is to take seven pairs of clean animals (Leviticus 11 describes which animals are clean and which unclean) and one pair of unclean animals. Here is clear evidence that the version of the Flood story in Genesis is a combination of earlier stories. We can learn much from this. First, it alerts us to the fact that Bible stories existed before the Bible and nurtured the faith of a people before they were written down. Secondly, similar stories can be told for different purposes and in different circumstances. One version of the Flood story of Genesis wishes to call attention to the distinction between clean and unclean animals; the other is not concerned with the matter. The reader may be confused by such apparent contradictions but he should not be put off. The people who put the Bible together provide us with many rich traditions in order to preserve different points of views. To offer a familiar example, the miracle of the multiplication of the loaves and fishes is the only miracle of Jesus told in all four gospels. Yet it is told very differently in each and with different emphases. As the police know only too well, no two versions of a story are ever the same!

Chapter 9

The Flood: Everybody's story

God created people because he loves stories. And his people love stories, too. The world is full of stories and story-tellers. We tell stories to amuse and to entertain, to instruct and to teach, to warn and to encourage. Indeed, we tell stories for almost as many reasons as there are stories. But the most common reason for story-telling is, surely, to explain - to explain ordinary and everyday facts of experience and to explain much deeper and profound matters.

Why is there hunger in the world? Why must human beings work for a living? According to the Bini people of Nigeria, a woman is to blame. In the beginning people didn't have to till the soil because the sky was close to the earth and they were allowed to cut off a piece of the sky and eat it whenever they were hungry. But the sky warned human beings not to cut off too much because they would have to throw some of the sky away and the sky did not relish ending up on the rubbish heap. One day, however, a very greedy woman cut off more than she could eat and had to throw away what she couldn't. The sky became very angry and rose high above the earth, far beyond the reach of men and women. And from then on people had to work in order to eat.

Why is there suffering in the world? According to an Ashanti story from Ghana, it is because a man and a woman came together, against the will of the creator. Both were punished:

Here is the punishment for men: when a man sees a woman whom his heart desires he will have to give her gold, clothes and many things before he can possess her. And here is the punishment for women: since you also disobeyed, when you see a man whom your heart desires, you will have to keep it to yourself in your head! In addition, you will have to pound the fufu and do all the work, before eating it yourself... You will be with child nine to ten months and you shall give birth in great pain.

It is clear from this story that the man took the initiative and that he had "sinned" first. And yet the woman must suffer more than the man! It should be noticed that ancient stories appear to have been composed mainly by men and reflect a world dominated by men. This is as true of the Bible as of any other ancient collection of tales. However, there are some exceptions and I include the following story as a refreshing counter-blast to the stories told by men.

According to the Ekoi people of Nigeria, in the beginning the earth was inhabited exclusively by women. One day, God (known as Obassi Nsi) accidentally killed a woman. To make up for his carelessness, he told the women that they might choose whatever they wished from all of his possessions. He described everything he owned but the women could not find, among God's fruits, birds and animals, anything as beautiful as the sister they had lost. Finally, there was one possession left: man. The women agreed to take man as compensation:

> Thus men became the servants of women, and have to work for them to this day. For, though a woman comes under the influence of her husband upon marriage, yet she is his proprietor and has a right to ask any service, and to expect him to do whatever she chooses.

An important lesson

There are not many stories of creation and human origins which do not put women in an inferior position and, if there is question of some "sin" in the beginning, the woman is almost always to blame. But the important lesson to be learned from such stories is that they describe the way society is and not the way it was. Story-tellers used an imaginary past to explain life as they experienced it in their time and in their place. Women were (are) everywhere seen to be inferior to men and treated as male property. For example, in the Bible, only men were allowed divorce; when a girl was raped, compensation was paid to her father, not to her (see Deuteronomy 24:1-4 and 22:28-29).

The low esteem of women in the world was reinforced by

stories which explained why it was so: women are the source of all evil. Imagine a young person asking a wise elder, "Why is life so harsh for women?" The answer will be a story of some "sin" committed by a woman which explains and justifies her painful and lowly condition. The present subjection of women is explained by an appeal to an imaginary and distant past. When, very rarely, one finds a story praising women and exalting their authority in society (as in the Ekoi story above), then one can be sure that it comes from a tribe or a people in which women were equal, if not superior, to men.

Flood stories

The story of the Flood is one of the most important in the Bible, though it is often neglected and overlooked. But the fate of Mr and Mrs Noah is crucial, if we are to understand the God who speaks to us on our journey through the pages of Scripture. In the last chapter, we saw that there are hundreds of flood stories around the world, all answering some "why" question. We shall use these tales to help us to understand why the story of Noah and his family is told in the Bible and why it is of such importance for our understanding of God and, consequently, for our understanding of the life and work of Jesus.

Flood stories, we can summarise, are of three kinds. The first kind concerns itself with creation and is not really about destruction. The earth was pictured as being in chaos, covered in flood waters and otherwise lifeless. Then the god or gods dispel the flood waters and create a world of order and inhabitants. The first humans are rescued from the flood in the sense that only when the gods have abated the waters is human life possible. We can see traces of this type of flood story in Genesis 1:2: "The earth was without form and void, and darkness was on the face of the deep; and the spirit of God was moving over the face of the waters". In such stories we see the belief of ancient peoples that the gods or god created the world by rescuing it from catastrophic flood waters and that the gods must continue to hold back the waters if disaster is not to return. What is interesting is that the tellers of such tales clearly understood that there is a relationship between creator and creatures. Not only does the creator save but he must go on doing so by protecting his creatures from the chaos of flood waters.

A second type of flood story takes matters a little bit further. Here the world and its inhabitants are already in existence and, for some reason or other, the gods decide to destroy humanity. Often enough, the reason for the destruction is not very serious; in one famous account, the gods are unable to sleep because of the noise of humanity and they decide to end the disturbance by ending the cause! In such stories, sometimes one of the gods rescues a particular human family from the catastrophe and humanity survives; in every case, there has to be an escape, engineered by human ingenuity or by some friendly god. Clearly, humanity survives (or there would be no one to tell the story!). Such stories were told probably to explain the precariousness of existence in the world, the capriciousness of the gods and the need for human vigilance in dealing with the deities. Flood stories of this kind teach the art of survival in a hostile world.

A third type of flood story contains most of the ingredients of the Noah story. We may list them as follows:

a. Some kind of human revolt against the god(s);
b. A divine decision to destroy all humanity;
c. A divine change of mind which now decides that some human beings are to be saved;
d. Instructions to build a ship of some kind;
e. Description of the flooding;
f. Sending out birds to seek dry land;
g. A divine promise not to destroy humanity again.

In our next chapter, we shall come to grips with the story of the Flood in Genesis. For now, it is rewarding to ponder that all flood stories, of whatever type, indicate that humanity lives in a relationship with God, that our future depends as much on divine help as on human ingenuity and that, at least for some ancient peoples, hope in God was not wasted.

PRAYER

Psalm 33 seems an appropriate response to the God whose steadfast love endures forever.

Chapter 10

The Flood:
Violence and the God of peace
Genesis 6-7

When Charles Dickens wrote his novel, *Oliver Twist*, he did not have Harry Secombe in mind. He intended to attack the evil social welfare system of his day and, in his book, the workhouse and Mr Bumble stand for all that heartless institutions and mindless public servants can inflict on the poor. Dickens, I'm sure, would have been greatly surprised to find his hard-hitting novel turned into a West End comic musical. Lionel Bart's great hit, *Oliver*, is everything a good musical should be: it is funny, lively and full of glorious songs. But it is not an attack on the Department of Health and Social Security!

What has happened to the story of young Oliver Twist in the hands of Mr Bart may be of help to us as we journey through Scripture. He took a tale of horror and murder and dressed it up in memorable tunes and snappy dancing. In other words, he told the original story in a new way and for different purposes. Dickens wanted to change society's attitudes to the poor and the unfortunate; Lionel Bart wished to entertain and delight.

We have seen that there are many versions of the Flood story among the peoples of the world and we have seen, too, that the story is told for a variety of reasons. Like Lionel Bart, the genius behind the Book of Genesis has taken an old story and fashioned it to his own purposes. As we read through the story again, we shall try to discover why it is included in the collection of tales which makes up the first book of the Bible.

READING THROUGH

Our story begins with a sad observation: the earth is filled with violence (Genesis 6:11). When Adam and Eve attempt to usurp the power of God, they succeed in bringing the whole of creation into disharmony. Nothing is as it should be and the first child of the rebellion is a murderer. Violence is the way of the world; death is, therefore, the way of all flesh. Lamech boasts of his wives (Yes! Wives! – men now seize as many women as they wish) that he has killed a young man who dared to strike him. Anyone offending Lamech will receive seventy-seven times as much in return (Genesis 4:24 – compare this with Matthew 18:21-22). Noah, the child of Lamech, inherits what his father has sown, a world corrupted by human violence.

God sees

When God created the heavens and earth and set men and women in the midst of all that he had made, he saw that everything that he had created was very good. God's seeing that all is very good is a way of saying that God wants everything to be very good: he intends that only the good shall be present to his sight. In Genesis 6:12, God looks again and "behold, the earth was corrupt". Will God tolerate a world filled with violence?

God acts

God determines to destroy "all flesh", that is, he decides to do away with the men and women of the world because they have filled the earth with violence. We have seen, and we will see again and again if we journey through the whole of Scripture, that the Bible's final word about God is that he is the one whose steadfast love endures forever. How is it, then, that he decides on a destructive policy? Ought not God to forgive and forget?

Readers of the ancient stories in the Book of Genesis need to remind themselves that they are not reading a modern History book. The biblical flood-story is not an account of something that actually happened. It is a story told for a purpose. It demonstrates, as does the story of Cain, how seriously God takes the sinfulness of human violence. The violence of our world is an affront to God. We stand as in the days of Noah – we are in the days of Noah! A world on which God cannot bear to look is a dangerous place to be.

Noah is a righteous man, blameless in his time, a man who

walked with God. "To walk with God" is a biblical way of saying that Noah is all that Adam should have been and would have been if he had not sought to invade the domain of God and go beyond the limits of creatureliness (see and compare Genesis 5:22, 6:9, 17:1; Deuteronomy 13:5 and 1 Samuel 25:15-35). In contrast to everyone else, Noah is not a man of violence; by violence, "all flesh had corrupted their way upon the earth". Noah's is another way, a way of non-violence: he walks with God. Noah is a new Adam and God decides to begin again.

The boat

In our story, God determines to put an end to violent humanity. But, in the same breath, as it were, he plans for humanity's future. Noah will be the new beginning, the one just man will be God's hope for the future of humanity. Noah does "all that God commanded him" (Genesis 6:22) – he builds a boat.

Mr and Mrs Noah, with their three sons and three daughters-in-law, embark with the animals and birds and God battens down the hatches (Genesis 7:16). The rains come pouring down and "all flesh that moved upon the earth" (Genesis 7:21) is swept away.

The details of the sending out of the dove and the building of the altar to offer worship to God are found in other versions of the tale. Even the observation that God "smelled the pleasing odour" (Genesis 8:21) of Noah's sacrifice is found elsewhere. But the use to which the biblical writer puts these little details is instructive. The dove assures Noah that the land is drying up. God then calls the family of Noah from their boat to begin the human story again. It is the Adam and Eve story all over again. God sends a human family out into the world; he provides animals for their sustenance and he blesses them with abundance (Genesis 8:15-19).

Noah makes a sacrifice to God, that is, he kills some animals and burns them on a fire in token of his belief that everything he has belongs to God. This acknowledgment of God's authority is in contrast to Adam's attempt to usurp divine power. The action of the righteous man, Noah, wins from God a gift beyond all price: "I will never again curse the ground (*adamah*) because of man (*adam*)" (Genesis 8:21). Here is God's word that the world will not be destroyed because of human sin, because of human violence. In our day, with our weapons of war, we do not need God to destroy the world. We can do it ourselves.

To ponder

The rebellion of Adam and Eve, the attempt to be like God, to refuse to accept the limitations of creatureliness, is a recipe for disaster. Cain, the murderer, is the offspring of rebellion and his violence spreads like a cancer throughout creation. Lamech is the proud boast of humanity: he knows how to kill!

Noah is a righteous man, a just man, a man of peace. He does not walk in the way of all flesh, in the way of violence. Noah walks in the way of his God. Noah survives, with his wife, and with his sons and his sons' wives. To save the world, one man of peace is enough.

PRAYER

Psalm 57 is a prayer to God that the storms of destruction pass by. It is a prayer that God's steadfast love and his faithfulness be our constant companions. It is a prayer that the glory of God, not his anger, be over all the earth.

Chapter 11

Noah and the rainbow sign
Genesis 8-9

Isn't it amazing how words change their meaning? If I said to you, twenty years ago, that I had streaked across the pitch, you would have assumed that I was running to claim my seat before the kick-off. To-day, you would assume that I had been arrested. Streaking may not be as fast as it used to be, but it attracts more attention!

Take a rather everyday word like "curious". It means "eager to learn", "inquisitive", even "prying". But a seventeenth century English poet, Andrew Marvell (1621-1678), in a poem entitled "The Garden", speaks of the "curious peach". Now I have never come across an inquisitive, prying peach. What has happened is that the word "curious" has changed its meaning. In Marvell's day, it meant "exquisite, possessing qualities of unusual delicacy and fine craftsmanship". In a word, it meant "well-made". Behind the English word is the Latin word *"cura"* which means "care". So "curious" used to mean "made with care". The same Latin word, *"cura"*, gives us the English word "curate". Is a curate someone who is well-made or someone who takes care?

READING THROUGH

On our journey through the story of Noah, we meet the word "covenant". The word appears first in the Bible at Genesis 6:18, where God says to Noah, "I will establish my covenant with you." However, it is only after Noah and his family are rescued from the flood-waters that we begin to see what the word means. And it is here that we need to remember the lesson of curious peaches and arrested streakers. Words change their meaning.

To the average church-goer today, the word "covenant" means a signed agreement to pay so much money to parish funds in order that the parish receive tax-relief from the Inland Revenue. We may have come across the word in ecumenical circles as, for example, when one Church covenants or agrees with another to do something in common. In the first case, covenant refers to a monetary agreement, a cash transaction and, in the second case, it refers to a solemn, binding commitment to a particular action or policy. Notice, too, that, in each case, there are two parties to the deal. In the first case, an individual promises to pay a certain sum to the parish and the Inland Revenue promises to grant tax-relief on the promised amount. In the second case, one Church agrees with another to act in a certain way. Our use of the word "covenant" – and we don't use it very much – conveys the idea of two parties, entering into a mutual agreement of some kind.

In our English Bibles, the word "covenant" occurs hundreds and hundreds of times. It is one of the most important words in all of Scripture. Unfortunately, it is one of the most misunderstood. The reason for misunderstanding is that we forget that words change their meaning and the meaning of a word is often modified by the circumstances in which it is used. It is true that there are occurrences of the word "covenant" in the Bible where the meaning is "an agreement or a contract between two parties". You may read an example of this in Genesis 21:25-34. Abraham and Abimelech are in dispute over a well and, to resolve the matter, "the two men made a covenant", that is, they entered into a solemn agreement whereby Abimelech recognised that the well had been dug by Abraham.

Yet, for the most part, when the Bible says that God made a covenant with so-and-so, it does not mean that an agreement has been reached between two equal partners. Nor does it mean that a contract has been signed between two unequal partners, almighty God and not-so-mighty human beings. Most frequently, it means that God binds himself to do or not to do something. In a human agreement, if one person breaks a contract, the other can claim that he is no longer bound by it. Indeed, in early English law, an action-in-covenant was, in fact, a court action in which damages were sought for a breach of a sealed agreement. But when God makes a covenant, his commitment to his promise does not depend on the action or conduct of another party. It is of the utmost importance to be clear on this point. When the Bible says that God made a covenant with Noah (Genesis 9:9), it means that God undertook to do certain things on Noah's behalf. There is no question of a mutual agreement. We might say that a covenant, when God is involved, is a unilateral declaration of intent.

READING THROUGH AGAIN

We continue our reading of the story of Noah at the point where the rains have ended (Genesis 8:15). We are told that in the six hundred and first year, Noah looked out of the ark and saw that the ground was dry. The reference to the six hundred and first year may be to the age of Noah (read Genesis 7:11-13). The great age of Noah, Methuselah (the oldest of all at 969 years!) and the others mentioned in chapter 5, should not be taken as historical. The writer is telling a "once upon a time" story about mighty heroes of ancient days, "the great heroes and famous men of long ago" (Genesis 6:4). In "once upon time" stories you can have giants (the Nephilim of Genesis 6:4 are giants) and everyone can live for hundreds of years. The interesting thing is that the dry land appears on New Year's Day! A new age has dawned. God has saved the human family and is ready to begin the human story all over again. A Happy New Year, indeed!

A sacrifice

God commands Noah to leave the boat and to take with him all the birds and animals and creeping things. Straightaway, Noah builds an altar and takes one clean animal and one clean bird (unclean animals were not offered to God) and roasted them in a fire on the altar. This ancient practice of burning animals in honour of the gods is found among many peoples of the world. The idea is that some valuable possession, an animal or even a child, is presented to one's god. The word for this action is "sacrifice". We shall meet the phenomenon again and again on our journey through Scripture and we shall examine it in detail when we come to the story of Abraham and Isaac in Genesis 22.

85

Speaking to the heart

In Genesis 8:21, the writer imagines that God smells the roasting animal and makes a promise to himself. We know that God doesn't have a nose but the only way we can speak about God is in human language and we must learn to make allowances. When we read that "the Lord said in his heart" (Genesis 8:21), we are to understand that God made a firm promise to himself, he committed himself utterly to a new policy. This new policy is good news: "I will never again curse the ground because of man, for the imagination of man's heart is evil from his youth; neither will I ever again destroy every living creature as I have done" (Genesis 8:21). A momentous decision for every man, woman and child who ever lives on this planet!

In Genesis 2:16-17, God said to the man:

> You may freely eat of every tree of the garden; but of the tree of the knowledge of good and evil you shall not eat, for in the day that you eat of it you shall die!

The enjoyment of Eden was conditional: do this or else! And the disobedience of Adam and Eve, the subsequent tale of human violence (Genesis 6:11: "the earth was filled with violence"), must convince us that we cannot survive if survival depends on our goodness. If, to survive, we need to be saints, then the outlook is bleak: anyone who is a sinner knows that much. By Genesis 8:21, God knows it, too. That is why he speaks to his heart: only God can cope.

A unilateral declaration

God makes a covenant with Noah. He declares what he will bind himself to do. Unlike Genesis 2:16-17 (quoted above), this is a "no strings attached" promise. This is what God determines to do:

1. I will never again destroy every human creature (8:21).

2. I will cause the seasons to come in orderly fashion, the summer following winter, the day following night; seed-time and harvest-time will not fail (8:22)

3. I restore the blessing of fruitfulness with which I blessed Adam (Genesis 1:28): the world will not be without its children (9:1).

86

4. I restore to Noah and his descendants (that is, to all the human race) authority over creation so that there may be food (9:3).

5. I give you the rainbow as a sign that I will keep my word. When the rainbow appears in the clouds, "I will look upon it and I will remember" (9:15-16).

We must remember that God's promise is for everyone. He makes a covenant with the world, with men and women of every race, of every colour, of every creed. And God's solemn promise to Noah is still good. Nowhere in the Bible does it say that God has abandoned his promise to Noah. God does not intend to destroy us, even if we appear to deserve destruction.

In our nuclear world, where we live under the threat of instant and total annihilation, we need to remember the rainbow. The sign for sinners is there for all to see. We, in our stupidity, in our pride, or, God help us, by mistake, may destroy our beautiful planet. But not God. We have his word on that.

A warning

In his words to Noah God offers a warning. "Whoever sheds the blood of man by man shall his blood be shed." This is a statement of fact, not a threat. Jesus put it this way: "All who take up the sword, perish by the sword" (Matthew 26:52). Violence, bloodshed, death, that is what happens when we forget that we are brothers and sisters. We know this to be true. God knows it, too, for he made us in his own image (Genesis 9:6): we share responsibility with God; as he is responsible for us, so we are responsible for each other and for our universe. Even after the disobedience of Adam, even after we have sinned, we remain made "in the image of God". To destroy another human being is to break God's image. It is a dangerous undertaking.

IMAGES OF GOD

The God of the Noaic covenant is a God who saves unconditionally. The author of the Book of Genesis presents a man and a woman in a paradise. But it is a rented paradise:

they must pay with their obedience. This proves to be too high a price and Adam and Eve are cast out, the world is soon filled with violence and God sends the rains. What is remarkable about the Flood story is that, as a result of the destruction, God changes his mind. Human beings are sinners (Genesis 8:21: "a man's heart is evil from his youth"). Does God destroy sinners?

There is an old Jewish story about a man who died and found himself kneeling before God for judgment. God called upon the recording angel to bring the book and read out the man's doings. Page after page of sinful deeds were read. The man cringed before the Seat of Judgment where God sat uneasily. Then God said, as the sorry tale continued, "If I sit here and listen to this, I shall have to destroy this man". So God got up and moved over to the Seat of Mercy.

The God of that story is the God of the Noah story.

PRAYER

Some will recall that the "De Profundis" used to be said after Mass. This, of course, was the Latin version of Psalm 130, a very suitable psalm to pray when there are floods about!

Chapter 12

From Noah to Abraham
Genesis 10-11

The word "Bible" comes from the Greek language. In that language, the word for the Scriptures was *"biblia"*, "the books". Latin took over this word with exactly the same spelling but regarded it as singular, meaning "the book". So our word "bible" comes to us from Greek through Latin into English. In speaking of the seventy-three books which make up the Scriptures as *The Book*, believers wish to imply that the Bible is the book of all books, because of its origin, contents and purpose.

We divide the Bible into the Old Testament and the New Testament. The Old Testament, those books which were written before the time of Jesus, we inherited from the Jewish people. The twenty-seven books which were written by early Christians, we call the New Testament.

All the writings of the New Testament were written in the Greek language. Jesus spoke a language called Aramaic which was rather like the Hebrew language in which the Old Testament, for the most part, was written. It is possible that Jesus may have been able to speak some Greek but that would not be his everyday language. When the Church began to spread among non-Jewish peoples, it inevitably carried on its business in the Greek language, since that was the most common language of the Roman Empire. It is interesting to note that, for the first couple of hundred years, the Mass and all other Christian services were conducted in Greek, even in the city of Rome itself! Greek, not Latin, was the language of the first Christians!

And so it is that much of our Christian vocabulary comes from Greek. It is from Greek that we derive the word "Testament", which we apply to the two parts of our Bible. The Greek word which lies behind our English word refers to two things. First, it refers to the idea of "covenant", the idea that God has bound himself to love all creation. We have seen how

God did this in his covenant with Noah. Shortly, we shall look at God's covenant with Abraham and readers of the Book of Exodus will come to Mount Sinai, where God made his great covenant with Moses and the people of Israel. Christians must journey, too, to the hill of Calvary, where, in the death of Jesus, God made a covenant with all the peoples of the world. So we divide our Bibles into two parts: that part which describes God's covenant before the time of Jesus (the Old Testament) and that part which describes the covenant made by God through Jesus (the New Testament).

The second idea which lies in the Greek word behind our word "testament" is more familiar to us. It is the idea conveyed in the phrase "last will and testament". In this sense, a testament is a document which contains details of an inheritance. The Old and the New Testaments contain details of what the people of the world, the children of God, inherit from their heavenly Father.

The table of nations

We have arrived at a difficult part of the Book of Genesis. Chapter 10 contains a list of peoples, supposedly a list of all the peoples of the world. There is no need for us to deal with every name on the list; we will content ourselves with a few general remarks.

First, the writer presents the view that all the nations of the world originated from Noah's three sons (see Genesis 9:19 and 10:32). In this way, he demonstrates the fulfilment of God's blessing on Noah and his sons: "Be fruitful and multiply, and fill the earth" (9:1). The writer impresses on his readers the faithfulness of God to his covenant promises.

Secondly, while we know that the writer's list is not historical, we can learn from his intentions. Clearly, by presenting "all the peoples of the earth" as descended from Noah, he affirms the essential unity of the human family. The people of God is one family. We are all brothers and sisters!

A third point: hidden in the table of nations, among the children of Shem, are the sons of Eber, the Hebrew people. Far from being a great nation of the world, Israel was an insignificant people, lost in a sea of nations. It was God's free choice which created a holy people of Israel.

The third rebellion

We have witnessed the rebellion of Adam and Eve. We have read of the murder of Abel by his brother and the spread of violence over all the earth, the wholesale destruction of people made in God's image. We have seen the consequences of Adam's rebellion; we have seen what happened in the Flood. With Noah and his family, God begins again. But nothing seems to change. Humankind rebels again.

READING THROUGH

Shinar

The writer imagines all the people of the world migrating from the east and arriving at Shinar. This is the biblical name for the territory of the Sumerians. Here it is simply the land of Babylon, the whole of what we used to call Mesopotamia.

Babel

There was a huge ziggurat in ancient Babylon, one of its famous temple towers. A ziggurat was a kind of pyramid.

It may be that this old Hebrew story was inspired by the great ziggurat of Babylon. The ziggurats of Babylon were regarded by the Babylonians as links between heaven and earth. Thus *Esagila*, the principal ziggurat of the city and the shrine of its god Marduk, was called "the house of the foundation of heaven and earth".

READING THROUGH AGAIN

All the people of the world spoke the same language. There are many stories throughout the world which explain how one original human language became confused into many languages. Of course, there never was a time (as far as we know) when every human being spoke the same language. But when small social groups came into contact with other groups who spoke different languages, the question of the diversity of language arose and stories grew up to answer that question. Often the confusion is caused because humans try to invade the heavens, the home of the gods. That is the case here. The people of the world decide to build a city and a tower which will reach into the very home of God in the heavens. (Many ancient peoples believed that God or the gods lived above the clouds and the people of the Bible called this "space" Heaven.) They are determined to make a name for themselves. Here is another human attempt to "become like God" (Genesis 3:5).

Rather amusingly, though the people thought that their tower reached into the heavens, the Lord had to "come down" to see what they had built. All humanity, with one voice, seemed set on attempting to storm the heavens. God decides to scatter the people and to confuse their language. The great Tower of Babel is reduced to a babble of confusion! In a rather weak pun, the writer pictures God naming the abandoned city "Babel" because there he had confused (*balal* = to mix or to confuse in Hebrew) human speech. In fact, the Hebrew Babel comes from the Akkadian language where it would be Bab-ili or Bab-ilani (meaning "the gate of the god[s]"), and from which comes the Greek form of the name Babylon.

So the rebellion is crushed and God scatters the people over the face of the earth so that they will carry out his blessing to be fruitful and fill the earth. If God wants obedience from his creatures, he will have to try again. This he decides to do. He speaks to Abraham.

The family of Abraham

We have had a list of the names of the family of nations. Now, in Genesis 11:10-32, we have a list of the ancestors of Abraham. It is as if the whole of God's efforts were to be concentrated on one man. We leave the world stage and enter the domestic history of Abraham and his barren wife Sarah. You will notice that at this stage of the story Abraham is called Abram; his name will be changed in chapter 17. Notice, too, that Sarah's name is sometimes spelled Sarai, a more ancient form of the name.

MESSAGE

The first eleven chapters of the Bible serve as an introduction to the whole of Scripture. They tell of God's offer of blessings and care and of men and women constantly rejecting God's gifts. They tell of a God who is determined to care for humanity, even in the face of human rebellion and violent sin. When the peoples are scattered as wanderers over the face of the earth, it seems as if all is lost. But God has other ideas. He goes back to the drawing-board and makes a new plan. The plan begins to unfold in the story of Abraham.

IMAGES OF GOD

At this stage of our journey through Scripture it would be a good idea to recall the kind of God we have met in our readings in the Book of Genesis so far. We have seen the creator of the world, looking on all that he had made, and seeing that it was very good. We have seen the kindness of God in providing food and work for his human beings. We have seen a God who gives a man and a woman to each other for love and companionship, a God who sees loneliness as inhuman and intolerable. We have seen a God who saves rebellious Adam and Eve from the worst consequences of their folly. We have seen a God who continues to shower the sinners with gift and blessing. We have seen a God who pleads with the murderer Cain that he ought to have care for his brother. We have seen a God who protects even the murderer. We have seen violence spread over the face of the earth and we have witnessed the tragic consequences. We have seen a boat and a family and God's fierce determination to save the world from its sins. Every time the human story takes a turn for the worse, God is to be found putting things right. This is the God of the Bible, the God of Abraham, of Isaac and of Jacob, the same God we meet in Jesus of Nazareth.

PRAYER

Psalm 75 seems an appropriate response to the God who saves the world. The Psalmist tells that when the earth totters, it is God who keeps its pillars steady.

Chapter 13

The call of Abraham
Genesis 12

If at first you don't succeed, try, try, try again. A sound piece of advice, to which God obviously subscribes. For when his hopes for humanity were frustrated by the Adams and Eves of this world, he turned to Noah and his family. The blessings given to Adam and his descendants were restored to Noah and his children after the Flood.

But the new beginning proved as fruitless as the first. The whole earth tried to storm heaven, the citadel of God, by building the Tower of Babel, a monument to human pride (Genesis 11:1-10). Once again God resisted the rebels and the human family was scattered over the face of the earth. The image of men and women wandering over the world suggests a people wandering away from God. What is God to do? Try again! So he began, not with the whole of the human race, not with a representative nation. He began with one man. God called Abraham.

READING THROUGH

The story of Abraham begins in Genesis 11:27 and continues down to Genesis 25:11 when Abraham dies. We must journey through nearly fifteen chapters and meet many people and many strange customs and beliefs. We will need to be patient and not greedy to know everything at once. The Bible is a very crowded place and, on a first journey through its pages, we cannot expect to discover everyone and everything.

In this chapter we will endeavour to identify some of the more important men and women who fill the pages of Abraham's story. There are many, many more but we shall confine ourselves to the chief actors and actresses in the play.

Patriarchs and matriarchs

The word "patriarch" means "first or chief father". Thus Adam is the patriarch of all humanity because, in the biblical myth, he is the first father, the father of all human descendants. The word "matriarch" means "first or chief mother" and the Bible calls Eve "the mother of all the living" (Genesis 3:20). After the destruction of the Flood, Noah and his three sons and daughters-in-law become the ancestral parents of all the human race and may be called patriarchs and matriarchs of all the living. But the words are usually reserved for Abraham, Isaac and Jacob and their wives who are regarded as the first or chief fathers and mothers of the people of Israel.

Abraham

Abraham was the son of a man called Terah. The first thing we note about him is that when we meet him in Genesis 11:27 his name is not Abraham but Abram. God gave him a new name:

> No longer shall your name be Abram, but your name shall be Abraham; for I have made you the father of a multitude of nations.
>
> *Genesis 17:5*

The name Abram means "exalted father" and the new name, Abraham, is taken to mean "father of a multitude". The Bible regards Abraham as the father or patriarch of many nations. Indeed, both the Arabs and the Jews look to Abraham as their common father – they are both sons and daughters of Abraham, brothers and sisters of each other.

There are many instances of people in the Bible being given a new name. Jacob, Abraham's grandson, has his name changed to Israel, which became the name of all those who trace their ancestry back to Jacob and his twelve sons, that is, the people of Israel, the Jews. In the New Testament, Simon has his name changed to Peter (Matthew 16:17-18) and Saul, the one-time persecutor of the christian churches, becomes Paul, the founder of many churches. Names are very important in the Bible and often indicate the kind of person one is. Simon becomes Peter, the rock on which the Church is built (Matthew 16:18; the word *"petra"* in Greek means "a rock").

The son of Mary is called Jesus or Joshua, a name which was taken to mean "one who saves" and St Matthew tells us that he is so called because "he will save his people from their sins" (Matthew 1:21). Matthew gives Jesus another name, Emmanuel, which means "God with us", for not only does he save us but our God is with us even to the end of time! (Matthew 1:23 and 28:20).

A name may be changed to highlight the character of a person or to indicate a call to a new way of life, to a new adventure, to a new vocation.

Sarah

Sarah, the wife of Abraham, is the matriarch or great mother of many nations. When we first meet her, she is called Sarai, simply an alternative way of spelling her name. In point of fact, both Sarah and Sarai mean the same thing in Hebrew ("princess"). However, on first meeting Sarah, we meet her tragedy: "Now Sarai was barren; she had no child" (Genesis 11:30). The writer of Genesis seizes on the different spellings of her name to bring to our notice the graciousness of God for he sees in the apparent change of her name a change from tragedy to laughter. From being barren, childless Sarai, God declares that she will become Sarah, "a mother of nations" (Genesis 17:16).

After Eve, Sarah is the first great woman we meet in the Bible. It is a pity but it is true that the Bible is very much a man's book, about a man's world, enshrining men's values over against women. Moses, Joshua and David, Jesus, Peter and Paul: these are the heroes we remember in the Scriptures. Do you remember the heroines? Elijah, Isaiah, Jeremiah and Ezekiel are the great prophets of the Bible. Do you remember the great women-prophets? In our male-dominated Church and world we need to meet the women of the Bible for their stories are told, as much as the men's, to encourage us in the present and to furnish us with hope for the future.

Lot

According to Genesis 12:5, Lot is Abraham's nephew. We shall see that his role in the story is that of a contrast to his uncle for he does not have his uncle's strong trust in God.

Hagar

Hagar is an Egyptian girl, a woman enslaved to another woman, Sarah. She is a chattel to be passed around men but God does not forget Hagar (Genesis 21).

Ishmael

Ishmael is the son of Hagar and Abraham. His name means "God hears". God listens to the cry of a slave girl and her child as keenly as he listens to the barren wife Sarah.

Isaac

Isaac is the son of Abraham and Sarah. His name means "He laughs" because of the peculiar story surrounding his conception (Genesis 17:15-21). Little space is devoted in the Bible to Isaac but the story of the unbinding of Isaac in Genesis 22 is one of the most important in all of scripture.

Thus, the cast. Next we shall turn our attention to the stage, the places where the great drama of Abraham enfolds.

PRAYER

The story of Abraham and Sarah is a story of much faith and little faith. It is a story crying out for a God who has faith in us when we lose faith in him and in ourselves. Psalm 86 reminds us that God gives his strength to those who call upon him. For God is the only one whose steadfast love endures forever.

Chapter 14

The promises to Abraham
Genesis 12 revisited

Faraway places with strange-sounding names! The line of the old song could be taken as a description of the Bible. What do you make of Maher-shalal-hash-baz? That is the name Isaiah gave to one of his sons! Or how would you like to be called Nimrod? He was a legendary hunter whose prowess became proverbial and he is supposed to be the founder of the great cities of Babylon and Nineveh (Genesis 10: 8-14). How would you like your home-town to be called Beth-tappuah? It means "the house of apricots". Or what about Beth-shittah, which means "the house of the acacia tree". Perhaps you would prefer Beth-lehem, which probably means "the house of bread"?

READING THROUGH

The story of Abraham is a story of faraway places and strange-sounding names. We will journey with Abraham to these places and we will need to get some of the names into our heads. We must submit to a little geography.

Ur and Haran
Abraham came from Ur of the Chaldees. This was an ancient city on the Euphrates river in eastern Mesopotamia (present-day Iraq). His father emigrated from there and settled in Haran, a city of northern Mesopotamia (that is, present-day eastern Turkey). It was in Haran that the promises of God came to Abraham and he set out for the land of Canaan in accordance with God's command (Genesis 12:1-9).

Canaan
We need to be very clear on where and what the land of Canaan is. It is the name of the land of Israel before the Israelites invaded it and subjected its people. It has a number

of names in history. The ancient Greeks used to refer to the country of the Canaanites as Phoenicia and both Canaan and Phoenicia probably mean "land of purple". The purple industry was of great importance in the region, rare and expensive purple dye being extracted from a mollusc found in the sea (Mediterranean). So expensive was this dye that purple became the colour of royalty – only kings could afford it! Later, Phoenicia came to refer to a different region and Canaan came to be called Palestine. This name was used by the Romans and is derived from the name Philistia, a name given to the coastal plain of Canaan when occupied by the Philistine peoples. You will remember that David slew Goliath. Well, he was the hero of the Philistines, a very war like people who terrorised the Israelites for many a day. The name Palestine remained down to the creation of the state of Israel in 1948 when the Jews adopted their own ancient name for their country. The name Israel comes from the name given to Jacob. We shall meet the story behind the name in Genesis 32:22-32. But, of course, there still remains the Palestinian question. Many people call Canaan or Israel or Palestine the "Holy Land" and for many reasons. Unfortunately, this beautiful and most holy of lands is a place of suffering and much pain.

Far-away places and strange-sounding names! Please locate Ur of the Chaldees, Haran and the land of Canaan on a map (I hope your Bible provides you with good maps). Notice the huge journeys made by Abraham and his wife Sarah. They were nomads, wandering bedouin-like people, emigrating from one place to the next to earn a living. But before we journey with them we must look at the promises made to our father Abraham.

READING THROUGH AGAIN

The beginning of the story of Abraham and his family at Genesis 12:1-3 sets the stage for all that follows in the rest of the Bible. After God's command to Abraham to leave his adopted country (verse 1), God sets out a series of unconditional promises. Five times God says: "I will..."; what is promised to Abraham comes only from God and there are no strings attached. God's promises are:

1. "I will make you a great nation." This promise God fulfilled when he brought the people of Israel out of slavery in Egypt and settled them in the land of Canaan. The story is told in the Book of Exodus and the Book of Joshua. Of course, the Jewish people were politically a great nation only for the brief period of David and Solomon (and not all that great!). Perhaps, the greatness of God's people lies in the rich religious and intellectual inheritance they have given and continue to give to the world.

2. "I will bless you." The childless Abraham and Sarah will soon be blessed with a son, Isaac.

3. "I will make your name great, so that you will be a blessing".

In contrast to the people who tried to make themselves great at Babel, God, and God alone, will make Abraham great. This promise is completed when God enters into a solemn covenant with Abraham's descendants on Mount Sinai (Exodus 19) and creates for himself a holy people. It is only the family of Abraham which can call itself the elect people of God.

4. "I will bless those who bless you, and him who curses you I will curse". It is worth noting here that God uses the plural ("those") for blessing and the singular ("him") for cursing. Surely we are to understand that while there will be much blessing there won't be much cursing.

5. "By you all the families of the earth shall bless themselves". Jewish rabbis teach that God chose one people in order that we might understand that all peoples are chosen. The story that begins with Abraham is not simply a Jewish story. Blessings promised to Abraham are not only for the Jewish people. The first Christians were Jews and they agonised over whether it was right to preach Jesus to non-Jews, to Gentiles, that is, to us. Eventually, they concluded what their holy books had taught them: God is for all.

PRAYER

Psalm 150 combined with a meditative reading of Ephesians 1: 3-14 would seem an appropriate response for us who have been so blessed by God.

Chapter 15

Abraham the traveller
Genesis 13-14

The Bible is full of stories. Indeed, it is full of journey stories. Almost all the stories in the Book of Genesis involve a journey of one kind or another. Adam and Eve are driven out of the garden. Cain is condemned to wander over the face of the earth. The people are scattered over the face of the earth because of their rebellion at Babel. Noah goes on a cruise. Abraham and his family are almost constantly on the move.

How many biblical journey stories can you think of? The greatest is the story of the journey out of slavery to freedom which we read about in the Book of Exodus. You will recall that we started our journey through Scripture with the story of Jonah, a much-travelled man. You might recall, too, the journey of Jesus from Galilee to Jerusalem, and, for good measure, the three great journeys of St Paul. You ought to be able to recall at least twenty journey stories in the Bible and that won't nearly exhaust the number.

Why journey stories? Think of the literature of the world. It is full of journey stories. The *Odyssey*, the *Iliad*, *The Canterbury Tales*, *Pilgrim's Progress*, *Gulliver's Travels*, *Robinson Crusoe*, *Don Quixote*, *Treasure Island*, *Moby Dick*, *The Wizard of Oz*, *Around the World in Eighty Days*, *Dr Who*, *Star Trek* – one could go on and on. There is no end to journey stories. The reason is that a journey is an apt symbol of our lives. We speak of life as a journey. Journey stories are metaphors for life stories. We see in the journey our own story. We travel in order to find ourselves. In the journey of Abraham, the journeys of Isaac and all the rest, in the journeys of Jesus, we see our own life journey unfolded before us. Journey stories are the most popular of all stories because they tell us about ourselves.

Travelling people

When he had received the promises from God, Abraham hastened to obey God's word. With his wife, Sarah, and his nephew, Lot, and all their possessions, he journeyed into the unknown. God led them to Canaan, that is, to the land which one day would be called Israel, the home of Abraham's descendants. He came to the very centre of the country, to the ancient city of Shechem, and God confirmed that the land of Canaan would belong to his descendants one day. Abraham built a stone altar to God and moved south and built another altar between Bethel and Ai. (It is much more fun if you follow the journey on a good map.).

Abraham was a great builder of altars. People all over the world have always put stones in the ground (that's what an altar is) to mark sacred places (Stonehenge, for example), places where they felt they could communicate with their gods. Abraham's altars are signs of his faith that God would one day dwell in the Holy Land with his people.

Abraham journeyed further south into the Negev desert and famine forced him to make his way to Egypt. The River Nile ensured a constant food supply and, indeed, Egypt was known as the bread-basket of the world.

In Egypt

As the writer of Genesis continues his account of the travels of Abraham he relates a story told elsewhere (Genesis 20 and 26). It is not a very flattering tale. Abraham passes off his wife as his sister because she is beautiful and he fears that the Egyptian Pharaoh will kill him in order get her. Sarah ends up in the royal harem as a royal wife. When plagues afflict the household of Pharaoh, he discovers the truth of the matter and angrily expels Abraham and his wife from the country.

What are we to make of all this? When we notice that Abraham does the same thing when he meets the king of Gerar (chapter 20) and that his son Isaac does much the same with Rebekah, his wife, when he fears the lust of the king of the Philistines (chapter 26), we begin to see what is going on. Our author has taken an old legend and incorporated it into the stories of his heroes. The reason seems fairly clear. God has made great promises to Abraham but once he takes matters into his own hands, everything is endangered. If there are to be any descendants to inherit God's promised land, Sarah must have a child. But her husband places her and God's plan into grave danger. Only God can save the situation and he does. The lesson is that God's promises depend on God, not on Abraham who is a bit of a curate's egg, good in spots. Abraham is a man of great faith but he has other less than admirable characteristics, as this and other stories make clear.

Lot's lot

The great ancestors of the Jewish people who fill the Book of Genesis are called the patriarchs. The patriarchs are regarded as the founding fathers of the Jews. These men (and we should not forget the matriarchs, the founding mothers!) were ass nomads, not camel nomads, as is often supposed. Genesis 12:16 says that Abraham possessed camels but this is not likely to be correct. The effective domestication of the camel as a widely used beast of burden does not seem to have taken place before the twelfth century B.C.E., that is, about six hundred years after the time of Abraham.

Abraham and Lot were sheep and cattle raisers and not desert wanderers. They were not bedouin men of the desert. For the most part, their travels took place between great urban centres, moving from one grazing to another. They were tent dwellers, possessors of slaves and retainers, collectors of silver and gold.

We can see in Lot's determination to settle down the beginning of a move from the semi-nomadic life of a cattle and sheep raiser to the settled life of a corn-growing farmer. We will see that Isaac, Abraham's son, sowed the land (26:12) and that Jacob's son, Joseph, dreamt of sheaves of corn in a field, not of sheep gambolling about. Abraham does not settle down in the lush pastures of the Jordan valley. He continues to pick up his tent and move where God directs, content to trust in God's promises and to go on building altars.

A deviation

The story of Abraham's victory over an alliance of four Eastern kings deviates from the usual picture of the patriarchs as relatively peaceful semi-nomadic herdsmen. Abraham is pictured as a great military hero who overcomes far superior forces with a small army of his own.

103

This is how the Battle of the Kings came about. Five kings of Canaan had been paying allegiance for twelve years to King Chedorlaomer, ruler of far-off Elam (in modern Iran) and they decided to rebel. But a coalition of four kings from the East invaded Canaan and defeated the rebels, taking much booty, including Lot and all his possessions. Abraham organised the men of his own houschold, followcd the victorious monarchs and defeated them, recovering all the goods, including Lot, "with his goods, and the women and the people" (14:16). Sensitive readers will notice that the goods are mentioned before the women!

We know from archaeological evidence that there seems to have been some great military upheaval in the area covered in our story and the places and invasion route seem authentic. It may be that the author of Genesis was aware of this ancient destruction and that he retold the catastrophic events, making Abraham the hero. We all like our ancestors to be heroes!

Melchizedek

Melchizedek is presented in the story as a Canaanite king of Salem, which is probably Jerusalem. His name means something like "The king is righteous". We are told that he was a priest of "God the Most High". It is not clear to whom this refers. "El-Elyon", usually translated as "God Most High", is a compound of two names of gods of the Phoenicians who may have worshipped in Jerusalem. It is hardly likely that we are to understand that the title here refers to Israel's God (as it does, for example, in Isaiah 14:14).

Melchizedek will have been a pagan king who exercised royal and priestly duties in the city where one day the name of the Lord, the God of Israel, would dwell. To this priest and king, alone of the many and great kings mentioned in this chapter, Abraham submits (paying tithes). The sharing of bread and wine is a sign of friendship (see Ruth 2:14). Some Church Fathers (that is, scholars of the very early Church) saw in the bread and wine a prefiguration of the Eucharist.

The story of Melchizedek and Abraham is included here to foreshadow the great role that the holy city of Jerusalem plays in our Bible story. In Psalm 110, a psalm probably composed for a royal coronation in Jerusalem, the poet gives thanks that God not only appoints the king but makes him a priest as well.

All early Israelite kings also undertook priestly responsibilities, their coronation being, in effect, their ordination as well. The reference to Melchizedek in verse 4 shows that the story of that ancient king was remembered with honour in Israel.

PRAYER

If you have looked at Psalm 110, then you might go on to pray Psalm 111, a psalm praising God's faithfulness, a characteristic of God which shines through the story of father Abraham

Chapter 16

A word between friends
Genesis 16-19

In the sacred writings of Jews and Christians Abraham is the
man of faith. The words of Genesis 15:6, "Abraham believed
in the Lord; and the Lord reckoned it to him as righteousness",
are echoed by St Paul in Romans 4:9 and in Galatians 3:6. In
the Letter of James (probably the first New Testament document to be written), the author quotes with approval the words
of Genesis and explains the phrase, "the Lord reckoned it to
him as righteousness". It means, says St James, Abraham "was
called the friend of God" (James 2:23). In the Book of Isaiah,
the writer has God speak of "Abraham, my friend" (Isaiah 41:8;
see also the Second Book of Chronicles 20:7).

Abraham was God's friend. Not that he was without fault!
One would hardly approve of his deception of Pharaoh
(Genesis 12) and of Abimelech (Genesis 20) when he tried to
pass off his wife Sarah as his sister to avoid possible danger to
himself. Nor would one want to defend his treatment of the
Egyptian slave girl, Hagar, and of the child he fathered on her.
Yet Abraham was God's friend. As often among friends, a
timely word in the ear can prevent a wrong-doing. In this chapter, we shall listen to Abraham having a word in the ear with
his friend God, a timely word to prevent a divine wrong-doing.

THREE STORIES

The Bible has been called "the greatest story ever told" and,
indeed, it is a great story. We have discovered it to be made
up from a whole host of stories. It is a collection of stories,
welded together to make one story. We might imagine it to be
like a patch-work quilt: hundreds of different pieces stitched
together to form one glorious whole. And just as a quilt is often
made from bits and pieces collected over a long number of
years, so with the Bible. Its stories come from different times
and different places. We might say that each Bible story has its

own history and geography before it becomes part of the great story. This observation will help us to understand three rather strange stories about father Abraham.

We may look on these three stories as a sandwich:
Top slice: Abraham has a word with God (18:16-23);
Filling: A tale of two cities (19:1-28);
Bottom slice: Two childless daughters (19:29-38).

In any good sandwich the bread should enhance the flavour of the filling and the filling should blend with the bread. That is how it is in the story-sandwich of Genesis 18:16-19:38. Each story has something to contribute to the others. Especially, the top and bottom slices counteract the strong flavour of the filling.

Top slice
Chapter 18 opens with yet another reassurance that Abraham and Sarah will have a son. Three men (angels, surely? - see Genesis 19:1) come to confirm God's intention but Sarah, considering her age and that of her husband, regards the matter as laughable. She is reminded that nothing is impossible with God. The writer then continues to keep us in suspense and turns to another story and we have to wait until chapter 21 before the long-awaited son is born.

The men of God leave Sarah and set out with Abraham for the city of Sodom. Abraham acts as guide. Then the intentions of God are revealed. It appears that Sodom is a wicked city and God is determined to destroy it and the equally evil city of Gomorrah. But God has a problem. On the very day on which he called Abraham (Genesis 12), God had promised that Abraham and his descendants would be a blessing to all the nations. And now we have Abraham leading God's angels (avenging angels?) towards Sodom, apparently on a mission of destruction. God is aware of the irony and, at first, seems to consider concealing the matter from Abraham but, in the end, he decides to investigate further. At this point, Abraham has a word in God's ear.

The question is this: is God a destructive God or is he a saving God? Which has the final word, good or evil? Is God good news, even for Sodom and Gomorrah? Is the blessing promised to us through Abraham real or merely an empty promise? Is God full of mercy or merely out for revenge? Does God's steadfast love endure forever for everyone or only for saints? God commands that we love our enemies. Is he able to obey the command himself? In this daring story, the author has Abraham teach God a theological lesson! Abraham's is the voice of humanity, begging God to come up with a better answer to human wickedness than destruction.

Abraham points out to God that matters are never quite as simple as we would like. Suppose there are fifty good people in Sodom? Must they be destroyed with the rest? Suppose there are forty or thirty or twenty or ten? The numbers don't matter. It isn't necessary to go down to just one righteous person. Abraham has made his point and God has seen the light. Having spoken with Abraham, "the Lord went on his way" – with much to think about. God has a question to ponder: "Can God, if he is really God and not a tyrant, destroy an entire city?" Can a God who is genuinely God be content with an eye for an eye and simply inflict punishment on the evil-doers? Abraham puts the question clearly: "Will you destroy the innocent with the guilty?" (Genesis 18:23). Rather, "shall not the Judge of all the earth do right?" (18:25). Abraham puts it to God that he should act like God and not like someone out to get his own back.

In the Book of Ezekiel, the prophet discusses the fact that the people of Israel were no better than the pagan Egyptians when they were enslaved by the Pharaohs. Yet God intervened and led them out of Egypt to freedom. Why did God do this? The prophet answers for God:

> I acted for the sake of my name, that it should not be profaned in the sight of the nations among whom they dwelt, in whose sight I made myself known to them in bringing them out of the land of Egypt.
>
> *Ezekiel 20:9*

God set the people free so that all would know that is what God is about: he sets people free, free from slavery and free from sin. That is his nature. And that is what Abraham is arguing about. If God is to be true to himself, he can't go around destroying people. What Abraham is saying is that God has his reputation to think about!

The filling

The second story, the filling in the sandwich, has no time for the deep discussion of the first. Genesis 19:1-28 is, indeed, the tale of two cities and it is a tale of destruction. This story is older and comes from a different tradition than the other. Its view of God is sterner and harsher. It is also rather naïve: it does not consider the possibility that there may be some good people in the cities. It relishes in an avenging God, not a merciful God. Which God do you prefer?

The story of the destruction of Sodom and Gomorrah is a very difficult one and we must tread warily. Two angels come to Sodom. We must realise that for the peoples of both the Old and the New Testaments, angels were regarded as adult males. Lot, the nephew of Abraham, invites them to his home. All the men of the city congregate around the house and demand that the two men be given to them "that we may know them".

Lately, much attention has been paid to the nature of the sin contemplated by the men of Sodom. Apart from the popular name of "sodomy" (from the name Sodom), the text does not help us much. The fact that the men of the city seek to "know" the visiting strangers would seem to suggest some kind of sexual offence and the fact that many people are gathered would suggest some kind of "gang rape" but hardly private acts of a homosexual nature. Elsewhere in the Bible the sin of Sodom is regarded to have been injustice (Isaiah 1:10; 3:9), a variety of irresponsible acts (Jeremiah 23:14), even pride, gluttony and indifference to the poor (Ezekiel 16:49). What is important to note is that the text is not specific enough to be pertinent to contemporary discussions of homosexuality.

Another detail of the story that captures the imagination of the more blood-thirsty amongst is the fire and brimstone raining down from the heavens. The stricken cities smoke "like the smoke of a furnace" (a detail picked up by the Book of Revelation 9:2). We must realise that such language is poetic and must not be taken as a factual description. All such language in the Bible which seeks to picture the judgment day of God is imaginative and urges us to take God's judgment seriously. But we must not accept such imagery as literal truth. Hell may be real; hell-fire is not.

Poor Mrs Lot! There is a rock formation at the southern end of the Dead Sea which, at least at a distance, looks like a human figure. Guides point it out to tourists as the unfortunate wife of Lot. But the story of the destruction of Sodom (and the next story of Lot's daughters) cannot be regarded as anything other than legend. We cannot root these stories in history any more than we can the stories of Cain or Noah.

How can we decide which God to accept into our lives? Must we choose the God who is ready to jump on us whenever we stray or can we trust the God whose steadfast love endures forever? Surprisingly, the bizarre story of Lot's daughters gives a verdict.

The bottom slice

The first thing to notice is that the daughters of Lot are not condemned for their strange conduct. That is not to say that the Bible approves of the steps they take to get pregnant. The point of the story is not condemnation of these (incestuous) unmarried mothers. The emphasis is on their children.

The first of our three stories presented God and Abraham, as blessings for all peoples, not only for God's chosen people. God wishes us to know that all peoples are chosen for blessing. The second story suggests that Abraham is not, after all, a bringer of blessing but of destruction. So which is it to be? Well, from the family of Abraham, through his nephew Lot, come the families of the people of Moab and the people of Canaan (Ammonites is another name for Canaanites). The land of Israel and its surrounding lands are blessed with fruitfulness on account of Abraham, even before Abraham himself has a son by his wife Sarah. Blessing, indeed!

There it is! The filling in the sandwich would seem to be contradicted and cancelled out by the top and bottom slices of bread. Wasn't it Jesus who said that if we ask God our Father for bread he will not hand us a stone?

PRAYER

A very suitable prayer, in response to the God who decides not to destroy us, would be Psalm 25. The psalm points out that God is gracious to us, not because we are good, but because he is good.

110

Chapter 17

Abraham, Sarah, Abimelech
Genesis 20

Everyone loves stories. There is something about a story which captures our imagination and rivets us to the teller until we have heard the end. I suspect that what keeps us hooked on a story is the compulsion of curiosity. We long to hear "what happens next". It is suspense which keeps the soap operas on our screens; everyone wants to know who shot JR.

There are, of course, other reasons why everyone loves stories. A good story has more than suspense. It will have interesting characters, dramatic action, lively and entertaining dialogue. Stories can take us to exciting places, to wherever our imagination dares to travel. They can take us into the past and even into the future. A story is a time-machine; it can transport us to Alice's wonderland or beam us up to *Starship Enterprise*.

The Bible is a collection of stories, as we have observed often enough. The "way" we read modern stories or the "way" we follow a television soap-opera can help beginners to read biblical stories. When we concentrate on a story, in a book or on television, we follow the action carefully. We note the characters as they appear. We are quick to spot the heroes and the villains; we know soon enough who is on the side of the angels and who is out to make mischief. We follow the dialogue, listening to all that is said so that we can make sense of what is happening.

When we read biblical stories we should bring our natural talents with us. In this chapter we shall look at a very strange story with nothing much more than our native curiosity and human imagination.

Bible beginners often feel uncomfortable because they cannot see the wood for the trees. Yet concentration on detail at the expense of the whole is, to some extent, a necessary first step. Such is the case here. We have met this story before (chapter 12) and we shall meet it again (chapter 26) and we may very well ask why the same tale is told three times. For the moment, let us be content with the trees and leave the message of the whole book in abeyance. We must walk before we learn to run.

What happens

Abraham and Sarah journey to Gerar, a city near the Mediterranean Sea. Afraid that the local king would kill him in order to take the beautiful Sarah, Abraham passes off his wife as his sister. Abimelech the king duly takes Sarah into his harem. But God warns the king in a dream that Sarah is a married woman and Abimelech pleads that he is innocent: "In the integrity of my heart and the innocence of my hands I have done this." God advises that Sarah should be given back to Abraham who will pray for the king. This Abimelech does, complaining the while that Abraham should have acted so wickedly. The king even showers Abraham and Sarah with gifts to right the wrong he so nearly committed. There is a surprise twist in the tail of the story. We learn that God had inflicted infertility on Abimelech and on his wife and harem because of the danger to Sarah's honour. Through the prayer of Abraham the affliction is removed.

A strange story, indeed!

The characters

We know quite a lot about Abraham. He is the one chosen to be the father of a holy people. He is supposed to be God's obedient servant and, for the most part, he is. But here we find him living out a lie. Not only does he lie; he allows his wife to be taken into the harem of a pagan king. And all to save his own skin. Abraham ceases to trust in the God who has called him and promised him greatness. Sarah is no more than a chattel, to be used as men please.

It is the pagan king, Abimelech, who comes out of the story

with honour. We must not ask how he manages to know God; our story-teller does not explain such matters. The king is a man of "integrity", a word used to describe Abraham (17:1) and that great saint of the Old Testament, Job (Job 1:1). The word indicates that Abimelech is a man of great piety. Throughout the story, the integrity of the king is in sharp contrast to the deviousness of Abraham, God's chosen one.

As in all Bible stories, the chief character in this story is God. It is God who intervenes to warn Abimelech and thus to save him from wickedness. It is God who directs the king in what he must do. The God in this story is shown to be a God who cares about morality, even of pagans. He is concerned to see that right is done.

THE MESSAGE

The message seems clear. God has chosen Abraham, not because of the man's goodness but because He makes a free choice. Abraham does not get what he deserves; everything comes from God's promise. We are about to witness the beginning of the fulfilment of that promise. Isaac will soon be born. But before he is, our story-teller provides this strange story so that we might learn that all is due to God's providence.

BIBLE STORIES

We have attempted in this chapter to read one Bible story. We can learn from our efforts the characteristics of almost all Bible stories.

First, we note that the story is told with extreme economy. In the space of just two verses we have an account of a journey to Gerar, of Abraham's duplicity and of Sarah's abduction by the king. We are not told why Abraham makes his journey nor are we given much detail as to where Gerar is. Only the bare minimum about the physical setting of the story is provided. No reason (as yet) is given for Abraham's deception. Abimelech is simply introduced as the king of Gerar. But what did he look like? We are not told. Almost nothing is known about the physical features of characters in the Bible. We know that

Sarah was beautiful, that Saul was tall and handsome, that Absalom had long hair, but beyond such general descriptions, we have few clues as to how characters looked.

A second point to notice is that rarely do more than two characters converse in a biblical scene at once. Here we have a conversation between God and Abimelech, then between the king and Abraham and, finally, between Abimelech and Sarah. There are no three-way conversations and this is typical of nearly all biblical narratives. The reason may very well be that stories which originally were told around camp-fires or wherever had to be kept fairly simple. It is not easy to remember the complicated dialogue of many speakers.

Thirdly, rarely are a character's thoughts or motives explained. This story provides both the rule and the exception. We are not told why the king takes Sarah into his harem. We are not told how Abimelech came to know God, how he recognised the message of God in his dreams or why his action should cause death to himself and all his people. Abraham's explanation of his subterfuge to the angry and distressed king is unusually verbose, appropriately, perhaps, for one caught out in a lie and having to explain himself to one of higher social standing who possesses the power of life and death.

Fourthly, the narrator is absent. Rarely in biblical stories does the story-teller interject his own commentary on the action. He keeps his opinions to himself.

We should keep these four points in mind as we read Bible stories. Other characteristics of biblical narrative will be noted as we continue our journey and we will become familiar with how stories are told. Knowing how a story is told will, of course, help us to understand it.

PRAYER

Every Friday evening (the beginning of the Sabbath), religious Jewish families sit down to eat the Sabbath meal. Before the meal there are family prayers. The wife lights the holy candle. She and her husband bless each other and their children. The husband recites Proverbs 31:10-31 as a hymn of praise and thanksgiving for his wife. I wonder whether a Christian husband, following the example of Proverbs, might fashion a prayer for "a good wife"?

Chapter 18

To Abraham and Sarah – A son
Genesis 20

The four most beautiful women in the history of the world are Sarah, Rachel, Ruth and Abigail. At least, that is, according to the Jewish rabbis. Another instance, you may say, of men passing judgment on women. But it is of interest to consider why Jewish teachers chose these particular women. Why not Helen of Troy? Why not Cleopatra or the Queen of Sheba?

Abigail

We will begin with the portrait of Abigail. Her story is to be found in the First Book of Samuel, chapter 25, and a remarkable story it is, too. She was married to a very wealthy sheep-farmer, "a churlish and ill-mannered" fellow by the name of Nabal. In contrast, Abigail "was of good understanding and beautiful". The story tells of how David and his followers "protected" (Mafia style!) Nabal's shepherds and sheep on Mount Carmel, at a time when David was on the run from King Saul and living a life no better than that of a marauding bandit. When David asked Nabal for some food for his men, the man stupidly refused. But secretly Abigail delivered supplies to the future king and thus prevented David avenging himself on the tight-fisted Nabal.

Abigail displayed intelligence, wit, charm (her speech to David must be the longest attributed to a woman in the Bible and it is pure velvet), and a great deal of political good sense. She was inventive, daring and eminently practical; she knew how to survive in a man's world. Not surprisingly, her husband was called Nabal; as his name means, so was the man, a fool. Nor is it surprising that when he died, David wooed Abigail to wife. It is instructive to note that Abigail is first called a woman of good understanding and then beautiful. The beauty of the women in the Bible is more than skin-deep!

Ruth

We met Ruth at the outset of our journey. She was, we read, "a woman of worth" (Ruth 3:11). She was praised for her kindness and fidelity to her mother-in-law Naomi, qualities which took her from her own family, from her own religion, from her own country, and turned her into an immigrant in a foreign land. She was brave and inventive, a resourceful survivor in a hostile world (as a poor immigrant, she was, on one occasion, in danger of rape – see: Ruth 2:9). Yet, through her good sense and intelligent determination, the impoverished foreigner became the great-grandmother of King David and an ancestor of Jesus of Nazareth (Matthew 1:5). The Bible does not say that Ruth was beautiful. It doesn't have to. The ingredients of beauty are the qualities of Ruth.

Rachel

Rachel we shall meet in very romantic circumstances later on our journey (Genesis 29). She was "a beautiful and lovely" woman. Her husband worked for her father for fourteen years to win her hand and "they seemed to him but a few days because of the love he had for her" (Genesis 29:20). But it was not her beauty alone that won her Jacob's love. If we may judge her by the elder of her two sons, who resembled her more than he did his father Jacob, she was a discerning and prudent mother. Her son Joseph saved not only the whole family of Jacob but, indeed, the whole earth came to him for bread in the days of the famine (Genesis 41:57). Like mother, like son!

Sarah

We know on the testimony of her husband Abraham that Sarah was "a woman beautiful to behold" (Genesis 12:11). But Sarah "was barren; she had no child". Her life was emptied by childlessness. To Abraham God had promised a great nation of descendants and, though he had children by his other women, God was determined that the people of Israel were to come from the womb of Sarah. But the womb of Sarah was barren.

We have followed the story of Sarah, noting God's determination to be faithful to his promise. We noted, sadly, that as time went by, the obstacle of old age was added to sterility. Yet when Abraham was over one hundred years old and his wife was over ninety, God renewed his blessing-word to Sarah: "I will bless her, and moreover I will give you a son by her" (Genesis 17:16). Abraham and Sarah fell about laughing!

Old age and barrenness. Why? Because we must understand that God does not depend on human agency to bring about what he intends. Our story-teller, again and again (and, surely, with great exaggeration), reminds us of the advanced age of Abraham and Sarah. Jesus said that what was impossible for human beings was not impossible for God (Mark 10:27). It is God's purpose which is at work in the life of this odd couple and his purpose will not be gainsaid. The promised child is to be the beginning of the people from whom will come Jesus of Nazareth, another child of an unlikely promise: "How can this be, since I have no husband?" (Luke 1:34). The barrenness and old age of Sarah and the virginity of Mary seem to exclude the possibility of children. But to Sarah and to Mary God gave his word and his word was made flesh in them. Sarah was, indeed, beautiful but, one suspects, her beauty was beyond compare when suffused with the joy of an expectant mother.

A son

After all the waiting and wondering, the birth of Isaac is narrated with the brevity of a notice in *The Times*. Physical impossibility, human incredulity and cynicism are overcome by the quiet and determined action of God: "the Lord did to Sarah as he had promised" (Genesis 21:1), and she conceived and bore a son and Abraham called his son Isaac. God will not be frustrated by human failure and human disbelief. Rather, he can fill the emptiness and barrenness of human existence with the laughter of children. The name Isaac means "he laughs". God not only gets the last say. He gets the last laugh!

IMAGES OF GOD

What kind of God do we find in the story of Abraham's and Sarah's longing for a child? Surely:
  a God who offers a future when none seems possible;
  a God who overcomes all that human failure and disbelief
    can muster;
  a God determined to bless his people;
  a God who is on the side of his people.

A Jewish teacher once said that God made one day holy so that we might realise that all days are holy. He said that God chose one people so that we might understand that all peoples are chosen. The birth of Isaac is a great God-sign, a sign that the future of humanity is laughter, not the barrenness of despair. God made Isaac for laughter that we might understand that we are all made for laughter.

PRAYER

Psalm 34 is a prayer for one who finds refuge in God, who tastes and sees that the Lord is good, who looks to him and is radiant.

Chapter 19

Unbinding God
Genesis 22

Religious people use lots of special words. Many of them are big words and most of them are little understood. Take some of the words you will hear Christians use, words such as incarnation, resurrection, reconciliation, salvation, redemption, justification. Do these words mean anything to ordinary people? Do they mean anything to you? Perhaps there is need of a rehabilitation centre for our religious language.

When we made our way through the Book of Ruth we were able to rehabilitate the word "redemption". Now we will tackle the notoriously difficult word "sacrifice" in connection with a story about Abraham and his son Isaac in Genesis 22. The story is often called "The sacrifice of Isaac"; however, Isaac is not sacrificed in the story nor does the word "sacrifice" occur there. When we have journeyed through the story, we may wish to remember it by another, more accurate title, "The unbinding of Isaac".

A burnt offering

Our story begins with the strangest command issued by God in all of the Bible. God orders Abraham to kill his child:

> Take your son, your only son Isaac, whom you love, and go to the land of Moriah, and offer him there as a burnt offering upon one of the mountains of which I shall tell you.
> *Genesis 22:2*

We are faced here with a difficult tale, an uncomfortable tale of a God who commands the murder of a son! We shall have to proceed cautiously and we will begin by trying to explain what is meant by "a burnt offering".

An overdone Sunday roast, victim of some cooking disaster, is about as near as we are likely to get to a burnt offering. And the one who unkindly greets the unfortunate cook with

"Another burnt offering, I see", is not likely to be aware that he or she is using the Bible language of sacrifice. For a burnt offering was a sacrifice. We must ask ourselves what a sacrifice was and what role sacrifice played in the religion of the Jews. Jesus was born into the Jewish faith; he lived and died in it. He and Mary and Joseph had animals and birds killed to offer in sacrifice to God. What, we might ask, did they think they were doing?

Sacrifice

The word "sacrifice" has many meanings. We admire parents who make sacrifices for their children, that is, who give up their own comforts and pleasures in order to provide for the education and well-being of their sons and daughters. When a soldier is killed in battle we speak of the ultimate sacrifice of laying down one's life for one's country. Here, then, is the first element of sacrifice: it involves giving up something valuable, even one's life.

In the game of chess or draughts a player may sacrifice a valuable piece in order to gain some advantage over his opponent. What happens is that player A permits player B to capture a piece freely but in such a way as to prove advantageous to himself. A second element of sacrifice emerges from this example: a sacrifice is a surrender of something of value as a means of gaining something even more valuable or desirable.

Taking these two elements together and putting them into a religious setting, a sacrifice is a surrender of something to the gods in order to influence them or to gain their good pleasure. Ancient (and not so ancient) peoples offered their most valuable possession to their gods to win their favour or stave off their anger. Different peoples offered different things, depending on their circumstances, and some offered what is valuable everywhere, human life. In many primitive societies, children were sacrificed to the gods.

A sacrifice, then, is some valuable possession made over to the gods as a means of gaining something desirable from them. To go about offering a sacrifice one had to find a way of transferring the valuable possession from one's own control to the domain of the god. For most ancient peoples, the way to do this was to destroy the object in question, usually by killing it (if it were an animal or human being) and burning it. So, for example, when Noah emerged from the ark, he built an altar (an elevated stone structure on which sacrifices are offered) and he killed one each of every clean animal and bird and burned them on it. In this way the animals and birds were totally destroyed (burnt to ashes, we might say) and so beyond human use. The fire removed them to the realm of God; somehow destroying what was of very considerable value to people demonstrated belief in and reliance on the gods and won their favour. In the case of Noah, you will recall that his sacrifice pleased God to such a degree that he renewed his blessings on all creation. People imagined that the smell of roasting flesh (animal or human) or of grain parched with fire was pleasing to the gods and attracted their favourable attention. The story of Noah tells us as much: "And when the Lord smelled the pleasing odour, the Lord said in his heart, 'I will never again curse the ground because of man'" (Genesis 8:21).

There are many reasons for praying and there are just as many reasons for offering sacrifices. Ancient peoples prayed and offered sacrifices to beg for good weather, for healthy animals, for plentiful crops, for the gift of children; they prayed and sacrificed to ward off harm and evil spirits, to plead for protection on perilous journeys, to win victory in battle, to make amends for sins committed and to feel close to the protecting power of their gods. There are as many reasons for sacrifice as there are concerns of the human heart.

READING THROUGH

Back to the story in Genesis 22. A few details need to be cleared up before we advance.

Moriah
The land of Moriah appears (on shaky evidence, it must be said) to have been a very old name for an area around what came to be the city of Jerusalem. Indeed, in the Second Book of Chronicles (3:1), the writer identifies Mount Moriah as the exact location on which Solomon built his famous temple. Mount Moriah is sacred to three of the great religions of the

world. It is sacred to the Jewish faith, for on it God tested Abraham and saved Isaac and because on it was built the holy Temple – a building which Jesus called "My Father's house". It is sacred to Christians because Jesus was presented to God there (Luke 2:22) and was put to death nearby. It is sacred to Islam for the prophet Mohammed ascended into heaven from the summit of Mount Moriah. Today the summit is enclosed by an Islamic shrine called the Dome of the Rock, the jewel which crowns the beauty of Jerusalem.

Angel of the Lord

The phrase "the angel of the Lord" is familiar to Christians because that is how the heavenly visitor to Zechariah is described by St Luke (Luke 1:11). In the Book of Genesis and, indeed, for most of the Old Testament, angels are not beings distinct from God but simply a way of speaking about God. To say that an angel appears means that God has revealed himself.

READING THROUGH AGAIN

We are now in a position to attempt to read this most difficult of Bible stories.

The story opens with a helpful nudge from our story-teller: "after these things". What happens next follows on what has gone before and we are invited to recall all the stories of God's dealings with Abraham before he is invited to make the terrible journey to the land of Moriah. The faith of the great man had been sorely tested up to now; he had been required to leave his own country, his kindred and his father's house and travel with no more than God as his guide to an unknown land. Abraham might fairly claim that his faith in God's promises had been sufficiently put to the test; why should he now have to take to the roads again with nothing at the end but the death of his beloved son? What kind of a God is it who demands the last pound of flesh?

"After these things" – of all that had gone before the most important concerns the children. The hope for the future is centred in the children, as, indeed, it always is! And Abraham is given a child, the child of Hagar, the Egyptian slave-woman and that child with its mother is driven out by Abraham and Sarah because there is a new child. It is true that God had announced that the great promises would come through the new child but nowhere had he commanded that Hagar and her child should be abandoned. Indeed, earlier, when Hagar ran away, the angel of the Lord promptly ordered her to return to Abraham (Genesis 16). When the unfortunate woman is thrown out, God has to accept the stupidity of human jealousy and change his plans! When Abraham and Sarah fail, God must intervene to save.

The future of the child of Hagar had been sorely jeopardised by the command of Sarah to her weak husband. Now the future of Isaac, the beloved son, will be endangered by the command of God. Abraham will learn that the future of his child and the blessings tied up with the child are at God's disposal, not his. So God puts Abraham to the utmost test of his faith. Abraham knows, as we the readers know, that God abhors child sacrifice. How, then, can he ask such a thing? Of course, the reader knows that God has no intention of allowing harm to come to Isaac and can see that the heart of the story concerns Abraham's trust in God.

The heart of the matter appears in Abraham's assurance to Isaac as all is to hand for the sacrifice but there is no lamb. "God will provide himself for a burnt offering, my son", says Abraham, and soon Isaac is bound and laid on the altar. God provided for the child of Hagar who was cast under a bush in the desert; will he do as much for Isaac as Abraham puts forth his hand and takes the knife to slay his son? But the angel calls, the knife is stayed, the ram is found caught in the bushes, Isaac is unbound. On that very spot Abraham learned, because he was willing to trust to the utmost, that God does provide. The future of Isaac is in the hands of God and all the blessings on the world are secure. It is not Abraham who saves Ishmael; it is not Abraham who saves Isaac; it is not Abraham who saves the world. The future does not belong to Abraham; nor does it belong to bombs and bullets. It belongs to God. But it takes faith to see it, the kind of faith Abraham found on Mount Moriah.

Perhaps, as we read this story we can sense a much larger issue than the perfect obedience of Abraham. Are we not challenged here to be inquisitive about the word "God"?

Are we at home with a God who tests, who commands and who promises? Undivided loyalty to God is as necessary as it is rare. The testing is everywhere around us, the choices everyday offered. We pray, in the Lord's Prayer, not to be brought to the test lest we be found out. But the testing is inescapable.

A God who commands... and a world which demands! Blessed are those who hear the word of God and keep it!

A God who promises? It is not easy to believe in promises, especially those made by God. After all, he's not easy to pin down. We can't haul him off to court and make him pay up. In today's world, believing in a God-of-promises is a problem. A God who provides? The same prayer which prays to be spared temptation and testing prays for daily bread. Is the prayer heard?

Isaac had his hands tied behind his back. He was bound and thrown on the stones. Lazarus (John 11) was bound and buried in a tomb. Jesus was bound and led from the garden (John 18:12). And Annas sent him still bound to Caiaphas the high priest. And, in the end, they bound his body according to the burial custom of the Jews and put him in a tomb. End of story.

Not quite! God insists on the unbinding of Isaac. As Lazarus hobbles from the grave, his hands and feet bound, the cry goes up, "Unbind him! Let him go free!". And, on the third day, they came to the tomb and the binding cloths were folded neatly; they were set aside; the tomb was empty.

The story of the unbinding of Isaac tells of God who sets free. It invites us to look anew at our God, to unbind him from the narrowness of our conceptions, to set him free. Maybe then he might be able to go about unbinding us, setting us free?

PRAYER

Try Psalm 33. The eye of the Lord is upon us; he is keeping an eye on us, not to catch us out but to jump in when we slip.

Chapter 20

To Isaac and Rebecca – Twins

Genesis 25:19-27:45

"God created people to know love and serve him in this life and to be with him forever in the next".

Well, yes. But are other answers possible?

God created people because he loves stories!

At least, that is the impression you get as you journey through Scripture. The Bible is full of stories. The world of the Lord is a world of stories.

The story of Jacob and his family occupies the remaining chapters of the book of Genesis. It is not an edifying story, at least, not on the surface. It is a story of cheating, lying, stealing, rape, attempted murder and murder itself. Few characters emerge to claim our admiration. When Abraham died, the Bible could say that he "died in a good old age, an old man and full of years, and was gathered to his people" (Genesis 25:8). Of Isaac, it is said that "he died and was gathered to his people, old and full of days" (Genesis 35:29). At the end of his days, Jacob sadly writes his own obituary: "few and evil have been the days of the years of my life" (Genesis 47:9). From the womb to the tomb, the story of Jacob is fraught with conflict, of brother against brother and hardening of hearts.

READING THROUGH

In this chapter we shall follow the story from the conception of the twins, Jacob and Esau, to Esau's determination to kill his brother. We have to face some very difficult material and meet many strange people, customs and beliefs. We will need to be patient.

Rebecca

Otherwise spelled Rebekah, the name means, most probably, "cow". While the name of Abraham's wife, Sarah, means "princess", the names of other famous women in Genesis are not so flattering. Leah, the name of Jacob's first wife, also means "cow" and that of his second wife, Rachel, means "ewe". Another woman who bore children to Jacob glories in the name of Zilpah, which means a "short-nosed animal". While the meaning of these names ought not to be taken as a clue to their characters, we might contemplate the position of women in a society which confers on them the names of animals. Like cows and sheep, women were the property of men. Small wonder that they must live on their wits!

Esau

The Bible offers two explanations of this man's name. Either the name was given to him because he was a rather hairy baby, ("all his body was like a hairy mantle") or because he had red hair. Both explanations seem fanciful. But if you believe that people with red hair are fiery-tempered, you may feel that Esau's name just about describes the man!

Jacob

Such is the importance of this man, we must spend some time on the explanations of his name, and the change to it, offered in the Book of Genesis. As is usual in the Bible (see the case of Jesus himself), an explanation of his name is offered at the birth. The second twin is said to have grabbed his brother by the heel as he came from his mother's womb and so he was called "grabber". An entirely suitable name in the light of his subsequent career!

When Jacob steals his father's blessing from his brother, Esau affirms that Jacob is rightly named "for he has supplanted me these two times". Jacob's capacity to cheat his (perhaps, not very bright) brother is emphasised here.

However, these derivations have more to do with popular story-telling than with strict definition and "Jacob" is probably a short form of "Jacobel" which means probably "May God protect". This particular Jacob is going to need all the protection he can muster, not least from his own cheating self.

In chapter 32, Jacob's name is changed to "Israel", the name of the modern Jewish state. We shall attend to this change in due course.

126

First-born

Esau was the first-born son of Isaac and as such he had a special status based on the belief that the first-born was sacred, the exclusive possession of God. Often, in the ancient world of the Middle East, the first-born was killed in sacrifice to the gods but the people of Israel shunned human sacrifice (with occasional lapses). Nonetheless, the first male issue of the womb ("the first issue of his father's strength", Deuteronomy 21:17), had certain rights. He became the next head of the family and tribe and responsible for the family and tribal welfare. As his birthright, he was entitled to the family blessing and he received a double portion of the family inheritance. He was the family priest and offered sacrifice (at a later time this responsibility was handed over to descendants of one of Jacob's sons, Levi). All these rights and privileges were formally acknowledged by the father's blessing. The blessing was our equivalent of making a will.

READING THROUGH AGAIN

Like Abraham and Sarah before them, Isaac and Rebecca suffer from sterility. For twenty years the pain of barrenness was borne by husband and wife. Isaac prayed for his wife; twenty years of praying, twenty years of hoping. Even before Isaac himself was born, God had committed himself to a promise: "I will establish my covenant with him as an everlasting covenant for his descendants after him", God assured Abraham (17:19). And Sarah had laughed!

Again, after Isaac's birth, God renewed his promise: "through Isaac shall your descendants be named" (21:12). Now the promises are more than twenty years old and Isaac is still praying, still believing in the God who made them. Though Isaac is the special child of promise, though Rebecca is of good stock, there is barrenness. No human arrangement can secure the continuance of this family. Barrenness cannot be overcome by the ingenuity of the parents. It can be dealt with only by the God of life. And so Rebecca conceives. Twins!

The events surrounding the pregnancy of Rebecca are notable. We are told that the children struggled in her womb and she said, "If it is thus, why do I live?". It is not clear what

127

Rebecca meant by these words for the Hebrew original itself is not clear. It would seem that Rebecca had some foreboding that all would not be well between her children. She went to enquire of the Lord (again, we are not told how she went about doing this) and was told:

> Two nations are in your womb, and two peoples, born of you, shall be divided; the one shall be stronger than the other, the elder shall serve the younger.
>
> *Genesis 25:23*

The unease of the expectant mother is confirmed. The lives of her sons will be full of conflict. The children are a gift, but a gift which will be lived out in bitter conflict. The ambition of the younger child will be to rob his brother of his birthright, to cheat him, to dominate him.

The people of Israel must long have meditated on the career of Jacob, the man who gave them their name, the father of them all, and wondered how it was that God's favour and promises rested on the ambitious, grasping upstart. They concluded that it was all part of God's purpose which was destined from the beginning, even before the children were born. It is the shifty Jacob who will inherit the promises made to Abraham and he will be the father of God's chosen people.

The rivalry between the brothers and the grasping nature of the younger one is plainly illustrated by the picture of Jacob emerging from his mother's womb grasping the heel of Esau, as if making one last attempt to be the first-born.

Red pottage

The story moves quickly. Esau grows to be an outdoors man, beloved by his father because of his success as a hunter of game. One senses that Esau is a wild giant of a man. By contrast, Jacob is the quiet, stay-at-home, mother's boy.

Esau is hungry and cannot wait. He speaks over the rumblings of an empty stomach, with the smell of the lentil stew in his nostrils. His appetite is not for the future blessings which are his by right of birth. Immediate gratification is more to his taste. The clever Jacob knows his brother's impetuous weakness and Esau swears away his birthright. The foolish, precipitous character of the older twin is mirrored in the words,

128

"he ate and drank, and rose and went away". His hunger is satisfied but his inheritance now belongs to the brother who knows how to wait, knows the value of planning for the future.

A father's blessing

Chapter 27 is concerned with the story of how Jacob obtains Isaac's blessing. The blessing of an ageing father had the legal validity of a last will and testament in our society. The deception of Jacob is carried out with the help of his mother, angry, perhaps, at the Hittite wives Esau had married and who managed to make life bitter for the elderly couple. Whatever her motives, Rebecca is clearly helping her favourite son to steal the blessing.

We must understand the power of words in the ancient society of the East. Once the blessing was uttered, it could not be recalled. It had been said and that was that. The testament was final; it could not be revoked.

The story is strange to our ears. How can God allow the blessing of his promises to be settled on a cheat, a deceiver? The vocation to be the father of God's chosen people (for that is what the blessing entails) is God's call; he has chosen Jacob. But the manner in which Jacob comes into his calling is condemned and we will see Jacob paying for his duplicity.

IMAGES OF GOD

These stories of conflict and deception challenge our faith. We are challenged to see God working out his purposes in the world in the midst of conflict, hostility and human corruption. God has to cope with our world as it is, a world which is fractured by sin. The very choice of Jacob is itself a witness to God's determination to bring his purposes to fruition. God may well find it pleasant to work with saints. But most of the time he has to make do with sinners.

PRAYER

Psalm 37 sings of trust in God, of faith in his goodness, of waiting for the blessings to come. A psalm, perhaps, that both Jacob and Esau might have prayed with profit!

Chapter 21

An act of God
Genesis 23:1-20-25:1-8

An act of God: dread words on your insurance policy! The greatest of disasters – the erupting volcano, the fierce hurricane, the bolt of lightning – all are blamed on God. God, it would seem, is to be found only in the terror of the storm. When the news is big enough and bad enough, blame God.

The lesson of Elijah

Elijah was a prophet who lived about 850 years before the days of Jesus. He was a pretty fierce fellow betimes, predicting drought and famine on the land (First Book of Kings 17:1-2), fighting the powerful prophets of Baal with fire from heaven (1 Kings 18), standing up to the formidable Queen Jezebel (1 Kings 19 and 21). Such were the spectacular acts of God in the life and times of fiery Elijah that, like an insurance man, he, too, began to believe that God is to be found exclusively in the terror of the storm. Elijah needed a lesson.

Elijah had to walk for forty days and forty nights into the desert (1 Kings 19:4-18). Have you ever noticed the relationship between "forty" and "desert" in the Bible? The people of Israel had to spend forty years in the desert in order to come to know the God who had rescued them from slavery in Egypt. Against this experience, many other experiences in the Bible are judged. For example, Jesus had to spend forty days and forty nights in the desert meeting the challenge of the forces of evil (Mark 1:13). For forty days, in the desert of a hidden room, the disciples were schooled by Jesus after his resurrection (Acts of the Apostles 1:3). The desert is a place of retreat, a place to learn about God. So it was to prove for Elijah.

At the end of Elijah's journey lay Mount Horeb (another name for Mount Sinai), on which Moses met with God. In the Bible, and in the religious thinking of many peoples throughout the world, mountains are holy places where, as likely as not, one might come near to God. Think of Moses, receiving

God's teaching, including the Ten Commandments, on Mount Sinai (Book of Exodus 19-21); Jesus teaches his followers on a mountain (the so-called Sermon on the Mount, Matthew 5-7) and Peter, James and John are taught the true identity of Jesus on the mountain of the Transfiguration (Mark 9:2-8). Mountains are God's classrooms.

Elijah came to Mount Horeb and "the Lord passed by". When the Bible says that the Lord passed by, it means to suggest that in some manner God's presence was particularly felt. At first, a great and strong wind swept over the mountain, such that the rocks were broken into pieces.

But Elijah did not find God in the storm. An earthquake next, but no sign of God. A fire! – but "the Lord was not in the fire". And then, "a still, small voice". And when Elijah heard it, he wrapped his face in his cloak for he realised that he was in the presence of God.

Elijah had learned his lesson. God may be found in the little things of life as well as the great. He is as likely to be in the ordinary as the extraordinary. Insurance men, please note.

READING THROUGH

Our journey through Genesis now takes us to three very ordinary events:

(i)   the burial of a mother (23:1-20);
(ii) the marriage of a son (24:1-67);
(iii) the death of a father (25:1-18).

The following call for some explanation:

Hebron
Hebron is a very ancient city in southern Palestine. It is a city holy to Jews, Christians and Muslims. There are buried Sarah, Abraham, Isaac, Rebecca, Jacob and Leah. Hebron, sometimes called Mamre (for example, Genesis 23:19), has long been famous for its glass.

Hittites
The citizens of Hebron, with whom Abraham negotiated the purchase of a grave, are repeatedly identified as "the

children of Heth", called, in most modern translations, the
Hittites. These people were a non-Semitic people, located in
central Asia Minor (modern Turkey) and, at one time (say 1600-
1200 B.C.E.), had quite an extensive empire. Whether their
power ever extended as far south as Hebron may be doubted.
But the Bible does claim that there were Hittites in the land of
Palestine (Exodus 3:8; Deuteronomy 7:1) and we know that
the husband of Bathsheba, the woman who committed
adultery with King David and who became the mother of King
Solomon, was that brave and honourable man, Uriah the
Hittite (2 Samuel 11:1-27).

The Canaanites

We remind ourselves that the land of Israel, like most
countries, has been known by many names in its long and
checkered history. We know it as Israel (Palestine, before
1948) or the Holy Land. Before it was occupied by the
ancestors of Jesus, it was called Canaan, the homeland of the
Canaanite peoples (sometimes called the Amorites). These
people manufactured purple dye which they extracted from a
mollusc found in the eastern Mediterranean Sea. So rare and
expensive was this dye that only the very wealthy could afford
it and purple became the exclusive colour of royalty. Canaan
would appear to mean "the land of purple".

READING THROUGH AGAIN

The burial of a mother

The story of Abraham began in Genesis 12 with a promise
of land and many descendants. For all practical purposes, it
ends with the same promise in Genesis 22:16-18:

> By myself I have sworn, says the Lord, because you have
> done this, and have not withheld your son, your only son,
> I will indeed bless you, and I will multiply your descend-
> ants as the stars of heaven and as the sand which is on the
> sea shore. And your descendants shall possess the gate of
> their enemies, and by your descendants shall the nations of
> the earth bless themselves, because you have obeyed my
> voice.

Promises! Promises! As yet Abraham, who left his home, his family, his land, at God's invitation, has but one son and no land.

Indeed, Genesis 23:4 acknowledges Abraham's landless state. He describes himself as "a stranger and a sojourner" to the Hittite inhabitants of Hebron. That is to say, he is nothing more than an immigrant, without a secure foothold in his adopted land. The Hittites call Abraham "a mighty prince", a phrase which would be better translated "a prince of God". The man of God, great father Abraham, the prince of God himself, turns out to be the stranger, the immigrant without land! The man with all the promises and nothing to show for them!

Abraham the immigrant is permitted to buy a grave. We can follow with some delight the polite oriental bargaining where "I will give you" really means "I will sell you". At the end of the formalities, Abraham owns a grave.

It is a small thing that God has done. Yet from this small beginning, from this seemingly hopeless thing, from this grave, the descendants of Abraham, the immigrant people of Israel, came to possess the whole land; from a graveyard to a land flowing with milk and honey. Christians will notice that their story, too, begins with the possession of a grave and an only son, out of which comes a resurrection and a future.

It is a small thing that God has done. Out of the barrenness of Sarah, God brings a child. Out of the grave of Sarah, he makes a land.

The marriage of a son

The promise that Abraham will have many descendants and that all the world will be blessed because of them, depends on Isaac marrying and having children. Before he dies, Abraham sets out to find a wife for his son and he wishes that Isaac be married to one of his own people. The task is entrusted to a servant who has to swear faithfully to carry out his master's instructions. The peculiar gesture accompanying the oath, "put your hand under my thigh" (Genesis 24:2) is to be found only in the Book of Genesis (see 47:29). Scholars explain: "the thigh in biblical usage is symbolic of the reproductive organs, the seat of the procreative powers". The servant has doubts that God will match his words: "Perhaps the woman may not be willing to follow me to this land?" (Genesis 24:5). But Abraham is constant in his faith:

The Lord, the God of heaven, who took me from my father's house and from the land of my birth, and who spoke to me and swore to me, "to your descendants I will give this land", he will send his angel before you, and you shall take a wife for my son from there.

Genesis 24:7

These are the very last words spoken by Abraham in the Bible and they are in striking contrast to the first words he uttered when he heard the twofold promise of children and land. Concerning children, he said, "O Lord God, what will you give me, for I continue childless?" (Genesis 15:2). Of the land, he said, "How can I be sure that I shall possess it?" (Genesis 15:8). But for Abraham the journey from doubt to faith is over. Abram the doubter has become Abraham the father of faith.

And, of course, the match-maker is successful. The delightful story ends in the marriage of Isaac and Rebecca: "she became his wife, and he loved her" (Genesis 24:67). But in the joy of their wedding do not forget the match-maker. He is the first person in the Bible of whom it is expressly recorded that he prayed for divine guidance at a critical moment. It is worth noting that he did not pray for a great sign but rather for sound judgement. And his prayer is a "prayer of the heart", a private, personal prayer, displaying belief in individual, direct contact with God, the prayer of one who understands that God is approachable, that he listens to the simple prayer of a servant.

The death of a father

We will not dwell on the concubines of Abraham nor on the many children he fathered on them in his old age (175 years at his death!). Suffice it to say that he provided for them and that Hagar's child, Ishmael, and Sarah's child, Isaac, are united at the grave of their father. After a long and turbulent life, peace surrounds the tomb of Abraham and Sarah.

134

IMAGES OF GOD

Three acts of God – buying a grave to bury a mother, marrying a son, burying a father – are the stuff of ordinary people and everyday life. The workings of God are not always spectacular, not magical, not freakish. The Holy Land of God begins with something as ordinary as a grave. The future is established by a loving couple and blessed by a dying father. God, not in the wind, not in the storm, not in the earthquake, but in the still, small voice.

PRAYER

Psalm 67 speaks of the ordinary care with which God looks after our world every day. Praise be to him!

Chapter 22

The melody of the past
Genesis 24-26

One day, the French playwright, poet, novelist and film director, Jean Cocteau (1889-1963), returned, after a long absence, to the village in which he had grown up. He remembered how he used to walk up the street from his home on the way to school, trailing his finger along the wall that skirted the footpath.

On his visit to the place of his childhood, the old man walked the once familiar street, trailing his finger along the wall. But the gesture did not summon up for him any sense of the past. Suddenly, he realised that he had been smaller then. So he bent down, closed his eyes, and again traced his finger along the wall – this time at the level of a little boy.

Cocteau later wrote of his experience: "Just as the needle picks up the melody from the record, I observed the melody of the past with my hand. I found everything: my cape, the leather of my satchel, the names of my friends and those of my teachers, certain expressions I had used, the sound of my grandfather's voice...".

So it is with us when we gather to share the Scriptures. We exercise our collective memory and discover the youth days of our faith.

We trail our finger along the foundations laid in the Bible and we bring back the sights and the sounds, the fears and the failures, the hopes and the triumphs which make us what we are. We listen to the melody of the past.

The melody of the past... the proclamation of the Scriptures. As the needle picks up the melody from the record, as we listen to the words, we hear again the stories; trailing our finger on the ancient walls of our world, the foundation stones of our faith, we trace the path along which we have come.

Family stories

The God of Abraham, of Isaac, of Jacob: the stories which now preoccupy us, concern families and their God. We have made our way through the story of Abraham. It is a family story, a story of infidelity and love, of barrenness and child-bearing, of despair and hope. In the next chapter, we will turn our attention to the history of Jacob and his family, which, surprisingly, takes up twenty-five chapters (exactly half) of the Book of Genesis. Between the great sagas of Abraham and Jacob lies the short narrative about Isaac. The brevity of the account leads the reader to believe that the traditions about Abraham's son were not very exciting or, at least, did not capture the imagination of the ancient story-tellers of Israel. Isaac does not appear to have had the stuff of heroes and there is little more than one chapter devoted to his tale. But it will reward careful reading.

There is a lesson in the very fact that the Book of Genesis is a collection of family stories: the God of creation is not to be found outside the human story. If we are to hear the melody of God, we must sing human songs. The melodies of the past sing of men and women, fathers and sons, wives and mothers. As we trace our finger along the foundation stones of our faith, we discover God, the God of Abraham, of Isaac, of Jacob, the God in human stories. This is the lesson of Christmas, too; the foundation-belief of Christianity is this: if we are to see God we must look no further than Jesus, the man from Nazareth.

READING THROUGH

The following details should be noted:

Laban

Abraham sent to his own people for a wife for his son and his servant found Rebecca. There is some confusion as to whether she was the daughter of Bethuel, the son of Nahor (who was Abraham's brother) or the daughter of Nahor himself (as Genesis 25:27 and 25:48 suggest), in which case, Isaac and Rebecca were first cousins. Such slight confusions need not unduly concern us. But we ought to remember Laban, the brother of Rebecca, the man who welcomes Abraham's messenger and arranges the marriage of his sister to Isaac. His hospitality to the stranger matches that of his beautiful sister, except that the impression is given that Laban is motivated by greed. He is not above noticing the rings, the bracelets and the fine camels. The story-teller is here preparing us for the character of Laban as it reveals itself later in the stories dealing with his nephew Jacob and his daughters, Leah and Rachel. For the moment, his conduct is perfectly straightforward and honourable. But he is a man to watch.

The Philistines

The Philistine people lived on the mediterranean coastal plain of the land of Israel and were a constant thorn in the side of the Israelite people. Bible readers will readily recall the battles between Samson and the Philistines and the rousing story of young David who slew the Philistine champion, Goliath of Gath, with a stone from his sling.

Abimelech the King

Chapter 26 of Genesis records a story we have heard twice before concerning Abraham (chapters 12 and 20): the attempt to pass off one's wife as one's sister. Rather than suppose that Abraham and Isaac were constantly in danger because of the beauty of their wives, it is more likely that ancient legends which grew up around Abraham were attached to his son as well. This is not uncommon in the Bible and elsewhere among ancient story-tellers.

Take, for example, the famous story of David's duel with Goliath (1 Samuel 17). Actually, a more ancient and more reliable tradition assigns the defeat of Goliath to Elhanan, son of Jair, who, like David, came from Bethlehem (2 Samuel 21:19). It is reasonable to believe that the victory of an obscure warrior has been attached to the stories of the more famous son of Bethlehem, David the King. Another example is to be found in the Gospel of St Mark. There are two accounts there of Jesus feeding a multitude of people in the desert and it is difficult to believe that he worked the same miracle twice (how do we explain the surprise of the disciples on two identical occasions?). We must accept that the Bible sometimes narrates a single story in different circumstances and for different purposes. We must not expect ancient writing practices to obey

138

the rules of modern historical research. Ancient writers had their rules; we have ours.

Wells

Wells feature prominently in the Bible. The Book of Genesis mentions many wells dug by the patriarchs. These sheep-farmers needed wells to water their flocks and their families as much as settled farmers had to have water. There was often tension between the nomadic herdsmen and the crop-growing farmers.

Wells played an important part in social life, too, as a meeting place. You will notice that many men met their wives at wells – Abraham, Isaac and Moses are examples. The most famous meeting of a man and a woman at a well took place at Jacob's Well in Samaria. The story is told in St John's Gospel, chapter 4.

READING THROUGH AGAIN

The birth of the twins, Esau and Jacob, is the most prominent feature of chapter 25. We shall pay attention to it when we come to the story of Jacob and his family. Three features of the Isaac story, brief though it is, will concern us here.

First, we notice that the life of Rebecca is dominated by men. The conspicuous place accorded to her brother Laban in her marriage arrangement is an all too common instance in the Bible of the lack of freedom afforded to women in the ancient (and not so ancient) world. Fathers, and if not fathers, then brothers, treat women as property and dispose of them as they will.

Take the case of rape. The Book of Deuteronomy lays down the penalties for seizing a woman and raping her:

> If a man meets a virgin who is not betrothed, and seizes her and lies with her, and they are found, then the man who lay with her shall give to the father of the young woman fifty shekels of silver, and she shall be his wife, because he has violated her; he may not put her away all his days.
>
> *Deuteronomy 22:28-29*

The rapist must pay the silver shekels to the father, not to the young woman. She is then married off to the man who raped her – she has no say in the matter. The severest penalty on the man is that he may not divorce his wife, a right he would otherwise normally enjoy. Women, of course, were not allowed to divorce their husbands. A man's world, indeed.

All the more reason, therefore, to notice the surprising touch added to our story by the response of Laban and his mother to the servant of Abraham who wanted to return with Rebecca as a bride for Isaac. They said, "We will call the maiden and ask her", and Rebecca gave her answer, "I will" (Genesis 24:54-58). What is refreshingly unusual about this incident is that the woman is given a say in her own destiny. Not a very common occurrence in the world of the Bible.

Secondly – and this is the most important feature of the history of Isaac – there is the renewal of God's promise. Apart from the mention of his weaning (Genesis 21:8), the story of the unbinding on Mount Moriah (Genesis 22), the search for a suitable wife (Genesis 24), little is told of the life and times of Isaac. In one verse (Genesis 25:21), we learn that Rebecca was barren, that Isaac prayed to the Lord, that the Lord answered his prayer and Rebecca conceived.

The only chapter in the Book of Genesis devoted exclusively to Isaac is chapter 26. Because of the famine in the land, Isaac moved to Gerar where Abimelech the Philistine was king. He is instructed not to go to Egypt (in contrast both to Abraham and Jacob) but to remain in the promised land as a sojourner, an immigrant stranger. But to this precarious, landless shepherd God repeats the blessing of a multitude of descendants and possession of the land:

> I will be with you, and will bless you; for to you and to your descendants I will give all these lands, and I will fulfil the oath which I swore to Abraham your father. I will multiply your descendants as the stars of the heaven, and will give your descendants all these lands; and by your descendants all the nations of the earth shall bless themselves.
>
> *Genesis 26:3-5*

There are two elements in the promise: a multitude of descendants and possession of the land. The story of Jacob and his large family will expound the multitude theme. Isaac, the man who remains in the land, even in the face of famine, is the sign that God will give the land to the descendants in his own good time. Of Isaac, alone of all the patriarchs, it is said that he sowed the land with great success: in one season he reaped an unheard-of harvest of one hundred fold. God's promise of a land flowing with milk and honey is symbolised in the fruitful fields of Isaac (Genesis 26:12).

Thirdly, the repetition of the old trick of passing off wife as sister in the face of covetous neighbours serves two purposes: (i) it demonstrates that Isaac, like his father before him, endangers God's promises by his lies. The reader is forcefully reminded that fulfilment of the promise is not dependent on human goodness or correct moral behaviour. The promises cannot be earned; their fulfilment cannot be merited. The promises are freely given; their fulfilment is entirely the work of God; (ii) the problem caused by the beauty of Rebecca leads to disputes over wells and these, in turn, lead to a covenant or agreement between Isaac and Abimelech to live together in the land in peace. In recording this agreement between the Philistine king and God's chosen bearer of the promises, the writer demonstrates that the promises are not for the exclusive benefit of the Hebrew people: "by you all the families of the earth shall bless themselves" (Genesis 12:3 and repeated at 26:4). In the perspective of the writer, God's promises to Israel are a blessing to all the peoples of the world. The great blessing is peace and that is what the blessed Isaac makes with the equally blessed pagans. If the Lord is with Isaac, he is with the rest of us as well.

IMAGES OF GOD

The very brevity of the tale of Isaac reinforces the picture of God which comes through in all the family stories in the Book of Genesis and, indeed, in all the stories of the Bible. The unremarkable character of Isaac and his story are still at the heart of God's promises and plans. Isaac is another example of "the still, small voice" of Elijah. God is as much at home in the little as the great. Out of the mouths of babes and sucklings...

141

God's capacity to further his purposes, with the least promising and uninteresting of material points to his way in our lives. The unflinching faith of Abraham (when at his best) may be beyond our ken. Isaac is more to our size. God is happy with both.

PRAYER

We are familiar with the prayer of Mary, the mother of Jesus, which Christians call "The Magnificat". It is to be found in Luke 1:46-55. The original version of the prayer was spoken by Hannah a thousand years before the time of Mary. She was barren (like Rebecca) and she prayed. You will find her story and her prayer in the First Book of Samuel chapters 1 and 2. It is a prayer for little people.

Chapter 23

Going into exile

Genesis 27:41-28:22

The Bible is a book of journey stories. Its people are forever on the move. Cain became a wanderer over the face of the earth and, after the Tower of Babel incident, all people were scattered to the four corners of the world. Abraham is called to leave home and travel to a distant land. Jacob is forced to flee his home by a brother's hatred. His descendants find themselves in a foreign land and seek to journey home. The very songs of the Bible sing of sad journeys to distant places and cry out in a longing for home:

> By the waters of Babylon
> there we sat down and wept,
> when we remembered Zion.
> On the willows there
> we hung up our lyres.
> For there our captors
> required of us songs,
> ... How shall we sing the Lord's song
> in a foreign land?

Psalm 137

The pain of the exile becomes intolerable when it is experienced as exile not only from one's home but from one's God.

Many of the stories of Jesus are journey stories: the Samaritan who was journeying from Jerusalem to Jericho; the son who left his father and brother to wander the world and squander his riches; the man who planted a vineyard and set out for a far country. Indeed, the story of Jesus himself is a journey story, the story of a man who travelled from his home in Galilee to his death in Jerusalem. To the mourner at the graveside there is no more final exile than the exile of death. Jesus on the cross prays the psalm, "My God, my God, why have you forsaken me?" Human journeys end in death. Only God can make resurrections.

Our exploration of the story of Jacob takes us to his uncle's house and to his marriage to two of Laban's daughters, Leah and Rachel. It is a journey into exile but it is not a journey into despair for (and this is the great lesson of all exile stories) God promises to be with Jacob and assures him of a safe home-coming. In its way, Jacob's story is a resurrection story.

READING THROUGH

Haran

We have come across Haran before, at the very beginning of the story of Abraham. When Abraham's father had moved from Ur of the Chaldees, he settled at Haran and it was here that God called Abraham and gave him the promises, directing his steps to Canaan. But other members of the family continued to live there and it was to these that Abraham sent when he sought a bride for his son Isaac. Here, too, among his own people, Jacob finds his brides. Indeed, all the fathers of the twelve tribes of Israel (that is, the sons of Jacob), except Benjamin, were born in the Mesopotamian city of Haran, in a region called Paddan-aram (now south-eastern Turkey).

Bethel

This city was about twenty miles directly north of Jerusalem and was founded about 4,000 years ago. It is a very important city in the Old Testament. Here Abraham built an altar; here Jacob had his famous dream; it is at Bethel, according to one version of the story, that Jacob's name is changed to Israel. Later on, the Ark of the Covenant was located at Bethel (Judges 20:18-28) and it was around Bethel that Deborah, the most praised of Israel's daughters, worked on behalf of her people (Judges 4-5). And there is much else besides, for Bethel has always been regarded as a holy place.

One can see why in its name. *Beth* means "a house" and *EL* is a name for God. So the name means "House of God". Another such town-name is Bethlehem which means (probably) "House of bread".

There are two reasons for packing off Jacob to his uncle Laban. One is the hatred with which Esau regarded his brother on account of the stolen blessing. Once again we meet brother against brother and are reminded of the cynical question of Cain, "Am I my brother's keeper?"

The second reason is to ensure that Jacob does not marry foreign women, as Esau had done to the great distress of his mother. Isaac sends his son on his way with a prayer that Jacob should inherit the blessings which God promised to Abraham. It is a prayer quickly answered.

When Esau saw that his wives did not please his parents, he marries into the family of Ismael, perhaps hoping to improve his standing in the family.

The story brings Jacob to Bethel, a place to excite the reader who knows the history of the place and the sacred associations suggested by its name. The lonely traveller builds himself a little camp and lies down to rest. He dreams. Dreams seem to run in the family of Jacob and play an especially important role in the story of Joseph. In the traditional stories about Jacob's family dreams are the means by which God communicates with people.

Jacob's ladder is a symbol of the closeness of God; the angels ascending and descending provide a vivid picture of God's constant concern for his people on earth. The purpose of the dream is to fulfil the prayer of Isaac: Jacob is to be the recipient of the promises made to Abraham. The land will be given to his descendants; indeed, later Jacob's name will be changed to Israel and that name will become the name of the country of his descendants. Through Jacob's descendants all the world will find blessings.

Along with the promise of posterity and the land, God gives Jacob an assurance of personal protection in exile and a guarantee of a safe return to the land of his birth. Here we meet one of the central concerns of the Bible: exile. Exile is at the heart of Jewish experience and so it is at the heart of the Jewish Scriptures. It is at once an experience and a symbol. The fact of the matter is that the descendants of Jacob, the people of Israel, have frequently been uprooted from their land and sent wandering in distant lands. Only for a very short period of their history have the Jews lived in peace in their own country. It has been their sad fate to be scattered, exiled far from their homeland. By the waters of Babylon, we sat down and wept!

And so exile became the great symbol of the human experience of the absence of God. Human tragedy seems to point to a distant God who is unconcerned by the pain and suffering of the world. The world which God blessed can seem a vale of tears. The promise to Jacob is God's assurance, an assurance to all who experience exile: I am with you and will keep you wherever you go... I will not leave you. The Christian sees the determination of God to keep his promise in Jesus, the word of God's promise taking flesh and dwelling amongst us, wherever we are.

When Jacob woke from his sleep he said, "Surely the Lord is in this place and I did not know it." And he was afraid. That is a constant theme in the Bible – experience of God leads to fear, to awe-struck reverence. For the Bible is clear: God is near to us but he remains God.

Jacob took the stone which had served him as a pillow and sets it in the ground and pours oil on it. He is, in effect, consecrating a little church and twenty years later he built an altar there (Genesis 35:7). The name he gave to the place, as we have seen, means "the house of God".

Finally, it is here at Bethel that Jacob decides to believe and accept the God of his father Isaac. There is a certain element of bargaining in the faith of Jacob: if God keeps his word and looks after me, then he shall be my God. Still the selfish Jacob! But as he journeys with this strange God he will change!

IMAGES OF GOD

This story of brothers divided by hatred, of family dissensions and storms, of sending into exile and strange dreams, presents us with a God we have met before. In the midst of the storms of life, God is to be found. We see again God's capacity to further his own purposes amidst the turmoil of human events. We see, too, a God who comes to us first – God was in Jacob's dream before Jacob made his act of faith. In our journey stories, God is ahead of us.

Psalm 22 was much used by early Christians in their contemplations on the death of Jesus for it tells the tale of someone who feels deserted by God and beset with enemies on every side. The prayer is for deliverance and it is answered. The psalm is about a death and a resurrection. It is an Easter psalm.

Chapter 24

A tale of two sisters
Genesis 29-31

King David and King Solomon led very merry lives,
With very many concubines and very many wives.
But when they both grew older and they were full of qualms
King Solomon built the Temple and King David wrote the
      Psalms!

Well, not quite!
   Certainly, Solomon built the Temple, a brand-new temple
for the people of Israel in their brand-new capital city of
Jerusalem, a city captured for the purpose by King David. But
it is not so certain that Solomon's father wrote the Psalms.
There are one hundred and fifty prayer-poems in "Songs of
Praise", to give the book of Psalms its proper title. About
seventy of these are attributed to King David but it is very likely
that later anonymous poets composed many of these and
tradition assigned them to the patron saint of the people, to the
king whom God called "a man after my own heart".
   And what of "the very many concubines and very many
wives"?
   King David married Michal, the daughter of his predecessor, King Saul. Of her it was said, "she had no child to the day
of her death" (2 Samuel 6:23). He married Abigail, "a woman
of good understanding and beautiful" (1 Samuel 25:3-42) and
also Ahinoam, from the fertile plain of Jezreel. When David
captured the city of Jerusalem, "he took more concubines and
more wives" (2 Samuel 5:13), to add to an expanding harem.
And, of course, there was Bathsheba, with whom David
committed adultery before murdering her husband, the brave
and honourable Captain Uriah (2 Samuel 11).
   Like father, like son! Solomon, we are told, "had seven
hundred wives, princesses, and three hundred concubines" (1
Kings 11:1). (A concubine, we should note, was not a mistress
but a secondary wife, usually of lower social rank.) Even

allowing for exaggeration on the part of the royal historians, Solomon's harem was a crowded place!

Yet, in the beginning, it was written, "a man leaves his father and mother and cleaves to his wife, and they become one flesh" (Genesis 2:24). How is it, then, that many of the great religious and political leaders in the Bible – Abraham, Jacob, Moses, David, Solomon – violate so flagrantly the teaching of Scripture? We shall attend to this issue presently.

READING THROUGH

Laban and Jacob

Laban, the father of Leah and Rachel, is Jacob's uncle and he welcomes his nephew into his home. It would seem that Laban adopted Jacob as his son and, before long, Jacob found himself a working member of the family, husband to two of Laban's daughters, and a shepherd of his sheep.

Jacob is a first cousin to the two sisters he marries. Marriage between cousins was not forbidden but the Book of Leviticus commands:

> You shall not take a woman as a rival wife to her sister, uncovering her nakedness while her sister is yet alive.
>
> *Leviticus 18:18*

How, then, was Jacob permitted to marry both sisters? Had their father no regard for the religious laws of his people?

Jacob's marriages

Legislation concerning marriage develops very gradually in all societies and, indeed, continues to develop, even in our own societies. The Bible reflects different stages of development. Even in the time of Jesus, when divorce was quite common, matters relating to marriage were confusing. For example, while it was agreed that a husband could divorce his wife (the legislation may be found in Deuteronomy 24:1-4), the reasons for which he could do so were by no means clear. Some said that a serious reason, such as adultery, was necessary; others maintained that a relatively trivial matter could be grounds for divorce. Indeed, even the recorded

149

teaching of Jesus is not without ambiguity. St Mark tells us that Jesus outlawed divorce on any grounds whatsoever (Mark 10:11-12). St Matthew, almost certainly writing later than St Mark, allows divorce on the grounds of *"porneia"*; unfortunately, there is no unanimous agreement as to what he meant by this ambiguous Greek word (see Matthew 5:32 and 19:9).

We must, therefore, be prepared to accept that, as in other societies, the marriage laws of the people of the Bible have developed over a long period. Different parts of the Bible reflect different stages of that development. So, for example, Abraham married his paternal half-sister (Genesis 20:12), although such a union was expressly forbidden by later law and custom (Leviticus 18:8-11; 20:17; Deuteronomy 27:22; Ezekiel 22:11). We have seen that Jacob's marriage to two sisters at the same time was repugnant to the sense of propriety of a later age (Leviticus 18:18). Reuben, the first-born of Jacob had an affair with one of his father's concubines (a secondary wife), who was the mother of his half-brothers, an affair clean contrary to subsequent teaching (Genesis 35:22; 49:4; 1 Chronicles 5:1; and the very peculiar story in 1 Kings 2:13-25).

The Bible writers saw fit to record the marriage practices of their ancestors even though they well knew that such practices were no longer tolerated in the society of their own time.

Rich and poor

There is a factor which governs marriage practices in ancient times and, indeed, in times not so ancient. There is, as our world knows too well, one law for the rich, another for the poor. The plain fact of the matter is that for most of the people of Israel marriage was monogamous, that is to say, one man/ one wife was the order of the day. The reason is simple: not many could afford more than one wife.

From ancient times, and down to our own day, in most parts of the world, women were classified with chattel property. The prophet Jeremiah, announcing an imminent attack by an enemy army, says that fields and wives will be seized; we notice that he puts the fields first (Jeremiah 6:12). Even in the Ten Commandments, woman is regarded as one item in a list of a man's property:

You shall not covet your neighbour's house; you shall not covet your neighbour's wife, or his manservant, or his ox, or his ass, or anything that is your neighbour's.

Exodus 20:17

A woman, to be sure, had some rights but these were only within the context of her husband's authority. The word a wife would use to address her husband was *"baal"* and it signifies "an owner of property" and "a husband" (the same word is used to indicate the authority or lordship of God or gods). A good wife, we are told, "is the crown of her husband (*baal*)" (Proverbs 12:40). St Paul speaks plainly: "The head of a woman is her husband" (1 Corinthians 11:3). Married women, even in the eyes of the Church's greatest theologian, are the property of men. St Paul was a man of his time.

Kings and princes are usually rich. The (vulgar) display of wealth has always been part of the pomp and circumstance of power. What better way to show off one's wealth than to display one's property to the best advantage? So rich men adorned (and still do!) their horses and their women for display.

Economics, then as now, determines, to a considerable degree, the marriage laws of society. Abraham had "sheep, oxen, he-asses, menservants, maidservants, she-asses and camels" (Genesis 12:16); he could afford many wives. David and Solomon were powerful and wealthy kings who displayed their power in the adornment of their women. In the political world, royal families often exchanged their women to cement alliances and treaties. Whether as property or pawns, women were the playthings of the rich.

For the less well-off, another contributory factor to monogamous marriage was the matter of a dowry. When Shechem wished to marry Dinah, the daughter of Jacob, he declared to the girl's father:

Ask of me ever so much as marriage present and gift, and I will give according as you say to me; only give me the maiden to be my wife.

Genesis 34:12

151

But not everyone could afford the market value of a second or third wife.

Yet there are voices in the Bible which speak of love and fidelity, of passion and permanence. Christians (eventually, but rather late in the day) came to share in the vision of the prophet whose little book is the last in the Hebrew Bible:

Has not one God made and sustained for us the spirit of life? And what does he desire? Godly offspring. So take heed to yourselves, and let none be faithless to the wife of his youth. "For I hate divorce, says the Lord the God of Israel, and covering one's garment with violence, says the Lord of hosts. So take heed to yourselves and do not be faithless."

Malachi 2:15-16

READING THROUGH AGAIN

Jacob comes to the end of his long journey into exile. He comes on foot and empty-handed, a refugee from his brother's anger. A state, perhaps, befitting one who sought to make his way in the world by deception and dishonesty.

But Jacob has learned from his dream at Bethel: there is a divinity which shapes our ends. The fact of his exile and the conditions of his future home-coming are God's doings. It is God, and not Jacob, who will cause blessing, who will forge history to his design.

A new chapter of Jacob's story begins with his meeting with Rachel, Laban's daughter, at the well. Welcomes and greetings are exchanged and Jacob enters his uncle's household to work for a month. When the question of wages is mooted, Jacob agrees to work for seven years for the hand of the beautiful Rachel. His love is beyond all telling:

So Jacob served seven years for Rachel, and they seemed to him but a few days because of the love he had for her.

Genesis 29:20

But the man who had exploited the darkness of his blind father is himself to be deceived in the darkness of his wedding night. The cheater is about to be cheated! The brother who substituted himself for his brother is about to have a substitute sister foisted upon him. Yet it is not simply a question of God balancing the scales of justice. Rather are we to understand that God alone is responsible for the blessings. If the treachery of Jacob cannot move the hand of God, neither can the deep and honest love he feels for Rachel. The unwanted Leah is part of the scheme of things, for from the womb of this unloved woman is to come, in God's good time, the two great institutions of the biblical story, the monarchy from her son Judah and the priesthood from her son Levi.

After another seven years, Rachel the beloved becomes Rachel the wife and from her, in the land of Haran, is born Joseph, the brother who will know what brotherhood means and save the family of Jacob from its sins. Thus, through human treachery and deception, God moves to fulfil his repeated promises. Through two wives and two maidservants the family of Jacob grows, well on the way to becoming a nation and a promise fulfilled.

Twenty years a-growing

After twenty years of service and the accumulation of wealth, Jacob decides to return home. Aware of the jealousy of Laban's sons (Genesis 31:1), he realises that it is time to assert his independence, to take his share of the flocks and to return, a prosperous but nonetheless prodigal son, to the land of his birth, to the homeland of his father.

Once again, Laban sets about cheating his nephew, the wicked uncle robbing his nephew of what is his due. But the return of Jacob to his home is a matter of divine policy:

> Return to the land of your fathers and to your kindred, and I will be with you.
>
> *Genesis 31:3*

Laban has pitted himself not only against his wily nephew but, unwittingly, against the determination of God to prosper Jacob and thus to fulfil the promises he had made to Abraham and Isaac. If there is to be deception – and with such a pair, it is to be expected – then, it will favour Jacob. Like Abraham

(Genesis 12:16,20; 20:14) and Isaac (Genesis 23:13-4) before him, now that God is with him, Jacob will receive fortune by means of what at best may be called sleight-of-hand. He turns the tables on his uncle:

> Thus the man grew exceedingly rich, and had large flocks, and maidservants and menservants, and camels and asses.
>
> *Genesis 30:43*

Jacob makes good his escape while Laban is occupied on a sheep-shearing expedition. An interesting but perplexing detail of the flight is Rachel's purloining of the images of her father's household gods. That these were small statues or figurines is clear from the fact that Rachel manages to conceal them in the saddlebag of her camel. Certainly, the objects appear to be of great religious significance, since Laban gives chase to recover them, but we are not told why they are important. What is certain is that Jacob refers to them as "your gods" (Genesis 31:32) and, dismissively, as "household gods" (Genesis 31:37). Clearly, the heart of Jacob is now with the God of Abraham and the God of Isaac (Genesis 31:42); whatever Rachel might believe, whatever power or solace she seeks from the gods of her father, Jacob acknowledges only the God of his family.

Uncle and nephew, after acrimonious words, decide to part in peace and amity. They conclude a solemn covenant or agreement to live in peace, Laban to drop all hostile action against Jacob, and Jacob to love and cherish Leah and Rachel, without ill-treatment and forsaking all others. Interestingly, the covenant is placed under the protection, not of Laban's household gods, but under the watchful eye of the Lord who sees all and will punish violations of the treaty even if they are undetected by human investigations (Genesis 31:50).

Jacob calls his kinsman to eat bread, to seal the covenant with the breaking of bread. The bread of friendship, the bread of brotherhood, the bread of reconciliation, the bread of peace. Jesus, too, took bread and gave it to his disciples. But, then, Jesus was a Jew and he knew well that the bread of friendship is the Bread of Heaven.

Twenty years a-growing! Twenty years from Jacob's meeting with God at Bethel to his return from exile in Haran. Twenty years coming to know and to love the God who caught the imagination of his father Isaac, the God who had won the heart of his grandfather Abraham. Twenty years of hard work, of love and marriage and children. Twenty years depending on the good-will of his uncle-employer. Only the eye of faith, only the ear of hope, can detect God working through life's storms, to accomplish his will, to fulfil his promises.

The lesson of Jacob's exile is the lesson of the Bible from the day of the creation of the world to the day of the incarnation of the Word. God may move in mysterious ways but he moves. "Thy will be done!" is not a pious hope but an acknowledgement of faith. To all who believe, to all who can see, God's promise to see the world as good and to bless it will not be thwarted. A cheating, treacherous, greedy, time-serving pair – for such are Jacob and Laban – cannot resist God's good work. Indeed, their very evil is turned to good purpose. The evil that men do lives after them, yes, but only that it may be transformed by a blessing, baptised to a new purpose, confirmed in a new hope.

In two verses, Genesis 31:42 and 53 (and only here in all of the Bible), God is described as "the fear of Isaac". It is difficult to know what this strange title might mean. On the face of it, it would appear to indicate "the one whom Isaac feared above all", that is, God. *The Jerusalem Bible* offers the translation, "the kinsman of Isaac", and this may very well be nearer the mark. In both verses, what is to the forefront is that the God of his family will not see Jacob sent away empty-handed. Like a good kinsman, God will secure protection and ensure blessing.

PRAYER

Through a life of treachery and cheating, a life of self-reliance and self-promotion, Jacob discovered that, for all his attempts to bluff and brow-beat his way in the world, he could not hide from God. Psalm 139 is a timely and prayerful reminder that the Lord knows us, warts and all.

Chapter 25

Wrestling with God

Have you ever prayed for the scholars who have spent their lives translating the Bible into English? We do well to remember those who have laboured that we might hear the word of God. To enter into the thought-world of another time and another place, to translate the words of that world to our time and our place, require the dedication of a saint and, betimes, the courage of a martyr. For the journey into the strange words and world of the Bible cannot be undertaken without passion, devotion and single-mindedness. It cannot be undertaken without the discipline of profound and prolonged study. It cannot be undertaken without the discipline of prayer. Such as have undertaken the journey on our behalf deserve to be remembered before the Lord.

Wrestling with strangers

The lot of the Bible translator is to wrestle with strange languages, strange customs, strange ideas, strange times and strange places. It is to wrestle with people who lived long ago and far away. How can he say to our time and in our words what the Bible writer said to his time and in his words?

The Old Testament was written in Hebrew, for the most part, with some few chapters in Aramaic, the language spoken by Jesus. Some two hundred and fifty years before the time of Jesus, a Greek translation was made which is called the Septuagint, believed (so the story goes) to have been the work of seventy scholars, working independently and coming up with the same translation! Whether the story is to be believed or not is beside the point. What matters is that the principle was established: it is right and fitting to make the Holy Book available to people who do not speak the language of Scripture.

All the material which came to be collected together (and it took over four hundred years finally to decide what to accept and what to reject) to form the New Testament was written in Greek. This was the common language of the Mediterranean world two thousand years ago as the first Christians began to move beyond the land of Israel and into the wider world of the Roman Empire. The first preachers, Peter, Andrew, James and the rest, spoke Aramaic but had to learn to share the message of Jesus in Greek, in order to make themselves understood by the peoples beyond the borders of Israel.

Over the next centuries, Latin became the dominant language throughout the Empire and St Jerome (?347-?420) produced the Vulgate or Common Bible. This Latin translation became, as its name suggests, the Bible of the Church in western Europe for over a thousand years. But it was not the Bible of the people; it was the Bible of churchmen and scholars. There was no Bible of the people. Most people did not read and, even if they did, they could hardly afford to buy enormously expensive hand-written books. Until the invention of printing, ordinary people did not read the Scriptures, nor were they encouraged to do so. They listened, without understanding, to readings in church from the Vulgate Latin translation of St Jerome and heard explanation in their own language by the deacon or priest, if either actually understood what they had just read to the congregation.

The situation in England was more or less the same as elsewhere. Most people, whether rich or poor, did not have access to the Scriptures. Bibles were produced by monks for use in monasteries and universities as instruments of study and veneration. Latin was the sophisticated language of study and, unless one was well skilled in it, learning was out of the question. The language of the ordinary people of England was not a fit instrument of learning. Most of the parish clergy did not understand Latin and managed by mumbling the Mass in a language they little understood. It is unlikely that even the Gospels were read in English at Sunday Mass. For the most part, sermons were merely stories culled from the lives of the saints. As a body the parish clergy leave almost no mark on the history of the English Bible.

Two forces were against the production of a Bible in the language of the people. First, the Bible was dangerous. The Church had long been accustomed to withholding the Scriptures from those who were ignorant of Latin. Secondly, the

Bible was the word of God and only the most sublime language was worthy of it. The "holy" languages of the Scriptures, Hebrew and Greek, could, in short, fittingly be translated only into the perfect Latin language. English was deemed too crude to be worthy of such honour.

John Wyclif

So there were religious reasons and cultural reasons for withholding the Bible from the people. Who would wrestle with the language to make it fit to carry the word of God? And who would wrestle with the authorities to enable the word to come to the people?

Geoffrey Chaucer (?1340-1400) wrote *The Canterbury Tales* and thereby broke the monopoly on learning controlled by the charmed circle of clerics and their Latin tongue. He and his fellow writers showed that English was as subtle as Greek, as clear as Latin, as beautiful as both. English had come of age as a fit language to express the most sublime ideas. Chaucer's portrait of the parish priest praises the parson,

> Who truly knew Christ's Gospel and would preach it
> Devoutly to parishioners, and teach it.
>
> Prologue to *The Canterbury Tales*

But the reality was a parish clergy who did not know, still less taught, the Scriptures. There was, however, a growing desire throughout Europe to have the Bible available in the languages of the priests and people. Often this desire was expressed by devout women, with no knowledge of Latin, but with a deep longing to know Jesus Christ. In England, the movement for the translation of the Bible into English was led, not surprisingly, by a contemporary of Chaucer, John Wyclif (?1330-1384) and his companions at Oxford and Lutterworth (Leicestershire).

Wyclif and his companions provided a translation of the whole Bible, much to the annoyance of Church authorities. His translation was condemned and his followers branded as heretics. In 1401 a statute "for the burning of heretics" was introduced. In 1407, meeting at Oxford, a synod of bishops, led by Archbishop Arundel, succeeded in having Wyclif's activities condemned. The Archbishop wrote to Pope John XIII in 1411:

This pestilent and wretched John Wyclif, of cursed memory, that son of the old serpent [has devised] a new translation of the Scriptures into the mother tongue.

Another writer of the period is more direct:

This master John Wyclif translated from Latin into English the Gospel that Christ gave the clergy and doctors of the Church... so that by this means it has become vulgar and more open to lay men and lay women who can read than it usually is to quite learned clergy of good intelligence. And so the pearl of the Gospel is scattered abroad and trodden under foot by swine.

The opposition of the Church to translations of the Bible was inevitable. First, the authorities believed that the proper understanding of Scripture was reserved, by the grace of ordination, to clerics and particularly to those who understood Latin. To hand over the Scriptures to ignorant priests and lay people in their native language was to promote heresy. Secondly, one could never be sure that a translation in the native tongue was accurate. For example, Wyclif translated certain Greek words of the New Testament as "congregation" and "senior" rather than as "church" and "priest" as the Latin translations had long agreed. The inference was that, when the New Testament spoke of "church", it didn't mean the officially organised Church but rather a community of Christians and when it spoke of a "senior" or "elder", it didn't mean an officially ordained priest, but a local leader. The fact that Wyclif was right is neither here nor there; to English bishops of the time he was plainly a heretic, undermining legitimate authority in the Church of God.

William Tyndale

Two things happened which favoured the spread and final acceptance of an English Bible. The first was the invention of printing which made books much more accessible to the public and more difficult to control, even if it did not immediately lead to a cheap and plentiful supply. The second was the rise and spread of Protestantism.

William Tyndale was educated at Oxford and was well

capable of translating the Hebrew and Greek of the Bible into memorable English. In 1524 he published his English New Testament on the continent but it was soon available in England. The Church authorities condemned it and it was publicly burned at St Paul's Cross in London. By 1531, he had published (at Antwerp) a sizeable part of the Old Testament. It was Tyndale's ambition to "cause the boy that driveth the plough" to know as much Scripture as any scholar. He was opposed by bishops and scholars, including Sir Thomas More, harassed by royal agents and burned at the stake in 1536.

But the winds were blowing in favour of the English Bible and its Protestant mentors. As Henry VIII found himself more favourably disposed to the ideas of the Reformers, English bishops found themselves more eager to support what the King permitted. Miles Coverdale (1488-1568) published the first complete Bible in English in 1535 and, on 5th September 1538, a royal command was issued which commanded the clergy to set up in every parish church "one book of the whole Bible of the largest volume in English". The war was effectively won, though there were still many battles to be fought.

The Rheims-Douai Bible

The opposition to the English Bible was based, as we have seen, on a misguided attempt by Church authorities to keep the Scriptures out of the hands of lay people and because of a genuine fear of the spread of Protestant ideas. But once the English Bible became readily available and promoted by king and bishop alike, English (Roman) Catholics began to see the need for a translation of their own. William Allen (later Cardinal), president of the English seminary at Rheims, set the project in motion. The translation was the work of Gregory Martin, assisted by Richard Bristow. The New Testament was published in 1582. Martin died in 1584 but his work facilitated the publication of the Old Testament in 1609-10, by which time the seminary had moved to Douai, which gave its name to the translation. Bishop Challoner completely revised Martin's edition in the eighteenth century, providing Catholics with the Douai version which served them into the present century. Unfortunately, Challoner did little to improve, and much to destroy, the excellence of Gregory Martin's rugged style. Martin should be remembered as the scholar who was responsible for such memorable and familiar English phrases as "to publish and blaze abroad", "the one shall be taken and the other left", "compassed about with an army", "to set at nought" and, most endearingly (though probably from Tyndale) "the fatted calf".

The Authorized Version of King James

In January 1604, King James I authorized work on a new translation because of complaints about the accuracy of the translations made in the days of Henry and Edward VI and which had served (with modifications) in the days of Elizabeth. Fifty-four scholars, of whom forty-nine are known, were given the task and the translation appeared from the press of Robert Barker, the King's printer, in 1611. The scholars drew on the Hebrew and Greek and on other ancient editions and they looked at translations in other European languages. They found much of their style in Gregory Martin's Douai. They produced the single most beautiful and influential book in the English language. To multitudes of English Christians it has seemed little less than blasphemy to tamper with the words of the King James Authorised Version.

Modern versions

Neither the King James nor the Douai are accurate translations, simply because the scholars who produced them did not have to hand the vast collection of ancient manuscripts now available to translators. A Revised Version was commissioned by the Church of England and published in 1881, an American revision following in 1901. The National Council of the Churches of Christ in the United States authorized a further revision and this was published as the Revised Standard Version of the Bible in 1952 (revised as *New Revised Standard Version* in 1989).

Roman Catholics of the present century have had available to them the translation of the New Testament by Fr Francis Spencer (1937) and the incomplete Westminster version which began to appear in 1913. Monsignor Ronald Knox published his own rather uninspiring translation between 1944 and 1954. By far the most influential translation has been *The Jerusalem Bible*, edited by Fr Alexander Jones at Upholland College and published in 1966. Few works have done so much to contribute to the rediscovery of the Bible by Roman Catholics in the English-speaking world. With the encouragement of Church authorities, Christians are now free to explore the Scriptures together in a vast array of excellent translations and, by so doing, come closer to the Word made flesh. But they would not have been able to do so were it not for those who have gone before, who have wrestled with the words and laid them before us in a language we can understand.

READING THROUGH

Jacob's return from exile has brought him to the land wherein dwells his twin brother Esau. We shall see how the deceiver fares in his meeting with the brother he so wrongly treated. Chapters 32 and 33 are given over to a series of encounters of one kind or another. Amidst the entanglements of personal affairs, there is one meeting, the meeting at the ford of the Jabbok, which is unparalleled in biblical stories and seems thoroughly bewildering.

Angels of God

As Jacob makes his way from his meeting with his father-in-law Laban, "the angels of God met him". When he had set out on his journey to Laban, Jacob had also encountered angels (Genesis 28:12). It is as if the everyday, mundane affairs of this man are surrounded by God and directed by him. In the midst of his comings and goings, we can detect a master-plan of God.

In the Letter to the Hebrews, the New Testament provides us with its definition of angels:

Are they not ministering spirits sent forth to serve,
for the sake of those who are to obtain salvation?
Hebrews 1:14

We are familiar with the idea of an angel as a messenger of God and, indeed, this is what the word means. An angel of the Lord appeared in the Temple to Zechariah to inform him that his wife Elizabeth would bear a son (Luke 1:11). The angel Gabriel appeared to Mary to announce that she, too, would conceive a son (Luke 1:30). Christians are familiar with the idea of a guardian angel, a belief which is to be traced to Matthew 18:10:

162

See that you do not despise one of these little ones; for I tell you that in heaven their angels always behold the face of my father who is in heaven.

The most ancient biblical narratives speak of "an angel of the Lord". For example,

The angel of the Lord said to her, "Behold, you are with child, and shall bear a son; you shall call his name Ishmael".
Genesis 16:11

A few verses later, Sarah says, "Have I seen God and remained alive after seeing him?". In Exodus 3:2, Moses approaches a bush which is burning furiously and yet is not consumed. "An angel of the Lord appeared to him in a flame of fire out of the bush" and then we are told that "God called to him out of the bush". In Judges 2:1, "the angel of the Lord" addressed the people of Israel and told them that "I brought you up from Egypt". We know that it was God himself who delivered the Israelites from slavery.

What is clear from these quotations is that the ancient phrase "the angel of the Lord" actually refers to God himself. The phrase is simply a polite and reverential way of speaking about God. We might recall, too, that the angels who accompanied Abraham to Sodom were regarded as men by the ruffians of the city (Genesis 19:1-14). So "men" can mean "angels" and "angels" can mean "God". The importance of this is that we will now realise that, when Jacob wrestled with a "man", he really had "striven with God" (Genesis 32:28).

Mahanaim

As Jacob is about to re-enter the land of promise after his exile in the country of his father-in-law Laban, he is accompanied by the angels of God. He interprets the heavenly vision as the armies of God and gives a name to the place of the apparition, "the place of the two (army) camps" (Mahanaim). Similarly, in Joshua 5:13-15, we read that when the people of Israel were about to enter the Promised Land after their exile in Egypt, they were accompanied by the army or host of the Lord. The reader realises that Jacob (soon to be re-named) and his descendants enter the land of Israel in accordance with

God's promise and under his divine protection. Mahanaim features in later history; the reader may wish to refer to 2 Samuel 2:8; 2 Samuel 17:24; 1 Kings 4:14.

Edom
The district known as Edom lies to the south-east of the Dead Sea. But the stories of Genesis 32 belong to the region on the east bank of the River Jordan. It must be that some stories concerning Esau were connected with the south-east region and some (such as we have here) were related to the Jordan region in the vicinity of the River Jabbok.

Jabbok
The Jabbok is a fast-running blue river flowing westwards into the River Jordan, some fifteen miles north of the Dead Sea. It rises near Amman and in all is over fifty miles long. Today it is called Nahr Ez-Zerqa.

Israel
The story of Jacob's wrestling with God offers an explanation of the name "Israel". It means "he who strives with God" or "God strives". But this is a popular rather than an accurate interpretation of the word. Scholars think that the name may be related to a Hebrew word meaning, "reliable", "happy" or "successful".

READING THROUGH AGAIN

Genesis 32:1-8
Jacob draws near to the land of promise, the land of his birth. The vision at Mahanaim is a further assurance that the Lord journeys with him. But the past is catching up with the cheating, crafty Jacob. Esau stands between him and safe return. Messengers are despatched to assure Esau of Jacob's wealth and to imply that gifts (bribes?) are readily available. It is impossible for the leopard to change its spots. But what is humanly impossible may prove to be possible with God. Ominously, the messengers report that Esau is on the march with four hundred men. Jacob splits his family and servants

164

into two groups in an attempt to cut his potential losses. A rather cynical procedure.

Genesis 32:9-12

Miracles will never cease. When Jacob met God in his dream at Bethel, he was willing to make a bargain. If God will be with him, protect him, provide him with food, lead him home in peace, then he would be willing to take God on board: "the Lord shall be my God" (28:20-21). Wouldn't we all?

At the Jabbok, Jacob realises that you can't bargain with God. You can only pray. For the first time in all the round of Jacob stories, we find the man on his knees. He acknowledges that all his prosperity had, indeed, come from the hand of God. More to the point, he admits (at last) that he was not worthy of all the steadfast love lavished upon him. He throws himself on God's mercy and reminds him of the promises. We are witnessing the beginning of the reformation of Jacob.

Genesis 32:13-21

But old habits die hard. Jacob lays out a series of impressive presents for Esau. He would buy his brother with gifts. Reconciliation is costed in terms of camels and sheep and goats. Jacob, as they say, knows the price of everything and the value of nothing.

Genesis 32:22-32

The story of the wrestling at the Jabbok is, indeed, strange. Jacob sends his wives and children across the river with all his possessions. He remains alone. Does he intend to spend a night in prayer? Suddenly a man wrestles with him but Jacob holds his own. His hip is put out of joint but his grip is tight. The man seeks to depart at daybreak. Jacob demands a price: "Bless me". Instead, he receives a new name and the identity of the wrestler is revealed: "You have striven with God and with men and have prevailed".

Perhaps, we can best understand the incident by looking on it as an imaginative dramatisation of what is happening in the life of Jacob. He is at a crisis point. His life, his family and his property are in danger from his estranged brother. He has made an effort to pray. His own resources are not sufficient to meet the circumstances. He must turn to his God and wrestle with him. His demand to know God's name is an attempt to retain control of the situation, to dictate terms. But that can never be. The blessing will have to do. Wrestling with God, trying to discover where he is in our lives and what he is doing there, is a dangerous business. But it is necessary, if we are to come to terms with his purpose. Jacob discovered that he could meet God face to face and be preserved. God does not destroy. But the possibility of acquiring a limp is high. Let the limp stand for the painful changes that must be made when we begin to take God seriously. The business about not eating the sinew of the hip is mysterious. There is no other record that this part of an animal was forbidden in Israel's dietary laws. But we don't know everything.

Genesis 33:1-11

The surprising thing about the reconciliation of Jacob and Esau is that Esau makes all the running. Jacob's reaction to his brother's approach is cowardly. He puts his secondary wives and their children up front, followed by the unloved Leah and her seven children. In the rear, he places his beloved Rachel and her son, Joseph. At least, he has the decency to walk ahead.

Like the father in the Prodigal Son parable (Luke 15:11-32), Esau, the wronged one, is the first to embrace, to kiss, to weep for joy. The wives and the children, far from being in danger, are welcomed. Jacob presses his gifts, explaining, "for truly to see your face is like seeing the face of God, with such favour have you received me". The father in Luke's parable is the God-figure. So, too, is Esau. Those who reconcile brothers are images of God. In the wrestling, Jacob may have seen God face to face and lived. Now, again, he sees God face to face in his brother and, despite all his misgivings, he and his family will live. It is fitting that Esau graciously accepts the gifts.

Genesis 33:12-20

Esau insists on accompanying Jacob. But the fate of the nations to spring from the two brothers will journey separately. Israel has a special role. Accordingly, Jacob, with his new name Israel, must move on alone. The story ends with the buying of

166

land and the building of an altar. The roots are laid in the land of promise. The altar is dedicated to El-Elohe-Israel. The name means "God, the God of Israel". Jacob has come home to his place and to his God.

THE MESSAGE

The journey of Jacob from the homeland of Laban to the land of Israel is a journey from exile. As such it belongs to the greatest of biblical stories, for they are all stories of exile and home-coming. The journey is fraught with danger but it is a journey in the company of God. It is, to be precise, a journey of faith. Somewhere along the way, God must be faced and that may well be a painful experience. It may well make demands and call for new orientation. It is instructive to realise that the journey with God must be a journey of reconciliation and that in the reconciliation of brothers we see the face of God.

IMAGES OF GOD

The image which stands out in these chapters is that of Jacob limping. The strange wrestling at the Jabbok haunts the mind. Is the effort to come to know our God full of danger? Is the struggle to find God in the hurly-burly of our lives a hazardous undertaking? Certainly, it is a matter of high seriousness. Everywhere the Bible tells of God's nearness. But, now and again, there is a reminder that we must not take Emmanuel, God-with-us, for granted.

PRAYER

Psalm 85 speaks of the restoration of the fortunes of Jacob, that is, of the people of Israel. It speaks of steadfast love, of faithfulness, of peace. It is a good prayer for limping people.

Chapter 26

The Joseph story
Genesis 37-50

Jacob dwelt in the land of his father, the land of Canaan, the land of promise. Abraham had travelled from his own country to "the land that I will show you" (Genesis 12:10) and, after much wandering, his grandson settled there. But it is not to be a final settlement. There is much more to be told. The writer moves on to "the history of the family of Jacob", a story which moves from the land of promise to Egypt, the land of oppression.

The story of Joseph, the husband of Mary, is the story of a dreamer. It is the story of a man to whom "the angel of the Lord appeared in a dream" (Matthew 1:20), a man who listened to his dreams and "did as the angel of the Lord commanded him" (Matthew 1:24). It is the story of a man with a family to care for, the story of a man forced by his dreams into Egypt, the place of oppression and slavery. But the story of this Joseph does not end in exile in a foreign land. Another dream, another command, and he and the child and its mother return to the land of Israel (Matthew 2:20).

Joseph, husband of Mary, father-figure to Jesus, dreamer of dreams, is not the first Joseph. He is not the original Joseph. The first – we might say, the mould of such Josephs – is Joseph, the son of Jacob. To understand the New Testament, we must understand the Old. The one is the indispensable key to the other. St Matthew pens his portrait of Joseph of Nazareth with his eye firmly fixed on the dreamer of Genesis, who listened to his dreams, who went down to Egypt, who cared for his family.

The "history of the family of Jacob" is told in the story of Joseph. It is the last great story in the Book of Genesis, the story to which all the others have been leading. It is the final word, the final lesson. At the greatest of all Jewish feasts, the Passover, there is a prayer which sings of the wonderful things that God has done in our world. As each new act of God's love is recalled, the family (for it is a family feast) respond, "That would have been enough for us!". But the litany of blessings goes on and on for there is no end to blessings. Likewise, if we listened to the story of creation and heard it rightly, we too would cry, "That is enough for us!" but hearts are hardened. If we listened to the story of Adam and Eve, the story of Noah, the story of Abraham, the unbinding of Isaac – each of these should have been enough for us. There is only one story in all the stories, one God, repeating again and again to us the great command "Listen!" But...

When St John came to tell of the death of Jesus, he tells that Jesus uttered his final words, "It is finished" and that he bowed down his head and gave up his spirit (John 19:30). It is finished, it is enough! It would be complete, it would be enough, if we listened. The story of Joseph, like all the others from Genesis to Jesus, would be enough. If only we listened. The Jews have a sacred prayer which they recite many times a day. It begins, *"Shema, Israel!"*, "Hear, O Israel!" It is not for nothing that the people of the Bible are commanded to listen.

READING THROUGH

There is much to excite in the story of Joseph and much to explain. We shall, initially, confine ourselves to the main characters in the drama, explaining detail as we go along.

Jacob
We have come to know wily Jacob and now we meet him as a loving, even doting parent who makes the mistake of favouring his younger children, particularly Joseph, the son of his old age (Genesis 37:3). Jacob had twelve sons and the twelve tribes of Israel spring from these sons.

Joseph
Thank goodness we don't need to have detailed knowledge of each of the twelve sons of Jacob to enjoy the story of Joseph. However, we need to know about some of them. Joseph, our hero, is the second youngest of Jacob's sons and the first child of Rachel. Throughout the story, it is emphasised that "the Lord

is with Joseph" (Genesis 39:2,23) and the man himself is deeply devoted to God.

Reuben

He is the eldest son of Jacob and his mother was Leah, Jacob's first but unloved wife. She bore her husband six sons and one daughter, yet she never won his heart.

Judah

He is the fourth son of Jacob, born to Leah. In the story, he acts, along with Reuben and Benjamin, as spokesman for his brothers.

The story of Judah and Tamar, told in Genesis 37, would appear to be an interruption of the Joseph story. It is an old tale, relating to the origins of the tribe of Judah and we might well ask what it is doing here.

In the Book of Ruth we came across the idea of levirate marriage and the strange custom of a childless widow having a right to marriage with a brother-in-law in order to have a son "to her dead husband's name". Tamar, a Canaanite foreign woman, was married to one of Judah's sons but he died. Another son, Onan, refused to give Tamar a child and spills his seed on the ground. He is punished, we are told, by death. Onan's sin, let it be noted, is his violation of the sacred levirate law and not the spilling of his semen.

Judah does not immediately take steps to provide Tamar with a husband and she dresses herself up as a prostitute and lures her father-in-law to her bed. When Judah hears of her subsequent pregnancy, he is full of zeal for the law: "Bring her out, and let her be burned". He does not even mention her name. Such is the world of women!

But Tamar, the pagan, knows that her cause is just and Judah is made to acknowledge it. And of this woman, of this part-time prostitute, in God's good time, was descended King David. And, in the fullness of time, of her stock was born Jesus of Nazareth, the Christ, the Son of God (see Matthew 1:3). What strange people one finds in the family cupboards of Jesus!

Tamar's story is told in the midst of the Joseph story to bring to mind the necessity of acting honestly and rightly, of abhorring duplicity and deception, above all of cherishing wisdom and the fear of the Lord. Death comes to the family of

Judah because it flouts the Torah, the wisdom of God. Even the pagan Tamar can see where justice lies. Joseph, the just man, is made of the same stuff.

Benjamin

Benjamin is the youngest son of Jacob, and his mother, Rachel, died in giving birth to him. His father's special devotion to the last of his children plays an important role in the story.

Ishmaelites and Midianites

Both of these peoples were nomadic traders, tent-dwellers and camel herders who traversed the desert regions of North Arabia. The fact that we are told that Midianites sold Joseph to Ishmaelites (when his brothers intended themselves to sell him to them) is confusing. But the confusion may indicate no more than that there were two versions of the story and the matter was no clearer to the author of Genesis than it is to us. Indeed, the Book of Judges 8:24 tells that the Midianites were Ishmaelites.

Potiphar

Though the story describes Potiphar as "the captain of the guard" (Genesis 39:1), we do not know what his precise duties in the administration of Pharaoh would have been. He seems to have had duties connected with the royal prison. A more correct form of his name, Potiphera, is that of the priest of the city of On, Joseph's father-in-law. On or Heliopolis was a centre of sun worship.

READING THROUGH AGAIN

The story of Joseph is one of the great Bible stories. It opens with a teenage boy enjoying the special favour of his father because he is the son of Jacob's old age. Jacob gives him a long robe with long sleeves, a sign of his doting affection. Naturally enough, Joseph's brothers resent this blatant favouritism; they, too, wish to feel the warmth of their father's love. Joseph brings "an ill report" concerning his brothers to Jacob and matters are not helped. When the dreamer recounts his dreams to his brothers, they hate him all the more. So our story opens with great love and profound hatred. Which will win out in the end?

171

The dreamer and his brothers

The opening of the story is ambiguous. Is Joseph a tell-tale or is he a responsible young man who knows that his first duty is to his father? In the matter of the dreams, are we to understand that Joseph is an arrogant fool who thinks that one day he, the second youngest of twelve, will rule over the whole family? When we recall that his father was a dreamer of dreams who, in his dreams, met the God of Abraham and of Isaac and saw the angels of God ascending and descending the ladder of heaven itself (Genesis 28:10-17), we may well ask whether there is more to Joseph's dreams than meets the eye. We note that Jacob rebukes the apparently presumptuous youth but that he "kept the saying in mind" (Genesis 37:11; and look up Luke 2:19). Crafty old Jacob knows a thing or two about the ways of God!

The hatred of the brothers spills over into action. When Jacob sends Joseph to see that all is well with his sons and the flocks, the brothers conspire to kill the dreamer. Reuben intervenes and, as befits the eldest of the family, intends to save Joseph and return him to his father. He suggests that they throw the lad into an empty water cistern rather than commit the dreadful crime of shedding a brother's blood. Later on, however, Judah convinces his brothers that it would be profitable to sell Joseph into slavery; that way they would be rid of him and avoid shedding blood. This they do and Joseph is brought to Egypt. There is some confusion in the text as to whether it is Midianites or Ishmaelites who buy Joseph but the main fact is that he is sold into slavery.

The garment which is the very symbol of Jacob's love for his son is used by the brothers in a cruel trick. They do not tell Jacob that his favourite child is dead; instead, they show him the robe and allow him to draw his own conclusion.

The "death" of Joseph knocks the stuffing out of Jacob and he foresees that the rest of his life will be spent in mourning for his beloved son. We know that Joseph is alive but that makes the mourning of Jacob all the more moving. "Sheol", as we have seen before, is the abode of the dead. The peoples of the Old Testament believed that all people, good and bad alike, existed after death in some underground region, bereft of God and with no memory of their former lives. It is well to remember that the very high moral demands made by the

Torah, including the Ten Commandments, were made with no thought of reward after death.

The interpreter of dreams

Joseph is sold as a slave to Potiphar. We cannot be sure what his precise duties were but it would appear he had some responsibility for prisons. In no time at all, Joseph is appointed managing director of all of Potiphar's domestic property and affairs. The reason for this sudden promotion must be carefully noted: "his master saw that the Lord was with him, and the Lord caused all that he did to prosper in his hands" (Genesis 39:3). Joseph "was a successful man" (Genesis 39:2), not because he passed all his examinations, but because God was on his side. Through him, the blessings of God were on Potiphar's household.

How is it that the pagan Egyptian and, later, even Pharaoh himself (Genesis 41:38), recognise that "the Lord was with Joseph"? The answer is: that is the way our story-teller planned it and it is impossible to know more than that. What the historical position might have been, we have no idea for we have no evidence. But we can see what the story-teller is about. What a contrast there is between the brothers who fail to realise the possibility that God might be revealing himself in Joseph's dreams and the pagan Egyptians who can see instantly that God is with Joseph! We are reminded of the sailors and Jonah, the pagans who prayed and the prophet who ran away.

Potiphar's wife desires to sleep with the "handsome and good-looking" Joseph. But he knows that such wickedness is a sin against God and his master. In the traditional manner of a woman scorned (at least, in stories!), she takes her revenge and Joseph is imprisoned. Has God abandoned the young man? Far from it! All is going according to the divine plan: "But the Lord was with Joseph and showed him his steadfast love" (Genesis 39:21). God's love is steadfast. Joseph is made prison governor – God is still with him.

The story of the chief butler and the chief baker serves several purposes. First, the writer informs us, through Joseph, that the interpretation of dreams belongs to God. Then Joseph proceeds accurately to interpret the dreams of the butler and the baker, proving (to us) that he is God's spokesman in the matter of the interpretation of dreams. Secondly, the butler provides the link between Joseph and Pharaoh so that when Pharaoh needs an interpreter of dreams the butler will be on hand to remember Joseph.

We come now to the third set of dreams (have you noticed that there are three sets of two dreams each?). None of the magicians nor the wisest men of Egypt can interpret Pharaoh's dreams. Joseph is sent for and again we are reminded that dreams are God's business and that Joseph is his interpreter (Genesis 41:16). He proceeds to explain the royal dreams. Note carefully: "And the doubling of Pharaoh's dream means that the thing is fixed by God, and God will shortly bring it to pass" (Genesis 41:32). We recall that Joseph's own dream was doubled and, therefore, "God will bring it to pass". Joseph had interpreted his dreams to mean that he would rule over his brothers; now we know that his dreams were God-given and Joseph's understanding of them correct!

Not only does Joseph interpret Pharaoh's dreams but he takes it upon himself to advise on what should be done. "A discreet and wise man" (Genesis 41:33) should be appointed to direct overseers who would collect a fifth of the harvest in the bumper years. We have seen Joseph achieve instant promotion before and so it comes as no surprise to us that there is no one "so discreet and wise" as himself.

The precocious young man is now Prime Minister of mighty Egypt with supreme authority (symbolised by the ring, the linen garments and the gold chain) over everyone except Pharaoh himself. A marriage to the daughter of Potiphera, a priest at the prestigious temple at On, confirms his position.

In ancient times, On was the centre of sun worship in Egypt and its priests were considered to be the most learned in the whole country. Incidentally, "Cleopatra's Needle" was originally one of the many obelisks erected in front of the temple at On. More interestingly, at this place, now called Matariyya, one of many legends places another Joseph after another flight into Egypt (Matthew 2:14). It is, after all, the same story!

The Prime Minister

At the age of thirty, Joseph finds himself the Prime Minister of Egypt. He is placed in charge of Pharaoh's palace, which probably means that he is given control of the king's personal estates. He is, too, controller of all the land of Egypt. "The chain

174

of gold" around his neck was a well-known Egyptian symbol of appointment, one of the highest distinctions in the land.

Joseph's chief task, and one to which he immediately gives his attention, is to lay up adequate stores of grain during the years of plenty to offset the famine of the lean years. It is one of the ironies of our story that the semi-nomadic shepherd of the family of Jacob should, along with his other duties, undertake the responsibilities of the Minister of Agriculture! Joseph's first dream, as you will recall, dealt with the binding of sheaves of corn in a field; perhaps that dream contained a hint of his future calling. In any case, Joseph assumes the duties of the ancient Egyptian functionary whose title is known to us: "Overseer of the granaries of Upper and Lower Egypt". Tax-collecting was one of the duties of the holder of this high office and we observe that Joseph, too, fulfils this task (Genesis 47:24).

It will be fruitful to reflect for a moment on some of the personal changes in the life of Joseph. It was not uncommon for foreign immigrants to adopt an Egyptian name and this Joseph does. Pharaoh bestows on him the name Zaphenath-paneah, a perfectly good Egyptian name which means, "the god has spoken and he (the bearer of the name) shall live". Thus we are reminded that Joseph's life, so often under threat, is spared because it is under divine protection. His wife's name is Asenath and it means, "one who belongs to the goddess Neith". The names of Joseph's children assure us of his faith in God who has given him a heart to forgive and to come to terms with the sorrow and injury imposed upon him by his brothers. Like many an exile in foreign land, he rejoices that the God he carries in his heart has prospered him and alleviated the pain of exile.

Notice that Joseph names his children, thus recognising them as his own. Centuries later, another Joseph gives a name to a child – "and he called his name Jesus" – thus making Mary's child, not his adopted son, but his own child with all the rights inherent in that status.

The seven years of plenty give way to the seven lean years and the famine-stricken population turn to Joseph for suste-nance. "Go to Joseph", says the mighty Pharaoh and the whole people obey. The phrase, in Christian piety, has attached itself to St Joseph who provided for his family as the earlier Joseph is about to do for the whole human family, including his own. For we are told that "the famine was severe over all the earth" and, in the same verse, that "all the earth came to Joseph to buy grain" (Genesis 41:47).

The famine forces Jacob to send his sons to Egypt for grain. Joseph adopts a hostile attitude to his brothers in order to set in motion a train of events which will bring about the reconciliation of the whole family. He plans to keep one brother (Simeon) as hostage in order to ensure that all his brothers appear before him. Particularly, he wants to see his own (and only) full brother, the son of beloved Rachel, Benjamin. We know that Joseph has not set his heart on revenge because, for example, he weeps at the words of Reuben (Genesis 42:22-24).

The main interest in our story is now a complex series of events which will demonstrate the fulfilment of Joseph's dreams in a way that will display the real nature of Joseph's authority over his family. We begin to see the importance of brotherly love and family responsibility. These features will become clear as we move to the climax of a delightful story.

Jacob is distressed to learn that Simeon is imprisoned in Egypt and that the Prime Minister there is demanding to see Benjamin in return for Simeon's freedom. The old man, believing that the other child of his beautiful Rachel, that is, Joseph, is already dead, is unwilling to entrust this last son of his old age to the harshness of the Sinai desert and the uncertainties of the Egyptian royal court. But the severe famine forces the old man's hand and he must send his sons again for food. Tension is heightened by the argument about Benjamin. Finally, Judah promises personally to be responsible for the boy's safety (readers of Genesis 38 may wish to compare this with his irresponsible treatment of Tamar), pointing out that, without Benjamin, they could not hope to obtain food in Egyptian circles whose demands had to be met. When all the brothers appear before the Prime Minister, we can feel Joseph's love for them and especially for the weakest among them, little Benjamin. There is, after all, no need for Jacob and his sons to fear: Joseph is a dutiful son and a loving brother.

A brother's keeper

Our story is now near its conclusion. In chapters 44 and 45 we see how Joseph contrives a situation in which his brothers are placed in utmost danger, and, indeed, Benjamin faces death. The young lad is accused of stealing Joseph's divining-cup (trying to ascertain the divine will and purpose by means of pouring some liquid into a special cup was common-place in the ancient world – compare this with reading tea-leaves). Thus the initial situation is now reversed; all the brothers face slavery and, worse still, Benjamin faces the apparent fate of Joseph (everyone still believes he is dead). Again, notice the role of Judah: in his final speech, he is willing, as in chapter 38, to take responsibility for what has happened and to endure the slavery he and his brothers so callously forced upon Joseph. He is, as it were, willing to lay down his life for his brothers. Since, as we noted previously, Judah is a spokesman for his brothers, we may hope that his repentance for what has been done and his willingness to accept punishment is characteristic of all the brothers.

But Joseph is not like all his brothers. He is not planning revenge. He has power and authority to exact the harshest penalty from his treacherous family. But his authority comes from God; his rule in Egypt is grounded in love, compassion and concern. At last, we can see the authority of God, the dominion of God, promised in Joseph's dreams. At last, we can see that the authority of God, given to Joseph, given to all made in the image and likeness of God. It is the authority of brotherly love: "I am your brother, Joseph".

I am your brother, Joseph

Once Joseph reveals his true identity to his startled brothers, they set off to bring Jacob from Canaan to Egypt. The entire family returns to be received with honours by Pharaoh and given land in Goshen, an area in the Nile delta. Thus Joseph's actions, guided by the God of steadfast love, restore the unity of the family. Throughout the story, Joseph is the one who acts as the true brother. Jacob hastens to bless the sons of Joseph, thus accepting them into the clan and giving them a destiny in the family history. These blessings, and the subsequent bless-ing of all his sons (Genesis 49), are not part of the original story but they reflect later developments which highlight the characteristics of the tribes which sprang from the sons of Jacob. Nevertheless, we can see the blessings have been possible only because Joseph declares, "I am your brother" (Genesis 45:4). Without the brotherly love and compassion of Joseph, there would be no family, no tribes, no future for the blessings and promises. It is the solidarity of brotherhood (and sisterhood) that makes the future possible.

After seventeen years in Egypt (Genesis 47:28), Jacob dies and his body is embalmed, as is Joseph's when he dies. While embalming had religious significance in Egypt, indicating belief in immortality, in the case of Jacob and Joseph, it serves practical and religious purposes. Practically, the bodies must be preserved so that they can be taken across the desert and buried in the holy land of Israel. From a religious point of view, it is appropriate that they should be buried in the promised land (see Genesis 49:13 for Jacob; Exodus 13:19 and Joshua 24:32 for Joseph). It would be unthinkable to leave the bones of the ancient fathers of God's people to lie in foreign soil.

With these considerations, we move to the national concerns which emerge from "the history of the family of Jacob" (Genesis 37:2). Though Jacob resides in the land of Egypt for seventeen years and Joseph for a further fifty-four years after his father's death (starting with Genesis 41:46, see if you can work out the calculation for yourself – read carefully), the temporary nature of the Egyptian exile is repeatedly mentioned. As Jacob journeys through Beersheba to Egypt, God declares:

> I am God, the God of your fathers! Do not be afraid to go down to Egypt; for I will there make you a great nation, I will go down with you to Egypt, and I will bring you up again.
>
> *Genesis 46:3-4*

In this way, the family history is transformed into a national saga. The family story becomes the nation's story. The family must remain in exile until it becomes a nation (see Exodus 1:1-7). Then God will bring his people out of Egypt and into the promised land, the land flowing with milk and honey. The creation story of Genesis becomes the liberation story of the Exodus.

The Joseph story is, we have noted, the last of the great stories of the Book of Genesis. It is a summary of all those great stories, our last chance, as it were, to hear the message. God gave no answer to Cain's question, "Am I my brother's keeper?" Human experience must be the teacher. And so we journey in violence to the days of Noah, in pride and over-bearing ambition to the days of Babel. We travel with the family of Abraham and its faltering faith, we come to the crafty, cheating Jacob. Brotherhood, togetherness, solidarity – these are not in the stories. Finally, Joseph answers for God: "I am your brother, Joseph".

If we are to live together, as family or nations, we must be brothers and sisters of each other. Joseph is brother to his own and to all the peoples of the earth; he is brother to his own who sold him into slavery and he is brother to the Egyptians who enslaved and imprisoned him. He provides, not only for his own family, "and you little ones" (Genesis 50:21), but also for "all the earth" who came to Joseph to buy grain because the famine was severe.

That this is the way human relations must be is clear from an incident in Genesis 50. After the death of their father Jacob, the brothers fear that Joseph "will hate us and pay us back for all the evil we did to him" (Genesis 50:15). They send a message to Joseph saying that it was their father's dying wish that he should forgive them. This is clearly an unprincipled lie but it also indicates that the brothers have not learned the lesson. Joseph does not act as a brother because his father tells him; he does so because there is no other possibility in human affairs. Patiently, Joseph explains to them that all that has happened is in accord with God's way for the world; thus, and only thus, "will many people be kept alive" (Genesis 50:20). God works through the human story in order that we might come to understand that we will survive only if we come to the realisation that the way of Joseph must be the way of us all. Brotherly love, not revenge, is the basis of peace: "So do not fear; I will provide for you and for your little ones." "Thus he reassured them and comforted them" (Genesis 50:21).

A second lesson of our story, though not so immediately obvious as the first, is that God cares for all peoples. Notice how, through the pagan power of Egypt, provision is made for all who suffer from famine. We must be careful when, for example, we describe the Church as the "People of God". This is a special use of language and does not and cannot mean that only Christians are God's people. Every man, woman and child born on this planet belongs to the People of God. Every human being is God's responsibility and he carries us all in the hollow of his hand.

IMAGES OF GOD

Throughout the story, Joseph is the man of faith, confident that "the Lord was with him and showed him steadfast love" (Genesis 39:21). We have met this description of God as "steadfast love" many times. We know it to be the love which endures forever.

The God of the Genesis story, the God of the Joseph story, the God of every story, is a God who does not abandon. He is concerned to be with us. He will not be rebuffed by rebellion, overcome by pride, cheated by devious ways. Blessings are his business and he will not allow sin to win the day. The brothers make common cause against the young Joseph but they cannot destroy him. At the end of the story, Joseph asks his brothers, "Am I in the place of God?" (Genesis 59:19). Well, is he? Is Joseph not a human sign of how God acts towards all his people, even if they try to kill him? Is Jesus not a sign for how God acts towards us, even if we kill him?

PRAYER

Psalm 103 celebrates God's love for all people and his steadfast intention to forgive, no matter how great our rebellion.

Chapter 27

The Psalms: Passionate prayers

Humpty Dumpty sat on a wall.
Humpty Dumpty got a great fall.
All the King's horses,
And all the King's men,
Couldn't put Humpty Dumpty together again.

God could.

The Book of Psalms is the prayer book of the Jewish people
and the Christian Churches. Generation after generation of
people who hold the Bible sacred have turned to the Psalms
when they wished to talk to God about what matters most. The
Psalms are not frivolous prayers. They are not for the mealy-
mouthed or the chicken-hearted. The Psalms speak from the
human heart to the heart of God. They mirror the cost and joy
of discipleship, of life lived in conversation with God. They are
lovers' prayers, passionate prayers.

Love, hatred, trust, joy, sorrow, anger, pity, hurt, happiness,
contentment, rage, gratitude, resentment, despair, hope: such
are the realities of human experience. Consequently, such are
the stuff of the Psalms. There is a movement in the Book of
Psalms, a movement from trust to hopelessness and, with a
struggle, movement back to new hope and new beginnings.
Humpty Dumpty's career may serve to plot the rhythms of life
which run through the oldest and chiefest of our prayers. The
confident sitting on the wall, the unexpected catastrophe of the
fall, the despair of recovery: such is the pattern of life. Such is
the pattern of the Psalms.

PSALM 23 : SITTING ON A WALL

The Psalms are poems and employ all the subtleties of
language in the poet's arsenal. What is most needed to enter

into the world of a psalm is imagination, and imagination is the painter-in-residence in the human heart. Each psalm is part of a human story. We must try to imagine the life, the experience, which gave birth to the song.

READING THROUGH

Psalm 23 is rooted in the life and experience of a shepherd, a shepherd of the East. The shepherd's story is one of desert and little pasture, of burning sun and little water. It is a story of wandering in search of fresh pasture and, consequently, a story of danger. Shepherds, themselves by no means the most honest of men, were constantly beset by robbers who hid in dark valleys and swooped down "like a wolf on the fold". King David, once a shepherd and, therefore, knowing the ropes, at one time turned his hand to terrorising shepherds, or, rather, not doing so but demanding protection money for leaving them in peace (1 Samuel 25). There is a certain irony in the fact that Psalm 23 was either written by David or, more likely, dedicated to him.

READING THROUGH AGAIN

Humpty Dumpty's confidence was not in himself. It was in the wall. There is an act of faith, a supreme trust, that it will bear him up lest he dash his foot against a stone. Secure in the wall's solidity, Humpty need fear no evil.

Psalm 23 is a song of absolute trust. It sings of a love that has no fear. It is serene, peaceful, full of gratitude for gifts received and confidence for the days to come. Here is the human spirit at home with its God. In rich and, perhaps, deceptively simple images, the poet paints a picture of faith without fear.

Psalm 23:1-3

The plan of the poem hinges on three words: Lord – Thou – Lord. The poet begins with a declaration of faith: The Lord is my shepherd. Everything follows from that assertion of absolute trust. Jesus, a man of the country, well knew the depth of the true shepherd's concern: "The good shepherd lays down his life for his sheep" (John 10:11). Ezekiel, dismissing the kings who battened on the flock, looks to another Shepherd:

> Thus says the Lord: "I, I myself will search for my sheep, and will seek them out. As a shepherd seeks out his flock when some of his sheep have scattered abroad, so I will seek out my sheep, and I will rescue them from all places where they have been scattered on a day of clouds and thick darkness ... and I will feed them on the mountains ... I will feed them with good pasture, ... I myself will be the shepherd of my sheep, and I will make them lie down", says the Lord God.
>
> *Ezekiel 34:11-15*

With such a shepherd, there is simply nothing lacking. Life is full of every blessing, rich in every resource. The images come tumbling fast: green pasture, still, restful waters, life replenished by plenty, safe paths through life's ways. The Lord is the satisfaction of every need not because of who I am but because of who he is. He has named himself: I myself will be the shepherd of my sheep.

Psalm 23:4-5

To call to mind what the Lord is and what he does, to list the gifts of his steadfast love, compels intimacy. No longer "he" but "thou". The explanation for blessings in profusion is a holding of hands: "for thou art with me". The one who is Lord is Emmanuel, God-with-us.

Yet faith does not destroy terror. Evil lurks in the valley of deep darkness. Enemies threaten still. But there is no fear. To walk in the shadow of the Shepherd is to be without fear in the midst of danger. He is armed with the armoury of his craft, a rod to deflect the robber wolf, a staff gently to guide along the right and safe path. A comfort, an assurance, to know that the shepherd goes before. There is a solidarity here, a oneness of sheep and shepherd which casts out all fear.

Enemies must witness the Shepherd's care. Before their very eyes, a table is laid, a most royal banquet. Once Jesus sat at table in the house of a man called Simon. But there was no water to wash the feet of a weary traveller, no kiss to greet a welcome friend, no perfume to hail an honoured guest (Luke

183

7:36-50). When "Thou" prepares a banquet, the richest of perfume fills the air. The wine flows freely.

Psalm 23:6

The poet has looked into his heart and found contentment and trust. Life with the Lord has been richly blessed. The past holds out promise for the future: goodness and kindness shall follow for all of life's days. The metaphor changes: "I shall dwell in the house of the Lord all the days of my life". The psalmist is not thinking of heaven or life with God after death. Such ideas were yet not current in Israel. He means that such is his intense feeling of the Lord's goodness and kindness that he feels as if he were everyday in the Temple, the house where the Lord dwells among his people.

PSALM 13 : A GREAT FALL

The Lord is Emmanuel, God-with-us. But he is not always with us. Our relationship with God is founded on divine presence but is often experienced as divine absence. Humpty Dumpty woke up one day to find the wall had vanished. Psalm 13 is the cry of those who have had a great fall.

READING THROUGH

Many of the Psalms have an introductory heading. Psalm 13 is headed, "To the choirmaster. A Psalm of David". We know that King David wrote psalms (the word, by the way, means "songs") but it is not certain that he wrote all the poems ascribed to him in the Psalter (the Psalms arranged for liturgical or devotional use). It may well be that the heading means no more than "dedicated to David" or "a song in the manner of David's songs". The instruction, "To the choirmaster", may mean that the psalm was offered to the choirmaster of the Temple. Some psalms offer additional information. Psalm 45 describes itself as "a love song" and adds the phrase "according to the Lilies", which may mean that the psalm is to be sung to the tune "Lilies". There is much that we do not know about the Psalms.

184

Conveniently, Psalm 13 falls into three parts. Each is concerned with the basic issue in the poem: where is this God of mine? What has happened to our relationship? Why has he deserted me?

Psalm 13:1-2

The fault lies with God. He has forgotten me. He has hidden his face from me. God, how long must this go on? How long must I bear this pain? Must I carry this sorrow day in, day out? How long will my enemies rejoice at my downfall?

Whatever has happened here is God's fault. The emptiness is not due to my guilt, my failure. There are two lovers in this affair and the pain, the sorrow, the emptiness are not of my making. How long, Lord?

We are not used to such robust prayer. We seldom march before God in protest, banners waving, accusing fingers in the air. Israel's poets had no such qualms (Jesus on the cross: "My God, my God, why have you forsaken me" [Mark 15:34; see also Psalm 22]). There are times when there is nothing left but to scream.

It is told that during the horrors of Auschwitz a number of rabbis managed to come together in the camp. Their question was profound: was God responsible for such horrors? A venerable rabbi was appointed judge. A jury of twelve heard the debate of learned and pious men. The verdict was announced: Guilty! In deep shock, for these were men of deep and abiding love of God, they turned to the judge. What do we do now? "Now", said the judge, "we pray".

Psalm 13:3-4

The stricken poet turns to urgent appeal. The Lord is still "my God". He has a responsibility; only he can cope. He must be moved to consider what is happening. He must answer the case. If not, death will prevail and God will be diminished. Enemies will see that trust in the Lord is of no consequence.

Psalm 13:5-6

Surely, God will remember. Remembering is what he is famous for. When the slaves in Egypt were tried beyond endurance, look what happened:

And the people of Israel groaned under their bondage, and cried out for help, and their cry under bondage came up to God. And God heard their groaning, and God remembered...

Exodus 2:23-24

The poet reminds the Lord of his trust in the one whose steadfast love endures forever. Perhaps, God will not forget forever. Perhaps, one day, the scream will be heard and there will be a salvation. There may be a time for a new song, a new rejoicing "because he has dealt bountifully with me". Perhaps, there will. But can you be sure?

PSALM 130: ALL THE KING'S MEN

Humpty Dumpty is in the depths. What to do? Put not your trust in princes. All the king's men do not seem up to a rescue. To whom then shall he turn? What is required is a picking up of pieces, a kind of new creation. What must be assessed is the potential of the pieces: is it possible to put them together again? And there is need of a construction engineer who is willing to pick up the pieces.

READING THROUGH

Of the many psalms of brokenness, seven have a long-established pre-eminence. They are known as the Seven Penitential Psalms (Psalms 6, 32, 38, 51, 102, 130, 143). What happens when an individual or, indeed, the whole people, find themselves broken, disorientated, cut off, for whatever reason, from their God? The breakdown may be due to God's abandonment, or due to infidelity, or to some external pressure (war, exile, sickness, death of a loved one, allure of riches). What is clear is that there must be change on both sides; something new must be worked out by these one-time lovers if they are to love again.

Psalm 130 is entitled "A Song of Ascents". The best guess is that the psalm was intended to be sung during a pilgrimage making its way up to Jerusalem. It would appear, then, to be a communal rather than an individual prayer.

The eight verses of the psalm move through four moods. Two are concerned with the plight of the broken one and two with the nature of the God who must cope. Each must be attentive to the other if there is to be a "putting together again".

Psalm 130:1-2

The cry comes from out of the depths. In the first place, the prayer springs from the lowest point. God on high is addressed, not by one in Sunday best, but naked and unadorned. The poem does not spring from a prayerful one, from a holy one. It is not the prayer of the church-goer, the God-fearing, the obedient. It is the cry of the down-and-out, the prayer of the gutter-snipe. Secondly, the depths are the deep places of the sea wherein dwell the fiercest of demons. The prayer comes from the lowest place and from the midst of the greatest terrors.

This is a bold prayer, a prayer of sweeping audacity. From the depths of the deepest despair a voice is raised to the throne of God. Listen! Hear my voice! Pay attention up there! Moses gathered all the people of Israel and gave them the word: "Hear, O Israel!" (Deuteronomy 5:1). God demands that you listen to him. So ingrained in the mind of Israel is the injunction to listen that its daily prayer begins "Hear, O Israel!". And another voice in another time spoke from out of the clouds of heaven, "This is my beloved Son; listen to him" (Mark 9:7). But now the tables are turned. It's time for God to do some listening (for a change?). There is an insistence here: cries from the depths must be given priority.

Psalm 130:3-4

The word in the depths is that the Lord does not take notes. The first fact of life is that if evil doings are jotted down and reckoned up, nobody will be left standing. The first notion of God is that "there is forgiveness" with him. It is the story of a father, eyes strained with looking over the hills, who yet sees a wayward son afar off and who has compassion and runs and embraces and kisses (Luke 15:20). Forgiveness is where God begins. God begins with forgiveness for a purpose: "that thou mayest be feared". Fear is a wide-ranging word in the Bible. It can signify anything from terror to reverence. In the context of Psalm 130, however, fear is an understanding of the situation of being in the depths and of the possibility of being brought out to something new and unexpected.

Psalm 130:5-6

God begins with forgiveness. Fear issues in hope and waiting, in an expectancy of change. There is an intensity of waiting, like that of a night-watchman waiting for his relief to come with the dawn. What new thing will God make? The hope is in God's word, in the promise of forgiveness, in the certainty that there will be freedom from the shackles of the past.

Psalm 130:7-8

If there is hope for one, there is hope for all. Not only is there forgiveness with the Lord. There is steadfast love, love without condition, love without end. There will be new life, liberation, family-making redemption (see above, on the Book of Ruth) for all the people. Only God can put our friend together again. Only God can cope with sin.

THE MESSAGE

Three psalms which touch on the rhythms of all the psalms. The messages are as diverse as human emotions. But underlying the diversity is the instinct to pray from where we are. There is no false modesty in the Psalms. Neither is there false piety. When God is present in the calm of our lives, gentle words between lovers come naturally. But in the whirlwind, when we feel nothing so strongly as the absence of God, it is time to shout, to scream, to demand a hearing.

It would be pleasant to stay with Psalm 23. Remember the words of Peter: "Lord, it is well for us to be here" (Matthew 17:4). But life is not like that, at least, not always like that. The mountain of joy is all too often upended into the depths. The God of the Psalms, the God of the Bible, the God of Jesus, is the God who can cope. On the one hand, there will be tables spread out, perfume aplenty, wine overflowing. On the other, there must be rescue, rehabilitation and a new beginning. And there is the God who has to cope with all the little bits in between.

PRAYER

The Book of Psalms offers prayers for every mood and tense. Pray from where you are.

Chapter 28

A question of identity

When I was thirteen my bicycle was stolen. As I rounded the corner of the school bicycle-shed, I saw a distant but vaguely familiar figure hurtling down the hill. I went to the police. I cannot say that they alerted all ports and informed Interpol but two days later I found myself at the station. The sergeant showed me two bicycles.

"Recognise any of these?"

"Yes, sir. The black Elswick with the tape on the handle-bars."

I wish I could have claimed the metallic-blue racer. Mine was a woman's bicycle.

"Follow me", said the sergeant.

We went into another room. Three boys with frightened faces stood by the desk.

"Well, which one of these villains was it?"

My heart sank. I knew who it was. His father worked for my father. I lied.

"I don't know, sir. I didn't see him clearly."

I wheeled my bike out of the station. My first identity parade and I had told a lie. What would my father say?

Who do you say that I am?

The four Gospels are concerned with one question: "Who do you say that I am?" On one occasion Jesus took his disciples to a region in the northernmost part of Israel, near to a town called Caesarea Philippi (modern Banias) and there he discussed with them the question of his identity:

Jesus and his disciples went out to the villages of Caesarea Philippi and, on the way, he questioned his disciples, saying to them, "Who do people say that I am?" And they replied, saying to him, "John the Baptist; others, Elijah; still others, one of the prophets." But he asked them, "But you, who do you say that I am?" Peter answered him, saying, "You are the Messiah."

Mark 8:27-29

Everybody had a say. Some people seemed to think that Jesus was a reincarnation of John the Baptist who had been beheaded by Herod Antipas, the political ruler (under the Roman imperial power) of the territory where Jesus lived and worked. Others believed Jesus to be Elijah, the ancient prophet who was taken up to heaven in a chariot of fire, drawn by two horses and swept along by a mighty whirlwind (2 Kings 1:1-12). Some Jewish people came to believe that Elijah would return one day to announce the imminent arrival of the Messiah. To this day, when Jews celebrate the Feast of Passover, an empty chair stands at table, waiting to be filled by Elijah. Yet others thought that, if Jesus were not Elijah, he might be a re-incarnation of one other of the ancient prophets. But Peter, speaking on behalf of the other disciples, did not hesitate: "You are the Messiah".

What the evangelists say to us is this:

Look, we have put together, each of us in his own way, stories about Jesus, about what he did and what he taught. We haven't included everything. We were not writing biographies. But we think that we have put in enough to enable you to identify who Jesus is. If you can unlock the secret of who he is, you will have found a pearl of great price.

We shall journey through four Gospel stories, one from each Gospel. To each story our question will be, "What can you tell me about Jesus of Nazareth?" It is the question to ask all Gospel stories.

Chapter 29

Mark's Gospel:
A storm at sea
Mark 4:35-41

Have you ever noticed how incompetent fishermen are? I mean, of course, fishermen in the Gospels. At the very beginning of his preaching career, Jesus invited four fishermen to join him, to leave their nets and prepare to become "fishers of people". Mark does not relate that Simon (Peter), his brother Andrew, James and his brother John, had any previous acquaintance with Jesus, though we may presume they had. In any case, up they jumped (for Mark wishes to show his readers how immediately they, too, should respond to Jesus) and "at once they left their nets and followed him" (Mark 1:16-20). Here were experienced, professional fishermen (they were not poor; they employed paid workers and engaged in a lucrative exporting business), leaving all to follow an itinerant preacher. And that's when the rot set in.

Take the next time they ventured out on the lake. A great storm arose. And what do these experienced professionals do? Haul in the sails? Take to the oars? No! They scream for help from a sleeping carpenter (4:35-41 and 6:3).

On another occasion, Jesus went into the hills to pray and he instructed his fishermen friends to cross the lake to the village of Bethsaida. When evening came, looking over the lake, Jesus saw that "they were distressed in rowing, for the wind was against them" (6:45-52). These men, brought up on the lake? A bit of a head-wind? Distressed? Really!

The carpenter and the fishermen went out in a boat one day. Said the carpenter to the fishermen, "Row out into deep water, there's bound to be fish right there". Said the fishermen to the carpenter, "We've been at this all night with nothing to show for it. But if you say so ...". "And when they had done this, they enclosed a great shoal of fish, so that their nets were breaking" (Luke 5:3-6).

Worse still. The fishermen went out in their boat for a night's fishing and caught nothing. Just as day was breaking, Jesus stood on the shore and he called to them, "Lads, have you any fish?". They answered him, "No". Can you feel the frustration in that impatient "No"? And then the chap on the shore had the gall to tell them, "Cast your net over to the right, and you'll find fish". Wearily and, I suppose, to please the busybody, they threw out a net ... and caught one hundred and fifty-three of the very biggest! (John 21:1-11).

Who then is this?

Gospel stories are identity stories; they seek to reveal who Jesus is. However, we must remember that the gospel-makers assume that we come to their stories with minds steeped in their Bible, the Old Testament. They tell their stories in the light of that great reservoir of God's words. St Mark's story of the storm at sea well illustrates both points. It is concerned with the identity of Jesus, to be sure. But, as we shall see, that identity can be revealed only if the story is told by a story-teller steeped in the holy books of his people. This makes great demands upon the reader.

READING THROUGH

Superficially, the story appears simple enough and only a few details call for an explanation.

On that day

Mark was not in the business of writing a life-story of Jesus. He tells us nothing of when or where Jesus was born, what he looked like or whether or not he was educated. He tells us little about his family, except that they thought that Jesus was mad (3:21; and look at 6:3). Mark never provides a date, not even for the death of Jesus. Occasionally, however, he does furnish a time-indicator, ("Now after John was arrested", 1:14; "that evening, at sundown", 1:38), such as he does here: "On that day". The purpose of these indicators is to link what follows with what has gone before. In this case, Jesus had just been teaching a very large crowd beside the sea (4:1) and, having dismissed the crowd (4:10), he went on to explain his teaching to his special intimates whom Mark calls "the twelve", and to other disciples. But what authority does Jesus have to teach about God? What reason is there for Mark's readers to take his teaching seriously? Who is this teacher? By linking the teaching section with the storm at sea story, Mark supplies the answer.

The other side

The Sea of Galilee is a large fresh-water lake in the north-east of the province of Galilee (see map). It is about ten miles long and stretches to six miles at its widest point. It is exquisitely beautiful and full of fish. St John also calls it the "Sea of Tiberias", for that was (and is) the chief city on its shores (John 6:1). Locally, it is known as Kinnereth, a word which means a harp and that is the shape of the lake.

Jesus spent much of his public ministry around the lake and he had his headquarters at Capernaum, a town with a thriving fishing industry on the northern shore.

Jesus had been teaching on the Jewish side of the lake. Now he proposed to "go across to the other side," that is, to a Gentile, pagan region ("to the country of the Gerasenes" – 5:1). Who is this teacher who crosses from the country of the Jews into the pagan world? And what awaits him on the other side?

READING THROUGH AGAIN

Verse 35

It was Jesus who proposed to journey across the sea to the pagan country of the Gerasenes. Later on (7:24), he will propose going north-east "to the region of Tyre and Sidon" (cities on the coast of Lebanon), thus initiating another excursion into pagan territory. After the resurrection, when the apostles and disciples begin to spread the Gospel, they will remember these journeys and realise that the teaching of Jesus must be borne beyond the confines of Israel, even to the ends of the earth.

Verse 36

Jesus and his disciples left the crowd. This was not out of any lack of concern; for, indeed, on another occasion when Jesus saw the crowd "he had compassion on them, because they were like sheep without a shepherd", and he proceeded to feed the people with loaves and fishes (6:34-44). Throughout Mark's Gospel the crowd is the recipient of Jesus' teaching and healing. On this occasion, however, the instruction is for the twelve and, perhaps, for those other disciples who were in "the other boats with him".

"They took him with them, just as he was, in the boat." Mark seems to be suggesting that Jesus had been sitting in the stern while teaching the crowd (4:1) and that, at the word of Jesus, the disciples shoved off without further ado. The verse may be intended to convey the eagerness with which the disciples obeyed the command of Jesus. However, Mark may be hinting at deeper matters. He may wish to suggest that the disciples took Jesus with them to pagan territory, at his request, just as later they would take the word of Jesus to the whole world after the resurrection. The Teacher the disciples took to Gerasa is the Teacher they will one day take to the world.

"And other boats were with him." This is a mysterious observation, for the people in the other boats play no part in the story. Perhaps Mark means that these boats contain disciples other than the twelve (see 4:10 – "those who were about him with the twelve"). Is it significant that Mark relates that the other boats were "with him", that is, with Jesus, not "with them", as we would expect? If so, Mark may wish us to infer that the disciples in the other boats were not terrified of the storm because "they were with him", that is, had faith in him. He may be nudging the alert reader in the direction of Psalm 107:23-24:

Some went down to the sea in ships,
doing business on the great waters;
they saw the deeds of the Lord,
his wondrous works in the deep.

We shall return to this matter.

Verse 37
Sudden and severe storms are frequent and feared on Lake Galilee. However, it is not the storm itself which is Mark's chief concern; it is the meaning which the Old Testament gives to storms that is the primary focus of attention.

Many ancient peoples, including the Jews, believed that

God created the world by means of overcoming chaos and creating order:

> In the beginning God created the heavens and the earth. The earth was without form and void, and darkness was on the face of the deep; and the spirit of God was moving over the face of the waters.
>
> *Genesis 1:1-2*

The earth was chaotic. The waters of the deep covered the world; darkness was everywhere. To create order out of chaos, God had to struggle with the forces of evil which caused chaos by stirring up the seas. God had to engage in battle with evil in order to fashion order out of chaos. God was victorious and set the boundaries of the seas:

> And God said, "Let the waters under the heavens be gathered together in one place, and let dry land appear."
>
> *Genesis 1:9*

God sentenced the demons to dwell in the deep waters lest they attempt to return the world to primeval chaos. But what would happen if the demons broke loose? Were not storms clear proof that the demons were restless? In such a belief system, inevitably the control of the sea must be part of God's continuous care of creation:

> The floods have lifted up, O Lord,
> the floods have lifted up their voice,
> the floods lift up their roaring.
>
> *Psalm 93:3*

But creation need not despair because,

> Mightier than the thunders of many waters,
> mightier than the waves of the sea,
> the Lord on high is mighty!
>
> *Psalm 93:4*

The demons of the deep sometimes were given names – Leviathan, Rahab – and the Old Testament poets loved to sing of God's supreme ability to control such agents of evil:

The Lord with his hard and great and strong sword
will punish Leviathan the fleeing serpent,
Leviathan the twisting serpent,
and he will slay the dragon that is in the sea.

Psalm 27:1

Referring to the escape from Egypt through the Sea of
Reeds, in his imagination Isaiah sees God defeating the demon
of the sea so that the people may pass through to safety:

Was it not thou that didst cut Rahab in pieces,
that didst pierce the dragon?
Was it not thou that didst dry up the sea,
the waters of the great deep;
that didst make the depths of the sea a way
for the redeemed to pass over?

Isaiah 51:9-10

Towards the end of the Book of Job, the poet imagines God
pointing out to Job that human reasoning cannot hope to
fathom the mind of God. After all, mere humans cannot control
Leviathan, whereas God can play with it as if it were a tiny fish
on a hook:

Can you draw out (from the water) Leviathan with a fish-
hook, or press down his tongue with a cord? Can you put
a line in his nose, or pierce his jaw with a hook?

Job 41:1

For Mark's mind, then, steeped as it was in the poetry of the
Bible, the storm was an attempt by demonic forces to attack
Jesus and his band of followers. The winds swept up the sea
and the waves beat into the boat "so that the boat was already
filling".

Verse 38
"But he was in the stern, asleep on the cushion." If the
religious person believes that God will not allow the forces of
evil, symbolised by the storm, to overwhelm humanity, then
he will have confidence in God. In the Old Testament, such
firm trust in God was often expressed by saying that even in

197

the most terrible storms the believer should not doubt God's power and determination to save:

> When you pass through the waters
> I will be with you;
> and through the rivers,
> they shall not overwhelm you.
>
> *Isaiah 43:2*

> He [God] reached me on high, he took me,
> he drew me out of many waters.
> He delivered me from my strong enemy.
>
> *Psalm 18:16*

The fact that Jesus was asleep on the helmsman's leather seat in the stern is a clear illustration, not only of his perfect confidence in the sustaining and protective power of God, but also of his supreme authority over the powers stirring up the deep. The Psalmist sings:

> I lie down and sleep;
> I wake again,
> for the Lord sustains me.
>
> *Psalm 3:5*

> In peace I will both lie down and sleep;
> for thou, O Lord, makest me dwell in safety.
>
> *Psalm 4:8*

"And they awoke him and said to him, 'Teacher, do you not care if we perish?'" The trust of Jesus was not mirrored by the disciples and they turned to him for help. Here the story begins to take on mysterious depths. Again, it is the Old Testament which comes into play. There were times in Israel's history when the sustaining and protective power of God seemed to be absent, when it seemed God had abandoned his people and lost interest in their welfare. At such moments of national crisis, the poets of Israel imagined that God had fallen asleep and they urged him in their prayers to awake and redress the evil they were enduring:

Awake, awake, put on strength,
O arm of the Lord;
awake, as in the days of old,
the generations long ago.

Isaiah 51:9

This is a particularly homely image. The poet imagines that God's arm has fallen asleep and urges that God shake off the pins and needles and use his "mighty arm", as he did long ago when delivering the people from slavery in Egypt (Exodus 6:6). Lamenting the destruction of Jerusalem in 587 B.C.E., the psalm-writer cries:

Wake, O Lord! Why are you asleep?
Awake! Do not abandon us for good.
Why do you hide your face,
and forget we are wretched and exploited?

Psalm 44:23-24 (JB)

Instead of addressing their rebuke to God, "the Lord, the God of heaven, who made the sea" (Jonah 1:9), the frightened disciples turn to Jesus: "Teacher, do you not care if we perish?" But what can a mere teacher do in the face of a great storm of wind?

Verse 39
"And he awoke and rebuked the wind, and said to the sea, 'Peace! Be still!' And the wind ceased, and there was a great calm." Mark's secret is nearly out. By his choice of words here, he directs us to Psalm 107, the Old Testament once again providing him with an interpretative key with which to unlock the secret of Jesus. Pay close attention to the following lines:

Some went down to the sea in ships,
doing business on the great waters;
they saw the deeds of the Lord,
his wondrous works in the deep.
For he commanded, and raised up the stormy wind,
which lifted up the waves of the sea.
They mounted up the heaven, they went down to the
    depths;

199

their courage melted away in their plight;
they reeled like drunken men,
and they were at their wits' end.
Then they cried to the Lord in their trouble,
and he delivered them from their distress;
he made the storm be still,
and the waves of the sea were hushed.

Psalm 107:23-29

What the Psalmist envisages God doing in his care of his faithful ones who are in distress in a storm at sea, Mark sees Jesus doing on behalf of his disciples. Note, too, that Jesus rebuked the wind. The word "rebuke" is everywhere used by Mark when Jesus is casting out demons (1:25; 10:25; see also 8:33-34). Thus Mark makes us aware that Jesus of Nazareth has control over the demon forces of the deep, the very control the Old Testament describes as the prerogative of God.

Verse 40
"He said to them, 'Why are you afraid? Have you [still] no faith?'" The twelve in the boat had witnessed the casting out of demons: "And he healed many who were sick with various diseases, and cast out many demons" (1:34). They had seen the leper cleansed (1:40-45) and the lame walk (2:1-12). But still they had not realised that they had nothing to fear from demonic powers while Jesus was with them. Several times throughout Mark's Gospel the most intimate disciples of Jesus stand accused of failure to understand and consequent lack of faith (7:18; 8:17-21; 9:19). Mark deliberately pinpoints the weakness of the disciples in order to challenge the faith of the reader. Would we have done any better in the circumstances? Do we do any better now? The story stands, not just as a rebuke (that word again) to the disciples, but as a potential rebuke to the reader.

Verse 41
"And they were filled with awe, and said to one another, 'Who then is this, that even the wind and sea obey him?'" The meaning is that the disciples were overcome with a feeling of reverential awe. In the Book of Jonah, when the pagan sailors discovered that Jonah was God's prophet and, moreover, a

disobedient one, "the men were exceedingly afraid" (Jonah 1:10).

Fear of God in the Bible has more to do with awe and reverence than with a state of dread or alarm. The implication is that one has come to understand something of the power of God. The impulse to reverence may be the beginning of faith: the fear of the Lord is the beginning of wisdom.

The question with which the story ends is the clue to its meaning. It is the identity question. Even the least attentive reader of the Old Testament knows well that God is the controller of the wind and the sea. He it is who is responsible for confining the demon world and curtailing its power. But here we have a teacher, Jesus of Nazareth, rebuking the winds and commanding the stormy sea.

Jesus is doing God-work. So who then is Jesus?

THE MESSAGE

First, the story offers a challenge to faith. Can we believe that, in the work of the carpenter from Nazareth, we encounter the work of God himself? Mark does not force the answer on his readers. The Christian must answer for himself and herself.

This story, as all Gospel stories, asks, "Who is this?" and directs the question personally to the reader: "Who do you say that I am?"

The second point has to do with all those stories of fishermen disciples losing their competence when Jesus puts in an appearance.

The gospel-makers wish their readers to understand that, once one commits oneself to discipleship, then it is the power of Jesus which is paramount.

Peter may be a great fisher of fish; only God in Jesus can make him into a fisher of people.

Thirdly, it is not fanciful to imagine early Christians reading or, more likely, listening to St Mark's story and seeing themselves in the boat of the Church, tossed about by persecution and wavering in their faith in Jesus. Was it true that he promised to be with them always? Is he asleep in the stern of the Church? Will our prayers wake him? Will the storms of persecution be stilled by him whom the wind and sea obey?

The habits of the eagle are described in the Book of Deuteronomy:

> Like an eagle that stirs up its nest, that flutters over its young, spreading out its wings, catching them, bearing them on the tip of its wings...
>
> *Deuteronomy 32:11*

This description of the mother eagle, whereby she destroys her nest, disturbs her young out of their resting place, even before they can fly, forcing them to take to the air with untried wings, and then flies under them to catch them on the pinion of her own wings, should they fall, and carry them to safety, is a delightful and engaging image. The writer of Deuteronomy wants his eagle to symbolise God. God weans his people from their rest, forever calling them to new places ("Let us go to the other side"); he forces them to try their own strength, even through affliction and danger ("the boat was already filling").

He stirs up the nest; he sometimes lets them fall. But his sustaining strength and mercy are always there to carry them to safety.

St Mark's story of the storm at sea offers in Jesus a God who may appear to sleep but who, at the end of the day, catches us on his wing and brings us to "a great calm".

PRAYER

Though long, Psalm 107 is a perfect prayer to the Lord whose steadfast love endures even in the tumult of the storm.

Chapter 30

Matthew's Gospel:
Crumbs for dogs
Matthew 21-28

Matthew's Gospel has long been the Church's favourite. Mark, the first Gospel to be written, was swallowed up by Matthew. Why read Mark when almost every line of his is in Matthew and much else besides? Mark tells us nothing about the origins of Jesus. Matthew has the excitement of dreamy Joseph, of wise men and their star, of flight into the land of Egypt, of the murder of children and the death of the king. Again, Mark has little of the teaching of Jesus. Matthew took what little he found there and added a great deal from his own rich sources. Such is the extent of the teaching material in Matthew that his Gospel has long been regarded as the catechism of the Church. And the passion and death of Jesus is narrated more extensively in Matthew than any of the others Gospels – another reason for its popularity.

For all that, we do not know very much about when or where Matthew's Gospel was written. There is a strong suspicion that it was written after the destruction of Jerusalem and the burning of the Temple in 70 C.E. There is, too, considerable agreement that it was written somewhere in Lebanon or Syria. Most scholars agree that it was written for a community of Christian Jews who were admitting pagan Gentiles into their ranks and wondering how to cope with the newcomers who did not have the rich religious traditions of Judaism behind them. Matthew begins his story with the Jewish family of Jesus, stretching back through the great King David to Jacob and Isaac and Abraham himself. At the end of the story, Jesus gives his disciples the task of teaching all nations (28:20). In between the first and last chapters Matthew explains how the Jewish family of Jesus can extend into the Gentile family of the Church. The story of the Canaanite woman (15:21:28) perfectly illustrates the issues at stake in the Gospel according to Matthew.

READING THROUGH

We need to pay particular attention to the geographical details which Matthew provides. These are the clues to the story's meaning.

Gennesaret

Jesus was at Gennesaret (14:34). This was the name of a small town and district on the northwestern shore of the Sea of Galilee. The point to grasp is that it is from the Holy Land that Jesus sets out on a journey, the second and last time he travels into the Gentile world (see 8:28-34).

Tyre and Sidon

Tyre is about thirty miles and Sidon about fifty miles from the Sea of Galilee. They are seaports of modern Lebanon. The Romans ruled the area at the time of Jesus and it was known as the province of Syro-Phoenicia. Earlier the region was called Phoenicia from a Greek word for "red purple wool". The local name was Canaan.

The Philistine people also lived in this region. They were the great enemies who so often inflicted crushing defeats on their neighbours in Israel. King David, you will recall, killed their champion, Goliath. Because Philistines and Phoenicians sold Israelites as slaves to Gentiles (Amos 1:9-10), Tyre and Sidon were roundly condemned by the prophets as pagan cities doomed to disaster (Joel 3:4; Ezekiel 26:28; Isaiah 23; Zechariah 9:2-4). What will Jesus do when he comes to the neighbourhood of these heathen cities?

A Canaanite woman

In St Mark's version of the story the woman is said to be "a Greek, a Syro-Phoenician by birth" (Mark 7:24-30). Mark means to convey that the woman was a Greek-speaking inhabitant of the Roman province of Phoenicia which was administered from Syria. In other words, the woman is a Gentile, a non-Jew. Matthew makes the same point by using the local name for the people of the region. The woman is from Canaan. She comes from an old enemy and, of course, she is a heathen. What will Jesus do when he meets a pagan woman?

Son of David

In Matthew's long list of Jesus' ancestors which opens the Gospel one man is mentioned three times (five times, if you count 1:17). In the opening verse, Jesus is called "the son of David" and, in verse 6, David is mentioned twice and we are reminded that he is David the King. There was a belief among the Jewish people that God would send a new David, descended from the old, who would rule over Israel and restore its fortunes. Here is how a poet wrote about the matter fifty years before the birth of Jesus:

> Behold, O Lord, raise up unto them
> their King, the Son of David,
> At the time in which thou seest, O God,
> that he may reign over Israel thy servant.
> *Psalm of Solomon 17:21*

The Magi come looking for the "King of the Jews" (2:2) and, at the end of the story, the sign on the cross reads "This is Jesus the King of the Jews" (27:37). Clearly, early Christians believed that Jesus was the longed-for King of Israel (see 27:11,29,42), descended from the royal family of David (12:23; 20:29-34).

Possessed by a demon

Have you ever been love-struck? Have you ever been awe-struck? For that matter, have you ever been stricken by a disease? If you have experienced any or all of these three, you are well on the way to understanding what the ancient world meant by demon possession. We know that our feelings and emotions, our moods and impulses, come from within us, that diseases come from organic disorder. But ancient peoples thought that such things were brought about by external forces. Such experiences are the result of a visitation by a spirit which may be said to take possession of the victim. One is struck by a spirit. You fall in love when Cupid strikes you with his arrow. Terror is not something which arises from inner fear:

The sinners in Zion are afraid;
trembling has *seized* the godless.

Isaiah 33:14

Good feelings and emotions come from good demons and
bad impulses and moods are caused by bad demons. So when
we speak of a person as stricken by disease, we are using the
language of demon-possession. The worst demon is the one
who strikes you dead.

READING THROUGH AGAIN

Verse 21

Our investigation into the exact location of the places
mentioned in this verse reveals that Jesus has moved into
pagan territory. Moreover, it is a heathen region long hostile
to the Jewish people. Once before Jesus travelled to a pagan
district, "to the country of the Gadarenes" and he cast out
demons from two men who were possessed (8:28-34). Going
on past experience, therefore, we have reason to believe that
the woman's request will be favourably received. But matters
take a strange turn.

Verse 22

Notice that Matthew again emphasises where the incident
takes place. This woman is "from that region". Moreover, she
is a Canaanite, a pagan. Yet look at her prayer! She begins with
"Have mercy on me, O Lord". Her words in Greek are familiar
to Christians: *Kyrie, eleison*. How is it that this pagan woman
calls Jesus "Lord", the very title which is at the heart of Christian
faith? And how is it that she is not simply speaking to Jesus? She
is praying to him!

The woman whose daughter is severely possessed leaves
no stone unturned. In her prayer, she recognises Jesus, not
only as Lord, but also as Son of David. Jesus is the new longed-
for king. The king is the shepherd of Israel. His task was "to
seek the lost, bring back the strayed, bind up the crippled, and
strengthen the weak" (Ezekiel 34:15-16). But many kings of the
past fed themselves: "You eat the fat, you clothe yourselves
with wool, you slaughter the fatlings; but you do not feed the
sheep" (Ezekiel 34:3). The Canaanite woman clearly hopes

that this new Son of David will be a true shepherd, an answer to her prayer. "But he did not answer her a word". He did not so much as look at her.

Verse 23

The disciples will have no truck with the pagan woman. They are for sending her away since her loud prayer is a public nuisance and an embarrassment. Some would suggest that the disciples mean, "Give her what she wants, and let her go", but it is not likely that Matthew would present the disciples as more compassionate than Jesus himself. We shall see.

Verse 24

Still not looking at her, Jesus explains that he is from God ("sent" = sent by God), that he is the shepherd who must seek out the lost sheep. But only the lost sheep of Israel. Pagans need not apply.

Verse 25

The woman comes up to Jesus and kneels before him. The gesture is not simply that of one who is begging a great favour. What the woman is doing is worshipping Jesus. Matthew (like all the evangelists) is sensitive to words. Many people in his Gospel worship Jesus. The Magi declare, "we have come to worship him" (2:2 and 2:11). A leper worships him (8:2); a ruler, whose daughter has just died, falls before the Lord in worship (9:18); the mother of James and John kneels in worship to make her request (20:20). What these people have in common is an understanding of who Jesus is, a realisation that he has the power to help them, and a deep faith in his desire to do so. They are people of faith. When Matthew comes to narrate the mockery of Jesus, when he is stripped of his clothes and dressed up in a scarlet robe and a crown of thorns, he tells us that the soldiers kneel before him (27:29). But he uses a different word for this kneeling. These men are mocking, not praying. The woman worships and prays: "Lord, help me." Surely, she will be heard?

Verse 26

The reply of Jesus is not addressed to the woman. It is as if it were spoken over her head (she is kneeling on the

207

ground). He explains that it is not right to take bread from the children (the Jews) and give it to the dogs (the Gentiles). The message of God and the riches it speaks of are for the Jewish people and may not be taken away from them and transferred exclusively to Gentiles. Jesus is not ruling out the possibility that there may be some food for the Gentiles. But the bread is for his own. What are we to make of this?

Verse 27

Still the woman will not give in. A third time she calls Jesus "Lord" and claims the right of the Gentiles to the crumbs from their masters' table. The promises of God are given to his chosen people, fair enough, but not to the exclusion of all other peoples. Surely – the woman is saying – the heart of God is not closed to all but a few?

Verse 28

At last! At last! He speaks to the woman. Her persistent faith, her determination to receive of the goodness of the Lord, cannot forever be denied. Her great faith has won through and her daughter is healed instantly. Her recognition of Jesus as Lord and Son of David, her instinct to turn to him in prayer ("Lord, have mercy"; "Lord, help me"), her kneeling in worship before him, show that this Gentile woman is entitled to her place in the family of Jesus.

THE MESSAGE

The community for which St Matthew wrote was predominantly Jewish but it had begun to admit Gentiles. There must have been much heart-searching and misgivings about the matter. The attitude of the disciples – "send her away" – may well represent the view of those Jewish Christians who felt it best to have no truck with Gentiles. Almost at the centre of his Gospel, Matthew placed a story which squared up to the issue. Whatever the original incident may have been, he told the story to his local Church community, making a story from the days of Jesus relevant to his own time and place.

The message is clear enough. It is permissible to admit pagans to the Church. But care must be taken. Jesus did not rush to grant the prayer of the Canaanite woman. There was a pretty searching examination of her faith. Here, then, is a model for the Church. By all means, admit the Gentiles to the family of Jesus. But ensure that they are well instructed. Be sure they recognise Jesus as their Lord and know him to be king. Let them be people of prayer, persevering in it, confident that the Lord will hear.

IMAGES OF GOD

At the beginning of his Gospel, Matthew announced that Jesus was Emmanuel and explained that the name meant "God-with-us". All of his Gospel is an exploration of the person of Jesus to enable his readers to come to an understanding of who he is. At the end of the Gospel, Matthew declared that Jesus must be preached to all nations (28:20). These two issues dominate the story of the Canaanite woman. God-in-Jesus is Lord. He is the merciful shepherd king. His message is not exclusively for his own people. But it is to the Jewish people that he came and it is for his disciples to teach all nations. The Gentile must receive Jesus as did his Jewish brothers and sisters in Matthew's community, in faith, in prayer and in worship. At the end of the day, there are no favourites. Emmanuel is with us all.

PRAYER

Matthew gives us the prayer most dear to the Christian heart, the Lord's Prayer (6:9-13). He offers the prayer with simple instructions: "Pray then like this."

Chapter 31

Luke's Gospel:
Guess who's coming to dinner?
Luke 19:1-10

Luke's Gospel is full of surprises. Guess who's going to have a baby? Elizabeth "in her old age has conceived a son and this is the sixth month with her who is called barren" (1:36). Guess who else is going to have a baby? Mary "who has no husband" (1:34). Guess who is the first to preach Jesus to the people of Jerusalem? Anna, an eighty-four-year-old widow (2:37). Guess who proved to be a neighbour to the man who fell among thieves? The priest? The Temple official (Levite)? No! The Samaritan "who showed mercy on him" (10:37). And guess which son for whom the fatted calf was killed? For the one who squandered his father's money on harlots and loose living (15:11-32).

We might well ask what surprises are in store for us as we make our way through the story of Zacchaeus, the little man from Jericho (19:1-10).

READING THROUGH

The story of Zacchaeus is placed by St Luke in a particular position in his Gospel in order to help his readers to understand who Jesus is. As we journey through the story, we shall pay close attention to its position in Luke's overall design and reap handsome dividends.

The following call for explanation: Jericho; chief tax collector; son of Abraham; Son of man.

Jericho
The Second Book of Chronicles calls Jericho "the city of palm trees" (28:15). The ancient town took its name from the beautiful oasis on which it was founded. The oasis is five miles

west of the River Jordan and fifteen miles north-east of Jerusalem, not far from the northern end of the Dead Sea (see map). The oasis is 770 feet below sea level and offers a plentiful supply of water and fruit to the traveller who is bound for Jerusalem, which is 2,500 feet above sea level. The ancient city was long in ruins but, just before the time of Jesus, Herod the Great built a new town on the oasis and, indeed, he later died there. The old town was the first to be won by the people when they crossed into Israel after the Exodus and the wanderings in the desert. The commander of the invading army was called Joshua, which is a Hebrew name. Turn his name into Aramaic (the language which Jesus spoke) and you get Yeshua. This is what Mary would have called her child (Jesus is the English form of Yeshua). The ancient hero of Israel, Joshua/Jesus, entered the old town of Jericho and spared the prostitute Rahab and all her family (Joshua 6:22-25; read chapter 2 as well). What will the new Jesus/Joshua do when he enters the new town of Jericho?

Tax collectors

Zacchaeus was a tax collector. The Gospels lump tax collectors and sinners together as a pair:

> And as he sat at table in the house, behold, many tax collectors and sinners came and sat down with Jesus and his disciples. And when the Pharisees saw this, they said to his disciples, "Why does your teacher eat with tax collectors and sinners?"
>
> *Matthew 21:31*

Mark and Luke tell the same story (Mark 2:15-16; Luke 5:29-30) and, indeed, Matthew puts tax collectors in the same bracket as prostitutes (Matthew 21:31).

There are three reasons why every decent Jew treated tax collectors with contempt. First, and rather obviously, who likes tax collectors? Secondly, at the time of Jesus Israel was occupied by a brutal, coercive power, the Romans. The tax collector undertook to collect local taxes for the foreign power, hoping to make a profit by cheating and exorbitant demands. Zacchaeus, as his name implies, was a Jew, a Jew who collected stringent taxes from his people to hand on to the greedy fat cats of the Roman Empire. Imagine a Frenchman collecting taxes for the Nazis during the occupation. That was what Zacchaeus was doing. He and all his breed were the worst kind of traitors.

Tax collectors were outcasts for yet a third reason. The whole Bible speaks of Israel as God's holy land. The pious Jew regarded the land as God's precious and inalienable gift to his people. God dwelt in the land of Israel as nowhere else: Israel was God's little acre. When a Jewish traveller returned to the Holy Land (we still call Israel by that name), he would take off his sandals and slap the soles together over the side of the ship in order to "shake off the dust of his feet". In this way, he made sure that the holy ground of Israel was not contaminated by the dust and dirt of pagan lands.

The tax collector took the produce of God's acre and gave it to pagans. He took the holy gift of God's harvest and handed it over to the heathens. What Zacchaeus was doing was casting pearls before swine. He was committing sacrilege. He was giving what was holy to the dogs. For this, above all, he was a sinner.

Zacchaeus was, Luke tells us, a *chief* tax collector. But there was no such office in the tax career structure. The implications of this will be explored later.

Son of Abraham

In Luke's Gospel, Jesus refers to an infirm woman as "a daughter of Abraham" (13:16). He calls Zacchaeus "a son of Abraham". On one level, this means no more than that both were Jews, physical descendants of their forebear, Abraham. But, on another level, they are heirs to the blessings promised to Abraham and his posterity throughout all time (1:54-55; 2:73-75). Since the woman was unclean, that is, unacceptable to God, because of her infirmity, and since Zacchaeus was, by the very nature of his business, a sinner, both would have been regarded by their religious neighbours as outcasts beyond the pale of God's promised blessings. Will Jesus accept the orthodox view, the judgement of the religious establishment? In the eyes of Jesus, will they be beyond the pale of God's mercy?

Son of man

In the Bible and in the languages of the Jewish people (Hebrew, Aramaic), to say to someone, "You are a son of man", was to say, "You are a human being". A "son of man" simply meant a member of the human race, male or female. When people are in distress and their prayer is heard,

> Let them thank the Lord for his steadfast love,
> for his wonderful works to the sons of men.
>
> *Psalm 107:21*

"Sons of men" is clearly just another way of saying "people". However, in a very few passages of the Old Testament and other Jewish writings from before the time of Jesus, the title "son of man" seems to have been used to refer to a heavenly figure or agent of God who would receive power from God to overcome all who oppose the divine will. The most famous passage reads:

> I saw in the night visions,
> and, behold, with the clouds of heaven
> there came one like a son of man,
> and he came to the Ancient of Days [God]
> and was presented before him.
> And to him was given dominion
> and glory and kingdom,
> that all peoples, nations and languages
> should serve him;
> his dominion is an everlasting dominion,
> which shall not pass away,
> and his kingdom one that shall not be destroyed.
>
> *Daniel 7:13-14*

The prophet is recounting a dream which is subsequently interpreted for him as meaning that the enemies of God's people will be overcome and that the people will live in everlasting peace. We must not take all these poetic images at their face value; it is difficult to see how anyone could travel on a cloud! But the meaning is clear: the cruel empires of the world which terrify God's family will not have the last say. It is the power of God which will have the final say.

213

Many New Testament writers seized on this passage to refer to the future coming of the Risen Lord in glory:

And then they will see the Son of man coming in clouds with great power and glory.

Mark 13:26

And they will see the Son of man coming on the clouds of heaven with power and great glory.

Matthew 24:30

And then they shall see the Son of man coming in a cloud with power and great glory.

Luke 21:27

Then I looked, and lo, a white cloud, and seated on the cloud one like a son of man, with a golden crown on his head, and a sharp sickle in his hand.

Revelation 14:14

Quite clearly, all these passages (and look, too, at Mark 14:62; Matthew 26:64 and Luke 22:29) are based on the words of Daniel. One interesting feature is that the quotation from Daniel speaks of "one like a son of man" and the Book of Revelation follows Daniel faithfully in this regard. In the Gospels, on the other hand, passages always refer to the "Son of man" directly. Furthermore, in all of the New Testament, no one ever calls Jesus Son of man, except himself (with one exception, Acts 7:56).

There are three kinds of situations in which Jesus described himself as Son of man. First, he used the title when he spoke of his vocation to heal and to forgive:

"Why do you question in your hearts? Which is easier to say, 'Your sins are forgiven you', or to say 'Rise and walk'? But that you may know that the Son of man has authority on earth to forgive sins" – he said to the man who was paralysed – "I say to you, rise, take up your bed and go home." And immediately he rose before them, and took up that on which he lay, and went home glorifying God. And amazement seized them all, and they glorified God and

214

were filled with awe, saying, "We have seen strange things today."

Luke 5:22-26

Notice that the man who was healed and forgiven and the people who witnessed the healing glorify God, not Jesus. That is to say, they recognised that the power exercised by the mysterious Son of man is God's.

When Jesus was challenged to account for the activity of his disciples on the Sabbath, he pointed out that he had the (divine) right to decide what could and could not be done on the holy day, for

The Son of man is lord of the Sabbath.

Luke 6:5

In the Zacchaeus story, Jesus will claim that the Son of man is empowered to carry out God's plan to save all sinners:

For the Son of man came to seek and to save the lost.

Luke19:10

Secondly, Jesus calls himself Son of man when he wishes to remind his disciples of the human frailty he shares with all men and women:

Foxes have holes, and birds of the air have nests; but the Son of man has nowhere to lay his head.

Luke 9:58

Frailty leads to death, the unavoidable human destiny:

And taking the twelve, he said to them, "Behold, we are going up to Jerusalem, and everything that is written of the Son of man by the prophets will be accomplished. For he will be delivered to the Gentiles, and will be mocked and shamefully treated and spit upon; and they will scourge him and kill him, and on the third day he will rise."

Luke 18:31-33

The resurrection will come but only after the death. There will be no Easter Sunday for the Son of man unless there be a Good Friday.

The third and most difficult way the title Son of man is used in the New Testament is to express the role which the Risen Lord will play in the final destiny of creation:

And there will be signs in sun and moon and stars, and upon the earth distress of nations in perplexity at the roaring of the sea and the waves, men fainting with fear and with foreboding of what is coming on the world; for the powers of the heavens will be shaken. And then they shall see the Son of man coming in a cloud with power and great glory. Now when these things begin to take place, look up and raise your heads, because your redemption is drawing near.

Luke 21:25-28

The New Testament is full of this kind of poetic language, full of wild and startling images:

Then I looked, and lo, a white cloud, and seated on the cloud one like a son of man, with a golden crown on his head, and a sharp sickle in his hand. And another angel came out of the temple, calling with a loud voice to him who sat upon the cloud, "Put in your sickle, and reap, for the hour for the harvest of the earth is fully ripe". So he sat upon the cloud, swung his sickle on the earth, and the earth was reaped.

Revelation 14:14-16

The white cloud, the golden crown, the sharp sickle: these images are the stuff of imagination. They do not provide us with a ringside seat on eternity. They do, however, challenge disciples of Jesus to believe that the future belongs, not to human powers, but to God.

To meet Jesus in the Gospels as Son of man is to meet a Jesus in whom the power of God is at work, forgiving, healing and saving the world. It is to meet the weakness of one who is like us in every point except our sinfulness. To embrace the Son of man is to embrace the future, for he promises that the power of God is on our side and our destiny is safe in God's hands.

The story of Zacchaeus fits in extraordinarily well with what has gone before in the previous chapter. All the parables and teaching of chapter 18 throw flashes of light upon the story of the little man who shinned up a tree. The insistent woman is no more deterred by the heartless judge than is Zacchaeus by the crowds, his stature or his sins. Jesus addressed the parable of the Pharisee and the tax collector to an audience "who trusted in themselves and despised others" (18:9-14). The Pharisee takes pride in the fact that he is not an extortioner, unjust, an adulterer or "even like this tax collector" (18:11), the bottom of the pile. Poor Zacchaeus is a *chief* tax collector! Luke 18:18-30 narrates the story of the ruler whose attachment to riches keeps him from throwing in his lot with Jesus. Jesus observes that it is easier for a camel to pass through the eye of a needle than for a rich man to enter the kingdom of God (a phrase which means "to be where God's will is done"). An amazed crowd asks, "Then who can be saved?". The answer is that what is humanly impossible is possible with God. Again, what is to become of Zacchaeus, the *rich* tax collector?

We begin to see what Luke is about. Zacchaeus is not just another of the many sinners who pack the pages of the Third Gospel. His story is not just one more event on the journey of Jesus to Jerusalem. Zacchaeus is the last sinner Jesus meets on the way and he is the worst. He is, in other words, a test case. After all the teaching and healing, after all the forgiveness and mercy, is it really possible for God to do anything for the rich, chief tax collector, the sinner supreme? Is it possible for Jesus to reach the lost Zacchaeus?

Verse 1
St Mark records that Jesus healed a blind man, one Bartimaeus by name, as he left Jericho (Mark 10:46-52). St Matthew agrees but he has two blind men (Matthew 20:29-34). Luke's blind man is healed as Jesus enters the town and, as he is passing through, he encounters Zacchaeus. Clearly, he wanted Zacchaeus to stand out as the last sinner to meet Jesus.

Verse 2
It isn't often that the Gospels record the names of people

who meet Jesus and when they do it is worth paying attention. Zacchaeus, a thoroughly Jewish name, means "the clean one", "the innocent one", in the sense that one is acceptable to God. All the more damning, therefore, that this Jew should turn out to be a chief tax collector.

The fact that Luke calls Zacchaeus a chief tax collector is extremely important. The Greek word which he uses here is found nowhere else, either in the Bible or in any other piece of Greek writing in the whole world. There was no such office in the tax administration structure. Tax collectors collected the taxes and handed them over; there was no middle man, no supervisor. The tax collector was not a civil servant. He was an independent businessman who guaranteed to collect what was due and his profit consisted in what he could rake off over and above. In other words, he was a cheat. By inventing the office of chief tax collector for poor Zacchaeus, Luke is making the little man a chief sinner. What can God do about him?

The ruler in chapter 18 was described as "very rich". Zacchaeus is no less wealthy. Luke puts the word at the end of his sentence to catch our eye. It is as if he were saying, "Zacchaeus is rich, filthy rich". Once again, Zacchaeus is an extreme case. Is he an impossible case?

Verse 3

Zacchaeus seeks to see Jesus, to see who he is. This is not idle curiosity. He is not trying to see what Jesus looked like. He wants to discover the identity of Jesus. Discovering the true identity of Jesus can have far-reaching consequences, as the little fellow will soon find out.

Verse 4

Because of the crowd and his lack of inches, Zacchaeus climbs into a sycamore tree. One senses the eagerness of the little man as he shins up the tree, unmindful of the possibility of public ridicule and even violence (a hated tax collector, remember).

Verse 5

When Jesus arrives at the place where Zacchaeus was, he looks up. We are reminded of the look he gave to the rich ruler (18:24) and will give to Peter after his threefold denial (Luke

22:61). It is not an idle glance; it is a look of concern and compassion.

Jesus calls him by his name. We need not trouble ourselves to enquire how he knew it. In his search for sinners Jesus knows all our names. The announcement that he must lodge at Zacchaeus' house means more than "I would like to drop in". It is a way of saying that the whole point of being in Jericho on that day, at that precise time, is to be with Zacchaeus. That is what God had decided from eternity. Jesus could be nowhere else, if he were to be about his Father's business.

Verse 6
Zacchaeus instantly fulfils the word of Jesus and welcomes him into his home with joy. Joy fills the pages of St Luke's Gospel from beginning to end. The child to be born to Zechariah and Elizabeth will fill them "with joy and delight" (1:14) and, at the end of the story, the disciples return to Jerusalem from the Ascension "full of joy" (24:52).

Verse 7
Now the tax collectors and sinners were all drawing near to hear him. And the Pharisees and the scribes murmured, saying, "This man receives sinners and he eats with them."
15:1-2

Now it is everyone who complains. The verse has the quality of a depressing summary. After so much, so little is understood. There is a total failure to understand the extent of God's mercy. It is important to remember the significance of eating. Sharing food is sharing one's life. By eating with Zacchaeus, Jesus is affirming his solidarity with the sinful tax collector. Religious people don't like that.

Verse 8
Overwhelmed by Jesus' act of mercy, or, more properly, restored to wholeness by his graciousness, Zacchaeus sets out on a new way of life. He does what the rich ruler could not do and puts himself to rights with regard to his riches. Half of his goods he bestows on the poor. The letter of the law (Leviticus 6:1-7) requires restoration in full plus one fifth for defrauding; Zacchaeus is willing to restore fourfold. The little fellow is not

boasting. He is simply stating what his new life will be like, a new life that follows on the discovery that Jesus is his Lord.

Verse 9

According to 1:77, God's people will experience salvation "in the forgiveness of sins". The message of the first Christian preachers was, "let it be known to you, brothers, that through this man (Jesus) forgiveness of sins is proclaimed to you" (Acts 13:38). The people want to put tax collectors and sinners outside the pale, to exclude them from the blessings promised to Abraham and his descendants and now being fulfilled in the life and work of Jesus. They want exclusive rights on salvation. Jesus will have none of this. God doesn't put anyone outside. No one is excluded from blessing. No religious group can collar the market when it comes to God's mercy.

Verse 10

This verse provides the explanation of all that has gone before. What we have seen enacted in the story is reviewed and summed up in a single sentence: the Son of man came to seek and to save the lost. The language here reminds us of the shepherd who searches out the lost sheep (15:1-7). The lost is anyone separated from that which gives identity, meaning and value to one's life. The lost is personified in the rich chief tax collector, Zacchaeus. He had sold his soul to his country's oppressor; he had cheated and robbed his own people. He had gone into his own far country (15:13). But Jesus, God's good shepherd, sought him out.

THE MESSAGE

Luke's Gospel begins and ends with joy. Zechariah is told by the angel that the birth of his son will fill mother and father with "joy and gladness" (1:14). At the end of the story, as we have seen, the disciples return from the Mount of Olives to Jerusalem "full of joy" (24:52). And, in between, joy is to be found everywhere. The baby in Elizabeth's womb "leaps for joy" (1:44); Mary's soul "rejoices in God" (1:47); the angel brings the shepherds "the good news of a great joy which will come to all the people" (2:10); the seventy return from their

220

preaching expedition "with joy" (10:17); the shepherd who finds the lost sheep, the woman who finds the missing coin, call friends and neighbours to rejoice because they have found what had been lost (15:3-10); the father of the spendthrift son knows that it is fitting "to rejoice and be glad" on his son's return (15:32). And, Jesus tells us, "there is joy before the angels of God over one sinner who repents" (15:10). Zacchaeus welcomes his guest "joyfully" (19:6).

That is what Jesus brings to the world: joy. Jesus seeks out that which is lost in order to spread joy and gladness. He does not come to threaten; he does not come to condemn; he comes to fill hearts with joy. If Jesus can cope with the rich, chief tax collector, chief among sinners, he can cope with me.

IMAGES OF GOD

Zacchaeus sought to see who Jesus was and found salvation, the forgiveness of his sins. In the person of Jesus salvation enters his home. The image of God which shines through the person of Jesus in St Luke's Gospel is that of a God determined to give peace and joy to his people. The story of the Prodigal Son is the story of God, the story of a father forever on the lookout for a son or a daughter who is lost.

PRAYER

The prayer of Zechariah (1:67-79), which speaks of a God who seeks to rescue us from enemy hands and to set us free from fear, is an appropriate response to the story of the little man from Jericho.

Chapter 32

John's Gospel:
Come and see
John 9:1-41

To be a gospel-maker you have to be a Jack-of-all-trades. You have to be something of an historian, for Christianity is an historical religion. It claims to be founded on facts. But telling the facts is not enough. For example, here is a fact: Jesus died. To which I reply: So what?

Your gospel-maker must be able to interpret the facts. What do they mean? And here's another thing. It is not enough to give the meaning of the facts as they happened. The question is not, "What did it all mean?", but, rather, "What does it all mean?"

When the gospel-maker has shown how the death of Jesus in the past has the most profound significance for the people of his own time, how does he persuade them to believe him? How does he convince them to change their lives? Not only must he answer, "What does it all mean?" He must so tell the story that the reader knows the answer to another question, "What does it all mean to me?"

The people who put together the Gospel according to John towards the end of the first century had to face these questions. How do we tell the story of what happened then in such a way as to show its relevance for Christians of our time and place? And how are we to tell our story not only to convince them of the truth of what we say, but to move them to say, with Thomas the Twin, "My Lord and my God" (20:28)?

The story of the man born blind (chapter 9) will show us how the gospel-makers went about their work.

READING THROUGH

The following need explanation: Rabbi, Siloam, Pharisees, the Jews, the Messiah, synagogue.

Rabbi

The word means "my great one" and it is a term of respect given to Jewish scholars who teach the Scriptures and holy traditions to the people. There is little or no evidence that the title "Rabbi" was used at the time of Jesus. It seems to have come into use about one hundred years later. But scholars in Jesus' day were called "Teacher". So here we have an example of the gospel-maker taking the term used in his day and applying it to the days of Jesus. After all, Jesus was a teacher, so why not call him by the "modern" name for those who teach about God? The writer is interpreting the historical Jesus in the language of his own time and place.

Siloam

The pool is at the end of the Kidron Valley, outside the southwestern wall of the old part of Jerusalem. The name is interpreted for the reader as "Sent". It is not perfectly clear that that is what *Siloam* means but the name is sufficiently like the word for "sent" to enable the gospel-writer to call our attention to the similarity. What he is concerned to do is to interpret what is going on. Jesus is "he whom God has sent" (3:34).

Pharisee

As in the Christian Church today, within the Jewish faith of Jesus' time, there were many "parties", each claiming that their understanding in religious matters was nearest the truth. One such group was the clergy who emphasised the importance of worship in the Temple in Jerusalem. Another was the deeply religious Pharisees who stressed living out the religious prescriptions which were handed down in the Sacred Scriptures and ancient traditions. After the Temple was destroyed in 70 A.D., priests ceased to have any function. But the Pharisees had the holy books and were steeped in the old traditions. Their message was simple: "We may not have the Temple but we have the Law. By living the Law we will remain faithful Jews".

In the time of Jesus, the party of the Pharisees was but one of many contending religious strands within Judaism. By the end of the century, however, it was by far the most influential. The name Jew was now almost synonymous with Pharisee. In the Fourth Gospel, written towards the end of the century, the opponents of Jesus are either "the Jews" or "the Pharisees". This is an over-simplification of the realities during the life of Jesus but it made sense. Christian communities at the close of the century found themselves at logger-heads with Jews over the meaning of Jesus. These Jews were now mainly Pharisees. The quarrels which Jesus undoubtedly had with all sorts of parties among the Jews of his time were now interpreted in line with the Jewish-Christian quarrels at the end of the century.

The Jews

In John's Gospel the term "the Jews" is frequently used to denote those who are opposed to Jesus. This cannot have been the case during the ministry of Jesus. For example, most Jews lived outside of Israel and probably never heard of the young preacher from Galilee. Again, the disciples of Jesus were all Jews and many of the ordinary people listened attentively to him and were the recipients of his healing power. It hardly needs to be said that Jesus was a Jew who lived and died within the religion of his ancestors. But by the time the Fourth Gospel came to be written, hostilities between Jews and Christians were widespread and John appears to use the term "the Jews" to mean those who opposed Jesus when he was alive and those who are still opposing his followers. Later quarrels are being read back into earlier disagreements.

The Messiah

At the time of Jesus there was widespread expectation among the people of Israel that God would intervene to rescue them from Roman tyranny and to restore national dignity and well-being. There was no general agreement as to how God's intervention would come about and the ancient prophets were by no means clear on the matter. However, it would be fair to say that, insofar as there was a national expectation, it was that God would raise up a descendant of King David. The new David would overcome enemies and rule with justice and peace. Some believed that the rule of the king would extend beyond the borders of Israel and, indeed, encompass the whole world.

The expected king was called the Messiah. The word means "one who is anointed". In ancient times, at the coronation of a king or the installation of a priest, the individual had his head anointed with expensive oil as a sign of the new role he was to play in the life of the people (see 1 Kings 1:38-40, the coronation of King Solomon). In Israel, the king was sometimes called "the Lord's anointed", meaning that he was the one appointed by God to care for the people. When the Jewish people expressed a longing for a new king like David, they would speak of "the anointed one", the Messiah.

The Greek word for "anointed one" is *"Christos"*, from which we derive the word "Christ" and, of course, the name "Christians". Christians are anointed at baptism to indicate the task they are assuming as ministers of the Gospel. All Christians are messiahs.

Although Jesus did not claim the title of Messiah for himself and accepted the designation with considerable reluctance and only after redefining it in terms of his suffering, early Christians seized on "Messiah" as their favourite title. It soon became part of his proper name, Jesus Messiah, Jesus Christ.

Synagogue

While there was only one Temple where sacrifices were offered, there were many synagogues in Israel. The word means "assembly" and it refers to the building in which the people assembled for prayer, teaching, and reading the scriptures (read Luke 4:16-30) or to the congregation itself.

The first Christians were Jews who continued to frequent their local synagogues for prayer and worship. But gradually relations between Jewish Christians and non-Christian Jews became strained, especially over the Messiahship of Jesus. Relations were particularly strained towards the end of the first century and around 90 A.D. an attempt was made to drive out from their synagogues all Jews who believed that Jesus was the Messiah.

READING THROUGH AGAIN

The gospel-maker must move hearts. It is not enough to tell the story. It must be told dramatically, with all the excitement the writer can command. To be sure, each Gospel is concerned with the question of the identity of Jesus. But the bare facts won't do. The writer must attract me to his portrait of Jesus. I

225

must be brought to the point where I can say, "Lord, I believe". The story of the man born blind well illustrates the gospel-maker's art. It is a drama in four acts which carries intense emotional appeal. But it is a drama set in the wider drama of the whole Gospel. We must ask what Jesus had been doing in Jerusalem before he saw the man blind from birth.

Jesus was in Jerusalem to celebrate the Feast of Succoth. This was a seven-day autumnal harvest festival of thanksgiving for the wine, fruit and olive harvests and of prayer for rains to ensure the next harvest. People celebrated it out in the fields. They made huts of tree branches and spent the time in the open, reminding themselves of their ancestors camping in the desert after the Exodus. There were special ceremonies in the Temple. On the first night and, perhaps, every night, four huge golden lamps were lit on the outside walls of the Temple and their light was said to lighten the whole city. Each morning a procession went to the fountain of Gihon which supplied the pool of Siloam. A priest filled a golden jar with water, while the choir sang, "With joy you will draw water from the wells of salvation" (Isaiah 12:3). The procession made its way back to the Temple and, when it reached the main altar, the people sang:

Save us, we beseech thee, O Lord!
O Lord, we beseech thee, give us success!

Psalm 118:25

Then the priest poured the water on the altar and it flowed to the ground, a sign that the life-giving water of the new rains was a divine gift.

During the festival Jesus made two very significant statements:

If any one thirst, let him come to me and drink. He who believes in me, as the scripture has said, "Out of his heart, shall flow rivers of living water."

John 7:37-38

and

I am the light of the world; he who follows me will not walk in darkness, but will have the light of life.

John 8:12

226

The people prayed for rain. Jesus stepped forward to proclaim another water, more precious even than the rains which give such abundant harvest. It is a "living water" which he alone can give. It is the Holy Spirit, the Spirit of truth, the Spirit who will guard and guide, who will "bring to your remembrance all that I have said to you" (John 14:26; carefully consider 15:26; 16:7-11; 16:12-15).

Festival lights illuminated the city. But Jesus declared that he is "the light of the world", the one who brings light and life to all humanity. His is a message from God which dispels the darkness of our world. It is a message which leads out of darkness into God's vision for the world. This enlightenment comes in Jesus; to believe him is to be delivered from the darkness of confusion into the light of truth.

Darkness, water, light and truth: these are the issues which are at the heart of the drama of the man who was born blind.

Verses 1-7

Sometime after the Feast, Jesus saw a man blind from birth. Note that it was Jesus who found the man (the Good Shepherd, 10:11). The disciples asked whether personal or parental sin caused the man's blindness. The belief that sin and sickness went hand in hand died hard in Israel. The view that children were damaged from birth by the sins of their parents could claim scriptural support: "for I the Lord your God am a jealous God, visiting the iniquity of the fathers upon the children to the third and fourth generation... " (Exodus 20:5). In the case of the blind man, Jesus did not provide a solution to the problem but he did maintain that out of such tragedy God could work for good. The blindness of this man was to be a divine example; turning darkness into light is God's business. The words of Jesus in verse 4 are "we must work". It would appear that he is inviting disciples to participate in helping the blind to see.

Jesus had declared himself to be "the light of the world" (8:12). The reader is reminded of "the true light that enlightens everyone" (1:9). The purpose of the mission of Jesus was to lead the world from the darkness of error into the light of truth. In the beginning of the Bible, the great command was given: "Let there be light" (Genesis 1:3). We might have expected such a word here. But no. The "light of the world" spat on the ground and smeared the sightless eyes with the dampened clay. The use of spittle was commonly regarded at the time as curative but it was not the clay/spittle which brought about the cure. Rather, it was the washing: "So he went and washed and came back seeing". The reason for the physical activity of kneading clay emerges in verse 16. The work was done on the Sabbath and was a clear breach of Sabbath rest. The conclusion: this man is not from God.

The instruction to go to Siloam and the cure are quickly told. But the gospel-maker demands close attention here. The sight-giving water is called "Sent". But Jesus is the one who is "sent": "For God sent the Son into the world... " (3:17); it was "the Father who sent me" (8:18). The "Sent One" can provide the living water which turns the dark of blindness into light. The "light of the world" overcomes darkness in living waters.

Verses 8-17

Now the real issues begin to emerge. First, the evangelist establishes beyond doubt the reality of the healing. This will be emphasised again and again. The neighbours are called as witnesses. Is this the man who used to sit and beg? Yes! No! But the man himself has no doubt as to the reality of what has happened: I am the man. But how?

Several times throughout the story, the once blind man is prevailed upon to tell what happened. He never deviates, never contradicts himself, never doubts. For one born blind, he sees with perfect clarity.

The man called Jesus. The identity of the blind man is established. The method of healing is established. But who is the healer? If the story is to reveal the identity of the healer, it is starting in the right place. The *man* called Jesus. The Word was made flesh. We must begin with the flesh. But where is he? Even the keen sight of the healed beggar cannot see Jesus. But Jesus sees him.

The neighbours are not convinced. The man is hauled off to the Pharisees. They are expert in religious matters and zealous champions of the sacred laws and traditions. So it is only when they are about to interrogate the man that the gospel-maker drops a minor bomb. The healing had taken place on the Sabbath and had involved work clear contrary to the law. Of the thirty-nine forms of work forbidden on the holy day, kneading dough or clay was one.

Again, the sceptical question: how did it happen? Again, the straightforward answer. Again, the blind prejudice, the failure to believe what is in front of their eyes. This man is not from God. (We, the readers, know that he is, that he is the one "sent by God".) He does not keep the Sabbath; therefore, he is a sinner. But how can a sinner do such signs (notice the plural; it is as if all the work of Jesus is under scrutiny). There is a taking of sides. They turn to the voice of experience, to the man himself. Who do you say that he is? And he said, "He is a prophet".

Verses 18-34

The second interrogation is conducted by "the Jews". As we have seen, the term does not refer to the whole Jewish people but rather to those elements opposed to Jesus and to Christians.

The parents are summoned to confirm the identity of the blind man. This they do but, crucially, they do not know "who opened his eyes". On the one hand, we have the evidence of the man born blind. The one who opened his eyes is "the man called Jesus" and "he is a prophet". On the other hand, we have an official verdict from some Pharisees: "This man is not from God". The centre of the stage is beginning to be occupied by the one who isn't there. With the evidence of the parents the identity of the once-blind man and the reality of his cure are established beyond doubt. But who is this man "who opened his eyes"?

The parents are cautious: "He is of age, ask him". The reason is new to us: anyone proclaiming Jesus to be the Christ must be put out of the synagogue. Now we know that the decrees to this effect were not in place until the end of the century. Questions as to the identity of Jesus were, of course, key issues in his life-time. Answers to these questions were key issues in the subsequent history of Christians. John is kaleidoscoping the two times. Proceed with caution.

Jesus the man. Jesus the prophet. Jesus the Christ. Gradually his identity is coming to light. But there is none so blind as those who will not see. Praise God, they say, and avoid Jesus the sinner. The miracle is standing before their very eyes: "I know one thing, that though I was blind, now I see". Yes, but what did he do? This is too much: "I have told you already. Do

229

you too want to become his disciples?" Notice the "too". The man is growing in understanding of who Jesus is and is committing himself to discipleship. But not the disciples of Moses. Even when the blind see, the lame walk, the dumb speak. If this man were not a worshipper of God... the obvious conclusion, but only if you open your eyes. So the man born blind and Jesus are lumped together: two sinners. Peas in a pod.

Verses 35-41

Jesus the man. Jesus the prophet. Jesus the Christ. Jesus the worshipper of God. Jesus who does the will of God. Jesus the one to whom God listens. Jesus who looks for the one cast out and finds him. The once blind man is called upon to believe in the Son of man. Why this rather puzzling title? Who is this Son of man? Precisely the question raised in 12:34 and answered:

> "The light is with you for a little longer. Walk while you have the light, lest the darkness overtake you; he who walks in the darkness does not know where he goes. While you have the light, believe in the light, that you may become sons of light."

John 2:35-36

This is what the Fourth Gospel understands by Son of man. He is the one who has been sent into the world to shed light on the distress of the world. He is the man who is "the light of the world" and who invites all to come out of darkness into the light. The blind man sees with new eyes and new understanding: "Lord, I believe". And he worshipped him. Who is Jesus that those who see him as he really is fall down in worship?

Jesus has the final say. He comes into the world and the world is forced to make a judgement concerning him. Unfortunately, those who ought to see (religious authorities, for example) will be blinded because they refuse to look beyond their own noses. Some Pharisees object; they are not blind. That is true, Jesus concedes. If you were blind (physically, like the man born blind), you would not be guilty of sin (9:3). But you set yourselves up as spiritual leaders, people claiming to see the ways of God more clearly than the next person (9:34).

230

You see no reason to go to the One Sent, to wash in the living water he provides, to have your darkness enlightened by the light of the world, to come to a knowledge of the truth. He came to his own home, and his own people received him not (1:11).

THE MESSAGE

This is a two-tier story. The first tier is the level of what happened. On leaving the Temple, Jesus saw a blind man and restored his sight. His neighbours doubted the reality of the miracle and the man defended Jesus before them and before the authorities, represented by the Pharisees and "the Jews". Reluctantly, the reality of the healing was accepted but the man's determination to stand up for Jesus led to his expulsion from the community (synagogue). Jesus sought out the man once more and the man expressed his faith in his benefactor.

Such a summary of "what happened" might very well prove that Jesus was a great miracle-worker. But, then, so were (are?) many other people. It is difficult to see what relevance the restoration of sight to a blind man nearly two thousand years ago has for your life or mine.

The second tier builds on "what happened" to establish "what does it mean". Jesus leaves the Temple where he had declared himself to be the source of living water (giver of the Holy Spirit) and the light of the world (giver of God's truth). He sees a blind man and points out that he will be the means by which God's work will be made known. The blind man is told what to do: wash in Siloam/Sent. There is a pun here. Jesus is the One Sent by the Father. He is the source of living water, the Holy Spirit who "will guide you into all the truth" (16:13). The "blind" must come to Jesus.

But who is Jesus? In the first place, he is a man, the man called Jesus. Secondly, as the once blind man comes closer to the truth of the matter, he sees that Jesus is a prophet. The prophets of old possessed God's spirit, enabling them to speak and act on God's behalf. Jesus "must work the works of him who sent me" (9:4).

So far, then, we know Jesus is "sent", he is a man and he is a prophet. The gospel-writer adds to our store: he is the Christ, the longed-for king who would restore Israel's well-

231

being and dignity. But, by the time of writing, anyone believing that the man Jesus was the Christ of the Jewish expectation was scorned and expelled from the community and forbidden the synagogue. The faith of the once-blind man is put to the test: "He is of age, ask him".

With courage and insight (in-sight!), he takes on "the disciples of Moses", affirms his intention to be "his disciple" and invites all to do the same. For his proclamation of the truth, he is cast out. But Jesus comes to him and reveals himself more fully and the man enters the community of believers and worshippers who have found the Lord in the man called Jesus.

Not, then, a story of the past. Rather, an invitation in the present. Jesus seeks out the blind of heart and spirit. We meet the man and listen. If we listen, he would be our teacher ("Rabbi"). Gradually, the scales will fall from our eyes and we will come to see who he is. Discipleship is a possibility but at a cost. Yet, "Jesus said to the Jews who believed in him, 'If you continue in my word, you are truly my disciples, and you will know the truth, and the truth will make you free'" (8:31-32).

IMAGES OF GOD

There is one image of God in this story: Jesus. What he does is what the Father does. His works are the works of God. No one, we are told, has ever seen God; the only Son, who is in the bosom of the Father, he has made him known (1:18). No one has seen God. Everyone is blind.

At the beginning (1:43-46), Jesus found Philip and invited him, "Follow me". In turn, Philip found Nathanael and said to him, "We have found him of whom Moses and the prophets wrote, Jesus of Nazareth, son of Joseph". Nathanael would have none of it: "Can anything good come out of Nazareth?" Philip said to him, "Come and see".

Come and see.

PRAYER

The prayer of the One Sent (17:20-26) is "that they may all be one", that all may come to the light of truth.

Chapter 33

From slavery to freedom
The letter to the Philemon

Have you ever written to a newspaper? A daunting task! Letters
for publication must be carefully prepared. Thoughts must be
expressed clearly and, as editors constantly remind us, briefly
and to the point. The right word must be found, the right tone
established. The matter under discussion must be of interest to
the general public we seek to interest and influence.

A private letter is another matter. There is no need for
formality with family and friends ("Darling"; "Hi, Mom!"; "Dear
Fred"). Thoughts need not be well organised – we can break
off suddenly and go into a "By the way, did you hear about
Jane?", knowing that our friends won't lose track of what we
are saying. Our private letters presume an understanding
between sender and recipient. Friends and relatives know our
minds and have no difficulty reading between the lines.

Letters in the New Testament

Of the twenty-seven books of the New Testament, twenty-
one are called Letters. Of these, thirteen are alleged to have
been written by St Paul. Some of these genuinely were written
by the great apostle, but not all of them. Some were written by
his disciples and some were promoted under his name to win
more widespread approval.

We can draw up a table:

1. Written by Paul:
   Letter to Roman Christians
   Letter to Corinthian Christians
   Second Letter to Corinthian Christians
   Letter to Galatian Christians
   Letter to Philippian Christians
   First Letter to Thessalonian Christians
   (Letter to Colossian Christians?)
   Letter to Philemon

2. Written by disciples:
   Second Letter to Thessalonian Christians
   Letter to Ephesian Christians
   (Letter to Colossian Christians?)

3. Allegedly by Paul:
   First Letter to Timothy
   Second Letter to Timothy
   Letter to Titus

So, there are seven, possibly eight, genuine letters of Paul in the New Testament. By the way, the order of his letters in your Bible is not chronological but rather is a matter of length. The longest letter – Romans – is first and the shortest – Philemon – is last.

Paul's Letter to the Romans is a public letter. It is written to Christians in Rome who were not his converts and whose leaders were not personally known to Paul. It is a very formal document, outlining Paul's understanding of how, in Jesus, we are brought close to God. It is a carefully argued, carefully written piece of work. The remaining six (or seven) are personal letters to Christians who were, for the most part, Paul's converts in the various cities to which he travelled. These people were friends and Paul was passionately concerned for their welfare. Sometimes, some of his converts would write to him seeking advice on a point of his teaching; sometimes he had to write to call a halt to some unbecoming behaviour or to put his little Churches right on a matter of belief. Since these letters are personal, we must not expect that they read easily. As our personal letters are best understood by our friends, so, too, with Paul's. Often, we have to guess what he means, to read between the lines, as he jumps around from one topic to the next, without much connection between them. Remember, we are trying to read someone else's personal letters. At the same time, Paul's letters are not intended for one person (not even his letter to Philemon, as we shall see). They are sent to groups of Christians from an apostle who was deeply and personally concerned for the welfare of his people. His letters are more like family letters ("Dear All") and, since we are part of the Christian family, we may look over the shoulders of Paul's brothers and sisters and read their letters as if they were addressed to us. But we must make allowances: Paul is neither writing to us or for us. We are eavesdroppers on other people's conversations.

The Golden Rule is to begin small. To introduce ourselves to the writings of St Paul we can do no better than to start with his very brief Letter to Philemon.

READING THROUGH

If we omit God and Jesus Christ from the reckoning, there are eleven names in the letter. Who are these people?

Paul

Paul was a Jew, probably born in the cultured city of Tarsus (in modern-day south-east Turkey), at a guess ten years after the birth of Jesus. He was called by the Jewish name, Saul, but, as was often the case, he was also given a Roman name, Paul (compare Simon Peter, John Mark). He was brought up in a strict Jewish tradition, well-educated (possibly, partly in Jerusalem). He seems to have been a supporter of early opposition to the Christian movement within Judaism and to have accepted responsibility for its suppression. On his way to Damascus to arrest some Christians, he had an experience of the risen Lord which forced him to see that Jesus was the fulfilment of all that he stood for as a Jew. He wrote of this crucial turning-point in his life:

> For you have heard of my former life in Jerusalem, how I persecuted the church of God violently and tried to destroy it; and I advanced in Judaism beyond many of my own age among my people, so extremely zealous was I for the traditions of my fathers. But when he who had set me apart before I was born, and had called me through his grace, was pleased to reveal his Son to me, in order that I might preach him among the Gentiles...
>
> *Galatians 1:13-16*

Having spent some time in Arabia (on retreat in the desert?), Paul presented himself to Peter and to James, "the brother of

235

the Lord" (Galatians 1:18-19) in Jerusalem and, subsequently, undertook missionary activity in Asia Minor (that is, Turkey). Paul returned to Jerusalem again but how often is difficult to say. He appears to have engaged in three major missionary efforts in Asia Minor and in Greece. The first journey (46-49 C.E.) took him to Syria and eastern Asia Minor, after which he went to Jerusalem to report on his success among the Gentiles and to present the case for not forcing his new, non-Jewish converts to submit to the Jewish practice of circumcision. Paul won his case (Galatians 2:1-10).

Later in the same year (49 C.E.), Peter went to Antioch in Syria (Paul's base) and, though at first "he ate with the Gentiles" (Galatians 2:12), he withdrew from their fellowship. Paul regarded this as going back on a binding agreement and "opposed him face to face" (Galatians 2:11). A major crisis was averted when it was agreed not to impose Jewish dietary regulations on Gentile Christians, except that, in mixed communities, they should abstain from meat sacrificed to idols, from blood, from meat of strangled animals and from some undefined sexual misconduct. In the Acts of the Apostles, St Luke combines the two issues of circumcision and food regulations and has both issues resolved at his so-called "Council of Jerusalem" (Acts 15).

The issues at stake were immense, by far the most serious ever to confront the Christian Church in all its history. Simply stated, they amounted to this: was the message of Jesus for Jews exclusively or was it intended to be "a light for the Gentiles" as well? Paul's vision of the universality of God's mercy, his conviction of his vocation to tell everyone about the gospel of God's love for all and his personal courage in standing up to those "who were reputed to be pillars" (Galatians 2:9) saved the Good News for his beloved Gentiles and, thus, for you and for me.

Setting out once again from Antioch, Paul's second journey (50-52 C.E.) takes him through Asia Minor. His practice, on entering a town or city (interestingly, Paul was a city man, Jesus essentially a man of the country), was to go to the Jewish synagogue to preach Jesus there. Sometimes he had success, as often as not, failure. Then he would turn his attention to the pagan Gentiles. On this journey, Paul passed from Asia Minor into Greece, to the port of Philippi, a town called Neapolis.

There he founded a little community, the first christian church on the continent of Europe.

Paul was flogged and imprisoned in Philippi because he cast out a demon from a slave girl, causing a loss of profit to her controllers. On release, he moved south to Thessalonica, forming a little church there, and, eventually, pitching up in the great city of Athens. Here he was singularly unsuccessful in interesting the inquisitive Athenians in the strange story of a man who had been put to death and raised by God from the grave. So he went south-west to nearby Corinth, a bustling port with a notorious reputation. During his stay of eighteen months Paul converted many Jews and Gentiles and established a thriving, argumentative and utterly lovable community of Christians. Paul's two surviving letters to his new parish (three have been lost), not only confirm the liveliness of these new Christians but also the abundance of gifts showered on them by the Holy Spirit. When accusations were laid against him before the proconsul L. Junius Gallio, though acquitted, Paul found it necessary to retrace his steps to base-camp at Antioch. There he remained over a year, probably from autumn of 52 A.D. to spring of 54 C.E.

In the spring of 54 C.E. Paul set out from Antioch for various parts of Asia Minor, eventually arriving at the capital, Ephesus. For three years he preached the Gospel, not without opposition (read the account of Demetrius and the riot of the silversmiths in Acts 18:21-41) and, indeed, there is some evidence that, once again, the apostle found himself behind bars. It is probable that it is to this imprisonment that the Letters to Colossians and Philemon refer.

On release, Paul moved on to Greece, probably to Philippi and, more certainly, to Corinth where he settled the disputes and contentions so evident in his letters to those turbulent Christians. It was during this stay, in 58 C.E., that he wrote the Letter to the Romans. Later that year he returned, via many towns and cities where he had established christian communities, to Jerusalem, where he and his companions were well received. But James, the leader of the Jewish Christians in Jerusalem, aware that the old wounds concerning the admission of Gentiles might reopen, insisted that Paul should perform a public display of piety in the Temple. While doing so, some Jews who knew of Paul's activities in Asia Minor and

Greece set upon him with such ferocity that the Roman tribune of the guard had to rescue him. He spent the next two years in gaol on remand at Caesarea on the Mediterranean coast. Then, with no trial in sight, he used his privilege as a Roman citizen to appeal to the Emperor and he was shipped to Rome. On the way his ship was wrecked off Malta and he did not reach Rome until 61 C.E. where he spent a further two years under house-arrest. Apparently he was permitted to preach to Roman Jews and Gentiles and to convert them to faith in Jesus Christ.

Paul had hoped to go to Spain but there is no reliable evidence that his ambitions were fulfilled (Romans 15:24). Christian traditions suggest that he was put to death (beheaded?) during the persecution by Emperor Nero which lasted from July 64 C.E. to June 68 C.E. It is less certain that he was martyred with St Peter. Paul was buried, it is believed, on the site of the present-day Basilica of St Paul's-outside-the-walls in Rome.

Timothy

Timothy, whose name means "honouring God", was born at Lystra in Asia Minor of a Greek father and a Jewish mother called Eunice. His grandmother, Lois, had become a Christian (2 Timothy 1:5). He joined Paul on the second missionary expedition and was his constant companion for many years. He is mentioned in most of the genuine letters of St Paul. These references indicate that Timothy was amongst the most intimate and trustworthy of the apostle's associates. The Letters to Timothy in the New Testament are directed to this companion of Paul but were not written by Paul himself. Paul calls Timothy his "brother", both out of affection and in recognition of his status as a fellow Christian and co-worker in the task of spreading the gospel.

Philemon

Philemon was a gentile Christian living in the city of Colossae in Asia Minor. He was a man of substance and a leader of the Christian community which met in his house. As head of the household, he would have been the leader of the community Eucharist. Paul calls him a "beloved co-worker", implying that Philemon had ministered on his behalf in establishing the church community in the city. Philemon probably worked with Epaphras (see below) who is generally regarded as the founder of the church at Colossae.

Apphia

Apphia, almost certainly, was the wife of Philemon.

Archippus

Archippus was a member of Philemon's household and possibly his son. He was personally addressed by Paul at the end of the Letter to the Colossians: "See that you fulfil the ministry which you have received in the Lord" (Colossians 4:17). We have no way of knowing what this ministry might have been. It is quite likely that the Letter to the Colossians was written by Paul or on his behalf while he was imprisoned in Ephesus and that Archippus was given the task of attending to difficulties which had emerged in the church at Colossae.

Onesimus

Onesimus was a slave who had run away from his master Philemon. How he came into contact with Paul is not clear. It may very well be that he was imprisoned in Ephesus and was converted by St Paul in gaol. He is mentioned in Colossians 4:9 as a travelling companion of Tychicus who delivered the Letter to the Colossians. The name Onesimus means "useful" or "beneficial" and Paul makes a pun on the name in verses 11 and 20.

Epaphras

Epaphras was a native of Colossae and almost certainly the one who first evangelized in the city. He was "our beloved fellow servant" and "faithful minister of Christ", from whom the Colossians first "heard and understood the grace of God in truth" (Colossians 1:6-7). He reported to Paul about certain heretical tendencies among his converts; hence the Letter to the Colossians, an attempt to overcome the difficulties.

Epaphras was imprisoned with Paul and was unable to return to his church community and, therefore, joined with Paul in sending greetings to his brothers and sisters in the Lord.

239

Mark

The name Mark was so common in the Roman Empire (rather like Smith in England) that it is difficult to be sure that, whenever the name crops up in the New Testament, the same man is indicated. There can be no doubt that a man called Mark, a cousin of Barnabas, was a companion of Paul's, introduced to the great apostle by his cousin in Cyprus (Acts 13:5). Mark left Paul at one stage in acrimonious circumstances (Acts 15:36-41) and a coolness grew up between them. At a later stage, however, they were reconciled and Mark is mentioned in Colossians 4:10. Whether this Mark is the same Mark who wrote the Gospel or either of them is the Mark mentioned in 1 Peter 5:13 or, again, the John Mark of Acts 12:12, is an open question. Which Smith is Smith?

Aristarchus

Aristarchus was a Macedonian Jew from Thessalonica, a companion of Paul during his tribulations at Ephesus and on the third missionary expedition (Acts 19;20). Subsequently, he journeyed to Rome with the apostle (Acts 27:2). What became of him there, we do not know.

Demas

Demas, while given here the status of a fellow worker with Paul, is elsewhere in the New Testament charged with abandoning Paul during his imprisonment because of his love of the world (2 Timothy 4:10). But the Second Letter to Timothy, where the charge is laid, was not written by Paul and does not bear his authority.

Luke

All the names in Paul's final greeting occur in the Letter to the Colossians. There Luke is described as "the beloved physician" (Colossians 4:14). This is the same Luke who wrote the third Gospel and the Acts of the Apostles.

READING THROUGH AGAIN

When we write letters, no matter how informal, we follow a pattern. Our address goes at the right-hand top of the page.

We begin "Dear Aunt Jane" on the left-hand side. We tend to put personal well-wishing first ("I hope that you are keeping well, as I am, thank God") and then the news or main body of the letter. Finally, we end with greetings ("Give my love to Uncle Henry and the twins") and farewell ("Lots of love"). Similarly, although Paul's letters are, for the most part, personal, they follow a pattern or structure which helps us to understand what he is saying. We shall call each element of his pattern a section.

Section 1: Salutation (verses 1-3)

The salutation at the opening of all Paul's letters has three elements: (a) this letter is from Paul; often he will add some personal detail such as "a servant", "an apostle", "a prisoner"; (b) this letter is to Philemon, to the saints at Philippi, to the churches at Galatia or whoever; (c) a greeting: "grace to you and peace".

In Philemon, Paul announces himself as a prisoner for Jesus Christ. He does not appeal to his authority as an apostle but rather to his distressing imprisonment in Ephesus which may move the heart of Philemon in the matter of the runaway slave, Onesimus. He makes it clear that he is not a prisoner on account of some crime but because of his love for Christ Jesus.

Philemon is addressed as "our beloved fellow worker". Paul appeals to a shared experience as fellow workers in spreading the gospel and to the love which binds together those who labour on its behalf. But the letter is not for Philemon alone. Paul calls to his aid "our sister" Apphia, who is probably Philemon's wife and Archippus, their son, and all the christian community which was accustomed to assemble for the Eucharist in his house. Indeed, the letter would have been read during the Eucharist, thus heightening its emotional appeal. Paul intends the letter to carry a message for the whole community. The whole community must be involved in the decision concerning the runaway slave.

The formula "Grace to you and peace from God our Father and the Lord Jesus Christ" is found at the beginning of all his letters. But it is not a mere formula. Paul wishes the graciousness (love) of God on all so that they may live in peace. It is this love and peace which he wishes to see extended to Onesimus.

241

Section 2: Thanksgiving (verses 4-7)

"I thank my God always..." This section frequently reveals the tone of Paul's letter. It reveals Paul's present attitude towards the people to whom he is writing (joy, consolation, even anger - see Galatians 1:6). This part of his letters often provides rich insights into his temperament and personality.

Paul gives thanks (in Greek, the verb is our word "Eucharist") for Philemon's faith and love which is directed to our Lord Jesus and flows outward to all the community ("the saints"). This sharing (*koinonia*) of faith and love promotes a deeper understanding of the great goodness they have all received from Jesus. This mutual exchange of love is the source of much joy and comfort for Paul. Again, note that Paul emphasises those very qualities which will be needed if Philemon is to forgive and accept his runaway slave.

Section 3: The situation (verses 8-16)

"Accordingly, though I am bold enough in Christ to command... I prefer to appeal." This letter shows us something of the way Paul exercised his authority. We are never in doubt that, as an apostle, Paul had the authority to tell Philemon and his household how the gospel was to be lived in concrete circumstances. Since the letter is addressed to the church which gathered in Philemon's house, the whole community is called upon to recognise that authority. However, Paul does not choose to exercise his authority through command but makes his appeal on the basis of love, the very foundation of christian fellowship. He is not above introducing an emotional element: he is an old man (some translations have "ambassador") and he is in prison for the faith.

Paul attempts to explain why Onesimus ran away; the suggestion would appear to be that his running away was somehow God's intention in order that Philemon and Onesimus might discover their brotherhood (not master/slave) in Christian fellowship. Onesimus had grown dear to Paul and a great comfort during his imprisonment but Paul acknowledges that the slave belongs to Philemon and it is for his master to decide where his work shall be. If Philemon were to receive Onesimus, not as a slave but as a new brother in the Lord, he might see his way to allow Onesimus to return to be with the apostle in his distress.

Section 4: Exhortation (verses 17-22)

"So if you consider me your partner... refresh my heart in Christ." Paul exhorts Philemon to receive Onesimus for friendship's sake. Receiving the runaway as if he were a prodigal son rather than a slave will confirm Philemon's friendship with Paul. The apostle even offers to re-imburse his friend for any loss he may have sustained through the absconding of his slave. At the same time, he reminds Philemon of the great debt he himself owes to Paul – his own life as a Christian. Confident of Philemon's obedience, Paul need not appeal to his apostolic authority. He knows that Philemon will receive Onesimus just as he will prepare a room for Paul's forthcoming visit.

Section 5: Final greetings (Verses 23-25)

The final greetings at the conclusion of Paul's letters fall into two parts: (a) Greetings to and from individuals in the communities of the recipient and the sender. The greetings are important because usually they reveal Paul's relationship to various members of the Church and so provide useful bio-graphical material. Of course, such greetings let us see how small christian communities around the eastern Mediterranean world kept in touch and were personally concerned for each other's well-being. (b) Blessings provide a solemn closing and a prayerful wish. If you wish to see how an ordinary letter would end in Paul's day, look at Acts 15:29. Paul's last word is infinitely richer. He prays that the love of Jesus Christ may surround the lives of his brothers and sisters.

THE MESSAGE

The obscure story of a runaway slave may not seem the stuff of christian inspiration. What, we may ask, is in this letter to justify its inclusion in the New Testament, that is to say, to justify its right to be a foundation document of the christian Church? I suspect that there are three reasons why we ought to listen to the voice of this little letter of 335 words.

First, notice how authority operates in the letter. Paul could exercise his authority and command as an apostle. But he does not choose to do so. Rather, he appeals to love and friendship, to shared faith and fellowship, to move Philemon to accept a slave as a brother. There is much to ponder here: how ought authority in the Church minister to the community so that it is an expression of love, not an instrument of coercion?

Secondly, notice that the letter is addressed to the whole community which is, therefore, seen to have a role to play in the matter of reconciliation between master and slave. Paul shares his apostolic office with all so that all may contribute to good fellowship.

Thirdly, notice the tone of the letter. It is prayerful, friendly, full of praise and acknowledgement of goodness. The letter is a model of how "these Christians love one another".

A word about the question of slavery. Though Paul would appear to be appealing for the release of Onesimus from slavery, the letter is not an attack on slavery. For St Paul, slavery was an accepted institution of society. To question it would be to call into question the very foundations of the state. It would be an act of revolution and Paul was no political revolutionary. However, the matter was not simply a question of respect for social institutions. Paul believed that the world order was quickly to pass away: "For the form of this world is passing away" (1 Corinthians 7:31). In the same chapter of 1 Corinthians, Paul advises slaves to remain as they are, unless they can lawfully obtain freedom. There is, he is saying, little point in changing, for the whole world is about to change. His teaching on the married and unmarried is the same: stay as you are, the end is nigh! In this, Paul was wrong. He had, too, a rather naive view of political authority, as Romans 13 all too clearly demonstrates. But he was right about one thing. He believed passionately that in the new future created by God we will all stand equal. Baptism is the sign of the future:

For as many of you as were baptised into Christ have put on Christ; there is neither Jew nor Greek, there is neither slave nor free, there is neither male nor female: for all are one in Christ Jesus.

Galatians 3:27-28

The words of a man who struggled all his life to understand the Scriptures will serve us here:

> This epistle gives us a masterful and tender illustration of Christian love. For here we see how St Paul takes the part of poor Onesimus and, to the best of his ability, advocates his cause with his master. He acts as if he were himself Onesimus who had done wrong. Yet he does this not with force or compulsion, as lay within his rights; but he empties himself of his rights in order to compel Philemon also to waive his rights. What Christ has done for us with God the Father, that St Paul does also for Onesimus with Philemon. For Christ emptied himself of his rights (Philippians 2:5-11) and overcame the Father with love and humility, so that the Father had to put away his wrath and rights, and receive us into favour for the sake of Christ, who so earnestly advocates our cause and so heartily takes our part. For we are all his Onesimuses, did we but know it.
>
> Martin Luther, *Der Brief an den Philemon*, 1522

PRAYER

The letters of St Paul are full of wonderful prayers. Since the Letter to the Colossians is closely connected to the Letter to Philemon, it would be fitting to pray the great hymn to creation to be found in Colossians 1:15-20.

Chapter 34

The Apocalypse: God rules

Revelation 1:1-8

There are two attitudes to the Book of Revelation or the Apocalypse – you either like it or lump it. People who like it tend to become obsessed with it, even to the extent of regarding it as the key to the whole of the Bible. People who can't stand it at any price tend to regard it as an unimportant footnote to the New Testament that is best left alone. George Bernard Shaw called it "a curious record of the visions of a drug addict". On the other hand, St Jerome remarked that "Revelation has as many mysteries as it does words". The sensible view is that Revelation is like every other book of the Bible. It is an invitation to hear God's love-call, to respond to it and to live accordingly. It is not the message of Revelation which is the problem; it is the strange language and images which are used to convey the message.

APOCALYPSE

The author calls his work an "apocalypse". The word is Greek and means "a revelation", "a disclosure". The idea is that a secret is been shared by the writer with the reader. The secret, as the very first verse tells us, is about Jesus Christ, a secret first revealed to the author and now to be passed on to us. Why the secrecy? Did not Jesus tell his disciples to preach to all nations, not to hide their light under a bucket? To answer the question we must make two journeys, one into ancient history and another into an ancient book.

A History lesson

Nero fiddled while Rome burned. He had become emperor in 54 C.E. when his mother almost certainly poisoned his step-father Claudius. Five years later, Nero had his dominating mother put to death and embarked on an orgy of pleasure-seeking which demeaned the office of emperor and diminished the coffers of state. On 19th July 64, a disastrous fire broke out in the city of Rome. It raged for six days and reduced the greater part of the city to ashes. So quickly did Nero begin a rebuilding programme that a rumour that he himself had instigated the fire in order to erect for himself a more magnificent imperial capital began to circulate. In order to root out this suspicion, the emperor blamed the Christians, a religious group already suspected of devious practices because of their close community life and secret worship. Here is how a Roman historian described the incident:

Nero fastened the guilt (for the fire) and inflicted the most exquisite torture on a class of people hated for their abominations, called Christians by the populace... Accordingly, an arrest was made of all who pleaded guilty... then an immense multitude were convicted, not so much for the crime of setting fire to the city, as of hatred against humanity. Mockery of every sort was added to their deaths. Covered with skins of beasts, they were torn by dogs and perished, or were nailed to crosses, or were burnt to serve as nightly illuminations when daylight had expired. Nero offered his gardens (on the Vatican hill) for the spectacle... Hence, even for criminals who deserve extreme and exemplary punishment, there arose a feeling of compassion; for it was not, as it seemed, for the public good, but to satisfy one man's cruelty, that they were destroyed.

Tacitus, *The Annals of Rome*, XV 44

It is probable that the apostles Peter and Paul were among the victims of Nero's cruel persecution. Ironically, just a few years before, writing to Christians in Rome, St Paul had advocated submission to Nero and the imperial authorities:

Let every person be subject to the governing authorities. For there is no authority except from God, and those who exist have been instituted by God. Therefore he who resists the authorities resists what God has appointed, and those who resist will incur judgement. For rulers are not a terror to good conduct, but to bad.

Romans 13:1-3

However, the honeymoon was now over and, increasingly, Christians were to become victims of a brutal and brutalising imperial machine. Nero's despotic behaviour caused opposition to break out in Gaul, Spain and Africa. The Jews revolted in 66 and the city most sacred to Jews and Christians, Jerusalem, was under severe threat. Nero cut his throat in 68 but so feared and detested had he become that many, indeed, most people believed he had not really died. For another fifty years, people were terrified that Nero would come again.

The empire fell into anarchy and several emperors followed in quick succession. In 70, the general Vespasian hurried back from the siege of Jerusalem to become emperor, leaving his son Titus to capture and burn the holy city of God and the Temple to the ground. Titus followed his father on the imperial throne, to be followed in turn by his brother, Domitian (81-96).

Anarchy brought misery to pagan and Christian alike. The Empire had been founded and sustained on brutality and terror (most empires are). The subjugated peoples had no loyalty to Rome and its institutions; they were bound by fear, not love. Domitian realised this and, madman that he was, he decided to create a principle which would unite the disparate peoples of his vast domain. The principle was the universal acceptance of his own divinity. Let everyone recognise that the emperor was God, let them be united in one faith, surely then loyalty will be assured. And the new religion was neatly summarised in a single slogan: Our Lord and our God. Every citizen was required to appear before the emperor's statue and throw incense on the eternal flame burning before it. A certificate was issued as evidence that one had embraced the new religion. No one was allowed to conduct business without the certificate. And everywhere the question was asked: has Nero come again?

The Jews managed to win exemption. But Domitian was deeply suspicious of Christians and was especially insistent that they conform. What was to be done? Some looked on the matter as no big thing. Throw the incense, get the certificate and walk away, still believing in one's heart that God is God and the emperor has no clothes. But many, including the writer of the Book of Revelation, believed that such compromise was tantamount to a denial of God, a denial that Jesus is Lord. There was only one thing to be done: stand up and be counted.

An old book

Of course, this kind of thing had happened before and Christians (and Jews) knew well what to do. In a crisis, turn to the Bible. The writer of Revelation turned to his and this is what he found.

Alexander the Great became king of Macedon in northern Greece in 336 B.C.E. He was determined to put an end to the constant menace to Greece of the Persian Empire to the east. He set out in 334 and swept through Asia Minor, Syria, Israel, Egypt, Mesopotamia and on to the banks of the Indus river. A threatened mutiny by his weary troops prevented him from conquering India. On his way home he died in Babylon in 323. He was just thirty-three.

Alexander's influence was immense. For the first time, he introduced European (Greek) culture, language, religion and customs to the East. He founded the city of Alexandria (Egypt) and it became a scholarly centre for the known world. There Jews came into contact with the new ideas and style and there they translated their Sacred Scripture into Greek. Alexander himself is reputed to have had a great respect for the Jews and he allowed them to carry on their worship in Israel and wherever they were scattered throughout his empire. Indeed, one tradition has it that on one occasion he joined in worship of God in the Temple in Jerusalem.

The generals of Alexander's army carved up the empire and years of war and uneasy alliances followed. Small countries such as Israel were mere pawns in a never-ending power struggle. About one hundred and fifty turbulent years after Alexander's death, a descendant of one of his generals controlled Israel and much of the northern half of the old empire. His name was Antiochus IV, one of the nastiest dictators in history. He was determined that Greek culture and religion should dominate everywhere. Consequently, he had a particularly unfortunate relationship with the Jews and Jerusalem. In 168 B.C.E. he ordered one of his generals to attack Jerusalem. The attack took place on the Sabbath and the pious inhabitants refused to bear arms and most of the male inhabitants were killed, the women and children enslaved.

Worse was to come. Antiochus attempted to give his views the force of law. He issued a decree to the effect that throughout his kingdom all peoples were to practise one religion and culture. To such an edict the Jews could not submit. Antiochus proceeded to forbid circumcision, the observance of the Sabbath and dietary regulations, under pain of death. Anyone found with a scroll of the Sacred Scriptures faced execution. Worst of all, an altar to Zeus was erected over the altar in the Temple and Jews forced to take part in idolatrous worship and in heathen festivities of all kind. Resistance grew and the country was plunged into a dreadful guerrilla war that continued for years after the emperor died in 163 B.C.E.

It might not seem that writing a book was a useful response to the horrors of those wicked times. But that is what one man did and it must have helped for the book not only survived, it was so revered that it found its way into the Bible: the Book of Daniel. The author wrote to offer encouragement and hope to a suffering people. God will not abandon his people forever. The cruel empires which rule by terror will not have the final say. People must endure, must stand up for what they believe, even in the face of death. Compromise with the persecutor means abandoning God and runs the risk of being abandoned by God when the day of salvation comes.

But how can one publish such subversive ideas without endangering both writer and readers? Let the royal censor get his hands on scrolls that promise that the tyrannical king will get his comeuppance and heads will roll. Writings which subvert royal authority, undermine royal policy and advocate universal disobedience cannot be tolerated by tyrants. The first victim of tyranny is the writer.

Unless, of course, you write in such a way that you appear to be quite harmless. Pretend that you are writing about long ago and far away, about fictitious characters, about strange animals and beasts, about dreams and visions. Invent a code language which only writer and reader share. Juggle around with numbers, giving them a secret meaning. Paint fantastic and wild pictures of the future, with dragons and demons, fire and brimstone. Write under an assumed name, preferably one belonging to some venerable figure of the past. Such is the recipe for the Book of Daniel.

Here, then, was a model for the writer of the Book of Revelation. Just as the Book of Daniel addressed itself to the suffering Jews under Antiochus, so our unknown author undertook to warn, advise and comfort Christians caught up in the persecution of Domitian.

READING THROUGH

One short passage will illustrate how the writer went about his work. We will examine the prologue and opening greeting (1:1-8). On first reading everything would seem to require explanation. For the moment, a few key details.

An apocalypse (verse 1)

The writer opens by informing readers that his work is a revelation (apocalypse) concerning Jesus Christ and given by God in order to be shared with the faithful. The revelation concerns the future. Immediately we can see that the writer wishes to promote a God's-eye view of the fate of his people. Broadly speaking, then, the revelation, the message of the whole book, is that the future belongs to God.

Seven Churches (verse 4)

The first part of Revelation consists of letters to seven churches in Asia Minor (modern Turkey). But the message is not to be confined to these Christian communities for seven is a special number. It means "totality", "completeness". Thus the seven churches stand for the whole Church; the revelation is for all.

The alpha and the omega (verse 8)

These are the first and last letters of the Greek alphabet and to call God by them is to declare that he is the beginning and the end of all creation. The origin and destiny of creation are in the hands of God.

READING THROUGH AGAIN

The prologue (Verses 1-3)

The writer remains anonymous. He is going to reveal visions granted to a certain John, a name attached to many prominent people in the early days of Christianity. The visionary would be known in Christian circles and his authority respected. Giving him such a commonplace name conceals his identity from the imperial police.

The revelation has its source in God and it concerns Jesus Christ. The intention is to console God's people ("his servants"). What is to happen to the churches? Are we forever to be a prey to imperial power? Will there ever be a time of justice for the persecuted and final judgement on the persecutors? It is no less than an angel who reveals "what will soon take place". Thus, we have God's word for it, to which Jesus himself is witness. The news must be good, for whoever reads or hears and keeps the words of the prophecy will be blessed. The writer sees himself as a prophet who brings the word of God to people in distress. Moreover, there are seven blessings in Revelation (1:3; 14:13; 16:15; 19:9; 20:26; 22:7; 22:14). To listen to and to keep the words of this prophecy is to have all blessings, to be totally blessed. And the time of blessing is near. Conversely, those who neglect the words of this prophecy are warned of dire consequences. This book is a two-edged sword.

To the seven churches (verses 4-8)

There were, of course, more than seven churches in Asia Minor. But the writer is interested in the symbolic meaning of numbers. Seven, the sign of perfection, of totality, is everywhere. There are seven seals, seven trumpets, seven signs, seven bowls, seven stars, seven lampstands, seven stages in the fall of Babylon (Rome) and so on. Six falls short of the perfect seven and so stands for all that is imperfect, flawed. The number of the beast (Nero or Domitian?) is 666, the totally flawed, totally corrupt (13:18). Four, because there are four points on the compass, indicates "universal", "worldwide" (see "the four horsemen of the apocalypse" – Revelation 6:2-8). The number 1,000 stands for "infinity", "beyond numbering". Thus, the countless angels are "thousands of thousands" (5:11).

Like Paul, John sends greetings of grace and peace. Grace is God's steadfast love which endures forever. Peace is wholeness, that fullness of life which comes to all who are enfolded by God's steadfast love. In these two words the message of the book is contained. All that follows is an assurance that God's love and peace await all who suffer in the present persecution.

Grace and peace come, first of all, from the one "who is and who was and who is to come". That is to say, the blessings come from a sure source, from God, who existed before creation and after creation had come into being, and who will exist in the world to come. Unlike human emperors who, in the second half of the first century were short-lived, God endures for ever. Secondly, grace and peace come from "the seven spirits who are before his throne". These may be the seven angels who are mentioned in the Book of Tobit 12:15. These guardian angels of the churches stand in God's presence and may be counted on to know of the suffering of the churches in their care and, as messengers of God, to hasten to them with grace and peace. Or, since seven denotes totality and completeness, the reference may be to the fullness of spirit, the Holy Spirit, who gives seven gifts to the churches (Isaiah11:2). Thirdly, grace and peace come from Jesus Christ and three things are said of him. He is "the faithful witness", in the sense that he came into the world as a witness of God's love. But the Greek word for witness is "martyr" and so the idea of Jesus dying ("faithful unto death" Revelation 2:10) in order to bring to us grace and peace is hinted at and made explicit in the phrase "by his blood" (by dying). But the suffering and martyrdom of Jesus are not the end; he is "the first-born of the dead". The resurrection is sure proof of God's protective love of his Son. The reader can be assured that his own suffering and death in the persecution similarly will come to glorious resurrection. Finally, Jesus is "the ruler of the kings of the earth". For all their might and power, the emperors of the world are subject to someone else. Domitian is not Lord and God. Jesus is.

Jesus does three things for us. First, he loves us. The Greek word used for love here means an unquestioning love. It is a love that is not conditional. The good news for all is that Jesus not only loves the lovable. He loves the unlovely and unlovable as well. Secondly, and on account of his love, he "has freed us from our sins by his blood". In our journey through the Book of Ruth, we encountered the word "redeemer". In the Old Testament, whenever one was in difficulty, lost in slavery, in debt, in sin, in childlessness (as in Ruth's case), the nearest male relative had to act and put the situation to rights, to restore the wholeness of the family. Jesus is our nearest of kin, our redeemer, who came "to seek and to save that which is lost" (Luke 19:10). Thirdly, he has "made us a kingdom of priests to his God and Father". In the Book of Exodus 19:6, the people of Israel were told that if they listened to God's word and remained faithful to the covenant they would be God's own possession. Furthermore, they would be witnesses to all peoples that God was present in the world, that is to say, they would be priests. Similarly, in the New Testament, the people of the Church saw themselves as witnesses to the world of God's presence-in-Jesus. The whole people of the Church are, accordingly, priests for the world.

John responds to such love with a prayer of praise: "To him be glory and dominion for ever and ever. Amen." Jesus is for ever to be glorified in recognition of his love for us. All power and authority belongs to him. Jesus, not the Roman emperor, has dominion and power which lasts for ever.

The Christian must look to the future. Almost as if he were having a visionary preview, John sketches out what is to come. Jesus will come with the clouds, that is to say, he will come as the instrument of divine judgement. All will see him, and especially the very men who put him to death. All the nations shall mourn at such a crime. John here recalls the words of Zechariah:

...when they look on him whom they have pierced, they shall mourn for him, as one mourns for an only child, and weep bitterly over him, as one weeps over a first-born son.
Zechariah 12:10

The reader is asked to fix his eyes on this vision of the future. That is where hope lies. The one who died for love will return in love. God-in-Jesus has not abandoned his people. To this truth we must shout out, "Yes! Amen." So be it! Let it be!

The vision is guaranteed by the Lord God, the beginning and end of all, who always was, who is, and who will be. The Roman emperors used to call themselves "autocrat", that is, "absolute ruler". Nine times in Revelation God is called "pantocrat", which means "the one who rules over everything", the Almighty One. Once again, persecuted Christians are reminded that the future belongs to God, that it is God who is the powerful one. In time of stress, the beleaguered Christians may think that God has lost his power, that the forces of evil have gained the upper hand. But, says Revelation, God has not lost his power. He is Almighty.

254

THE MESSAGE

In the Prologue, the author sets out his purpose. He intends to reveal a message from God, to reveal heavenly secrets. The message concerns Jesus Christ. All that he witnessed (of God's plan for the future) is about to be told. All who hear and obey will be blessed.

The Greeting contains more than twelve quotations from the Old Testament (without appearing to do so). John's visions are couched in Bible language. It was the practice of this kind of writing to go back to the past and to seek solace and hope there. But, though the language is that of the Old Testament, the message is that of the New. There is reference to the Father, Son, and Holy Spirit. The death and resurrection of Jesus, the redemption which they bring about and the second coming of the Lord in judgement are affirmed to be the basis of lasting grace and peace. In this way the writer has given us the whole of the Christian message in a few sentences. The rest of his book will spell out the message in detail.

IMAGES OF GOD

The frightened Christian is offered a vision of God. Here is a God who is all-powerful, who is swift to act, who is in control of creation. No matter what the powers of this world do, they cannot put themselves beyond the power of God. In Jesus we see what God intends. The God whose steadfast love endures is the God who rescues his Son from death. What he does for his Son he will do for all his sons and daughters. All God's chillun got wings!

PRAYER

The Book of Revelation contains many fine prayers. The prayer at 11:17-18 is a hymn of thanksgiving which perfectly sums up what the book is about. It is a prayer of hope in times of distress. But it is a fine prayer for anytime. A prayer for all seasons.